Depression and Bipolar Disorder

Family Psychoeducational Group Manual

Therapist Guide

Christina Bartha, MSW, RSW
Kate Kitchen, MSW, RSW, LISW
Carol Parker, MSW, RSW
Cathy Thomson, MSW, RSW

Centre
for Addiction and
Mental Health
Centre de
toxicomanie et
de santé mentale

Depression and Bipolar Disorder
Family Psychoeducational Group Manual
Therapist Guide

Christina Bartha, MSW, RSW
Kate Kitchen, MSW, RSW, LISW
Carol Parker, MSW, RSW
Cathy Thomson, MSW, RSW

CAMH Development and Design Team for this manual:
Evelyne Barthès
Christine Harris
Caroline Hebblethwaite
Eva Katz
Nancy Leung
Norman Liu
Sue McCluskey

ISBN 0-88868-399-5

Printed in Canada

Copyright © 2001 Centre for Addiction and Mental Health

For information on other Centre for Addiction and Mental Health resource materials or to place an order, please contact:

Marketing and Sales Services
Centre for Addiction and Mental Health
33 Russell Street
Toronto, ON M5S 2S1
Canada

Tel.: 1-800-661-1111 or 416-595-6059 in Toronto
E-mail: marketing@camh.net
Web site: www.camh.net

A World Health Organization Centre of Excellence

ACKNOWLEDGMENTS

Dr. Joel Raskin
Dr. Sagar Parikh
Dr. Robert Levitan
Susan Dickens, MA
Theresa Knott, BSW
Families who participated in the group series

REVIEWED AND MADE RECOMMENDATIONS FOR TRAINING

Louise Jablonski
Dave Foster

MANUAL REVIEWERS

Annabel Bassin
Sheila Porter
Barb Tiessen
Ian Waters
Charmaine Williams

CONTENTS

INTRODUCTION

This group manual for therapists provides a framework for the delivery of an eight to 12-week series for families who require information and support in dealing with bipolar and depressive disorders. The manual includes process notes, lecture materials and content for eight to 12 educational sessions, and handouts for group participants.

The manual is written for clinicians/group therapists who have previous training and experience in facilitating clinical group process but who also require the content and structure provided in the manual to meet the specialized needs of this group.

The group program aims to provide the following:

1. Information and education
To provide up-to-date, empirical information about the etiology and treatment of mood disorders

2. Practical coping strategies
To provide family members with practical strategies to deal with the behavioural symptoms associated with these disorders

3. Strategies for reducing isolation and providing support
To provide a supportive environment where family members can share the painful feelings triggered by these situations and receive support and empathy from other people dealing with similar circumstances. The group is intended to have a therapeutic effect on family members; however, it is not a traditional group psychotherapy experience.

HISTORY OF THE MANUAL DEVELOPMENT

This manual was developed as part of a three-year project in the Mood and Anxiety Disorders Program at the Centre for Addiction and Mental Health. An eight-week group program was developed in response to numerous requests for practical assistance from family members struggling to manage the needs of relatives who were diagnosed with major depression and bipolar disorder. The goal of the group was to improve the family's ability to cope with the situation, rather than to focus on the ill relative's condition.

Families expressed the need not only for information about how these disorders are understood and treated but also for practical strategies and skills to better cope with their relatives at home.

Many of these families had been dealing with their relative's illness for many years. While family members were expected to provide ongoing care and support, they lacked access to information about medications, treatments or the prognosis of their relative's condition — even in cases where their relative consented to the open exchange of information between the doctor and family members.

The model and content of this group series was developed after extensive review of the literature and based on our conversations and clinical experiences with clients and family members. The series is based on principles drawn from the models of group psychotherapy, psychoeducation and adult education. It is important to note that although the manual addresses most issues, it is not intended to be an exhaustive source for every issue that may arise from group discussions. Depending on the constitution of each group (spouse/parents/siblings), different themes will arise and can be integrated into the group process. While the literature is well-developed in the area of psychoeducational interventions for families of people with schizophrenia, the literature is less developed for the disorders of major depression and bipolar disorder.

The absence of resources in this area was reflected by the overwhelming response from families in the community once the program was launched.

WHICH FAMILIES ARE APPROPRIATE?

This series was developed for adult family members who are dealing with adults (over age 18) diagnosed with mood disorders. Participants may be parents of adult children, partners or spouses, adult siblings, step-family members and even close friends who are part of the affected person's support system.

The model format is designed to be flexible.

This series can be presented over an eight-week period, which is both cost-effective and allows time for participants to establish a supportive environment and group cohesion. For therapists who are providing these groups for the first time, however, the content may appear overwhelming to present in only eight weeks. For this reason, we have developed a model that can easily be adapted and presented over a longer period, such as 10 or 12 weeks. In these cases, Groups 4 (communication strategies), 5 (problem management) and 6 (crisis management) can each be extended over two sessions.

Depending on the individual style of each leader and the needs of the community, groups may run for 90 minutes without a break, or for two hours with a short break.

GROUP SIZE

Ideally, the group should include 12 group members and two therapists. However, groups can also be highly effective with only eight or 10 members, or up to 16 members. Most members are extremely motivated and attend the complete series; however, dropout will sometimes occur due to unforeseen circumstances. For this reason, groups should start with at least 12 participants to avoid the possibility of an overly small group.

Optional follow-up group

You may also choose to hold a follow-up group approximately three months after the final group meeting. The follow-up session offers group members an opportunity to meet again and discuss how they have coped with their individual situations since the end of the formal series. It also encourages group members to stay in contact after the series closes, either through informal friendships or by means of a more formal continuing self-help group.

Previous experience facilitating groups

All leaders will need experience with managing and guiding group process, including an understanding of the stages of group process, dynamics of groups and the role of the facilitator in this process. The integration of practical information and processing the emotional reactions/responses of group members can be challenging. Factual information can often trigger strong and painful emotional responses in parents and partners. Disclosures by group members can lead to powerful exchanges between group members or between members and leaders. As a result, you must be skilled in managing and directing group dynamics before launching a series that requires the integration of both content and process. You should feel comfortable directing the group process to ensure that the content is covered throughout the series.

If you lack experience facilitating psychoeducational groups you should consider using the longer format (two-hour sessions held over 10 to 12 weeks), which allows more time for content and discussion. Ideally, the model requires two group therapists to facilitate the group; however, one experienced therapist can provide the service with the assistance of a family member who has had training and orientation in the running of psychoeducation groups, perhaps through a self-help organization.

In some areas, two therapists may offer the group in the first series, and a particularly effective family participant may be identified to receive some further orientation, and then work with the therapist to facilitate the next group series.

KNOWLEDGE BASE OF GROUP LEADERS

Typically, clients who attend psychoeducational programs tend to be well-read and well-informed before attending these groups. As a result, most group members are not seeking general information but rather to discuss various contradictions found in the literature, self-help materials or on the Internet.

This manual provides the core content required for groups in which participants have both basic and advanced knowledge. You should also be prepared do background reading on mood disorders in order to remain current regarding recent developments in the literature.

RECRUITMENT OF GUEST LECTURER FOR MEDICATION INTERVENTIONS (GROUP 2)

Although this manual can be presented by two consistent group facilitators, you will need to recruit someone with expertise in medication treatments to conduct Group 2 (a one-hour information session for families). This person may be a psychiatrist, pharmacist, clinical nurse specialist or registered nurse who has experience in the area of mood disorder medications. Please refer to Group 2 (p. 31) for more details. Because it may take some time to locate an appropriate individual, arrange this early in the planning process.

ADDITIONAL REFERENCES

Although comprehensive references are listed at the end of this manual, it is important to note that the literature is ever-changing. As a result, you will need to continuously update your knowledge by visiting academic libraries, as well as researching community resources in and around your area.

GROUPS FOR ETHNO-RACIAL/ETHNO-CULTURAL POPULATIONS

This manual provides the core elements to include in a psychoeducation series. If your group includes relatives from specific ethno-racial and ethno-cultural populations, you will need to be sensitive to the specific needs of these groups. For example, in some cultures, it is difficult to discuss mental illness because it is not considered to legitimately exist. Early in the process, group members may need the opportunity to address this issue and to address their subsequent discomfort even attending the group.

In these cases, you will need to be reasonably knowledgeable about specific cultural groups and how the manual content should be modified or adapted to meet their needs. This might involve adding or omitting content and substituting more appropriate role-plays.

Consultation with people from the particular cultural group, or consultation with people who are knowledgeable about the norms and values of the group, could facilitate the process.

RECRUITMENT OF GROUP PARTICIPANTS

Before launching this series, allow three to four months for planning purposes and for recruiting group participants.

Prepare and distribute advertisements/promotional brochures through general hospitals, community mental health centres, self-help organizations and community radio and television stations. (See **Appendix 1**, Sample Brochure) When answering inquiries about the group, emphasize that the program is a series with both an educational and therapeutic component, and that an intake interview is required. This interview is to provide information and determine the suitability of the group for a particular individual.

GROUPS FOR EACH DISORDER OR MIXED GROUPS?

Depending on location and resources, you can choose among the following group structures:

1. Groups specific to one type of disorder and one type of relative (e.g., bipolar group for partners only)

The most informative and satisfying model (both for participants and leaders) is when all group participants are dealing with the same disorder and have the same relationship with the ill person. For example, a group of partners of clients with bipolar disorder allows for not only a discussion of the illness but also how the illness has changed the couple's relationship. Issues faced by partners (such as companionship or deciding whether to separate) are often very different from issues faced by parents (such as coping with a dependent adult child) because the nature and expectations within these relationships vary greatly.

Although this type of group can be highly effective, it may be difficult to organize, particularly when resources are limited or where there is a high demand for the group from all types of relatives.

2. Groups specific to one type of disorder, but with a mixed group of relatives

These groups can also be effective because members are all dealing with similar symptoms exhibited by their ill relative. For example, a group focused on depression will provide necessary information to all members, but the discussion on the impact on family relationships will vary; this can include changes between spouses, between parents and adult children, and between adult siblings. In this area, you may want to focus on common themes. Regardless of the type of relationship, all family members will benefit from the practical coping strategies and ways of responding to their ill relative's behaviour.

3. Groups that focus on both disorders and may or may not include a mix of relatives

These mixed groups may be most suited to rural areas where resources are scarce, and the number of group members may be spread across a wide geographic area. In these cases, there may not be enough family members to fill either a depression or bipolar group. While there is more material to present and more variation across group members, these groups are still highly effective. It will be necessary, however, to modify the group format and accommodate a longer series, possibly 12 weeks, to allow coverage of all the material.

SCREENING AND INTERVIEW WITH PARTICIPANTS

An important component of all psychoeducational groups is the provision of an orientation and intake process for group members. This step is important for several reasons:

1. Ensuring the family member's relative has a primary diagnosis of a mood disorder

In some cases, family members are unsure of their relative's diagnosis because the relative has refused to disclose this information. In these cases, the intake should include the checklist of screening of symptoms observed by the relative to verify that the ill person is dealing with a mood disorder (see **Appendix 2**, Mood Disorders Screening Form).

Family members who would not be suitable for the group would include cases in which the ill person has a primary diagnosis of schizophrenia, schizoaffective disorder, psychosis, obsessive-compulsive disorder or other major mental illness that is not included in the mood disorder spectrum.

In cases where a mood disorder is the primary diagnosis, but treatment is complicated by secondary conditions such as anxiety or personality traits, relatives will benefit from and should be included in the group program.

2. Gaining information about the family member's situation

It is not unusual for family members to seek help through a group when they are in the midst of a crisis involving their ill relative or when a crisis is imminent. The intake interview screens for such crises and ensures that the family member has access to alternative resources, as the group program is not a crisis intervention. Information collected during the intake remains confidential. Once in the group, participants may choose to disclose this information themselves. Such disclosure varies widely among participants.

The assessment should cover the following points to gain personal information about the family member: (An example of an intake form is provided in **Appendix 3**, Intake Form.)

- What is the age, occupation, living situation of potential group member?

- Does the ill relative live with him or her? If not, how much contact do they have?

- How long has the relative been ill? When was he or she formally diagnosed?

- How much information about the condition and treatment of the patient has been shared with the family member?

- What type of treatment has been tried? What was the outcome?

- What was the level of compliance with treatment?

- Have there been any suicide attempts? If so, how many?

- For partners with children, how many children are there, and what are their ages?

- Does the potential group member have a history of either depression or bipolar illness him- or herself? If so, was he or she treated for the illness, and when was treatment received?

Given the prevalence of mood disorders in the general population, it is not unusual for family members to themselves have a history of depression or bipolar disorder. Knowledge of this allows the facilitator to be more sensitive to specific group members who may find the information presented and the comments of other members at times painful. The facilitator can reframe certain information or discussions in a more gentle or sensitive manner.

Allow one hour for each intake interview. This comprehensive interview process will ensure that only appropriate, group-ready individuals are accepted into the program and will also prevent crises from disrupting the group process later on.

3. Orientation to group process

During the interview, orient potential group members to the psychoeducational model. After presenting the information, provide the opportunity for open discussion. Address the fact that the initial groups are presented in a lecture format, focusing on the ill relative, while later groups focus on participants' needs and further developing their coping skills. This can be a difficult shift for family members because typically their focus is on helping the ill relative rather than taking care of themselves.

Inform potential members about the number and length of the groups in the series. Given the sequential nature of the group program, emphasize the importance of attending all group sessions. Ideally, none of the participants should miss more than one session.

Explain the supportive aspects of the group; members can choose to be as open or as quiet as they wish. Assure all members that any information discussed during intake remains confidential unless the group member chooses to disclose it during the group.

Explain that the group attempts to shift the focus from exclusively discussing how family members can help their ill relative to addressing various ways in which they can take care of themselves by adopting different strategies or perspectives.

Because psychoeducational groups are not widely available, many family members may find your resource only after having lived with an ill relative for many years (sometimes for as long as 10 to 20 years). Other group members may have only recently become familiar with the illness. Ideally, avoid mixing the newly diagnosed (under one year) with those relatives who are dealing with a more refractory or chronic course of an illness.

Given the scarcity of psychoeducational groups that are specific to mood disorders, families of the recently diagnosed usually want to participate. In these cases, you should explore with the family member what his or her level of tolerance might be when hearing stories of serious situations experienced by other family members. Some individuals find such experiences to be disturbing and frightening, while others are better able to set boundaries around this material and separate it from themselves. Their desire to attend such a group and have access to the material and general support may far outweigh the impact of hearing other group members' difficult experiences.

FAMILY MEMBERS WITH A HISTORY OF DEPRESSION/BIPOLAR DISORDER

Given the hereditary nature of mood disorders, it is important to explore with the potential group member whether he or she has ever been treated for a mood disorder. Where such a history exists, inform the person that, given the nature of the group, some of the information presented or some of the comments made by other group members may be disturbing. This may occur because family members experience the group as a safe place to express their anger, frustration and disappointment. In our experience, however, group participants with this history find the experience very positive. Each participant can decide whether to disclose his or her history of treatment to the group.

SEVERAL FAMILY MEMBERS IN ONE GROUP

In cases where several relatives from one family wish to attend the same group, limit the number to two to three family members per group. Otherwise, a large number of people from the same family can influence group dynamics and lead to the focus being on one family's set of difficulties rather than common difficulties shared by all group members.

OPTION TO BUILD A GROUP WITH THE "BEST FIT" OF GROUP MEMBERS

As with other types of therapeutic groups, you are able to bring together a "good fit" of group members based on age, relationships, issues, personality and interpersonal style.

During the intake, some family members may present with personality styles or personal issues that are not suited to a group format. Family members who are particularly angry or hostile and those who have a great deal of difficulty listening may find the group process unsatisfying. In such cases, use your discretion to refer them to other resources. Explain that the group format is not appropriate for everyone and that other options may better suit their needs.

It should be noted, however, that groups with a diverse membership have worked very effectively, with group members varying in age, gender and experience with mood disorders.

USE OF THE MANUAL

The manual provides information about the factual and emotional information required by families. Each group has content and process directions for group leaders, and each session builds on the work completed in the previous session.

The manual content is comprehensive and, depending on the needs of each group, may not need to be presented in its entirety. For example, if your group identifies that the management of mania is creating the most difficulties, place greater emphasis on this material. Other groups may focus on the impact of the disorder on the marital relationship.

Each group session offers direction as to when to distribute handouts (either before or after the formal group), but group leaders should decide how best to incorporate the use of handouts into their own presentation style.

In order to track themes and select appropriate content, after each group is completed note the following:

The themes/issues most relevant to the group discussion; this will guide the direction of each group and form the foundation for Group 8 (or the last group) when a summary of content and salient issues is reviewed.

The issues from each session that may require follow-up in later sessions. For example: further discussion on the management of suicide or how to explain mental illness to children.

Resources to plan in advance

- space for the meetings
- flipchart, markers, tape and name tags
- a list of local resources and a reading list to be handed out at last group, or earlier if requested
- a guest lecturer for Group 2, which focuses on medications and treatment modalities for mood disorders
- refreshments for the first and last group (optional)
- a satisfaction form (an example is provided in **Appendix 4**, Satisfaction Form)

CONVENTIONS USED IN THIS MANUAL

Throughout this manual we've used the following typographic conventions:

indicates material that is intended for the group leader.

Depression can take many forms

indicates material that is intended for participants.

in the margin alerts the group leader that a handout should be distributed to the group at this time.

D **B** in the margin indicates that the following material is intended specifically for either depression or bipolar groups.

OUTLINE

Introductions and Overview

HANDOUTS

HANDOUT 1.1: Schedule for Eight-Session Group
HANDOUT 1.2: Major Depression — Overview
HANDOUT 1.3: Bipolar Disorder — Overview
HANDOUT 1.4: Cause (etiology) of Major Depression
[for depression group]
HANDOUT 1.5: Cause (etiology) of Bipolar Disorder
[for bipolar group]

GROUP 1
Introductions and Overview

LEGEND:		
B		Bipolar Group
D		Depression Group
		Handouts

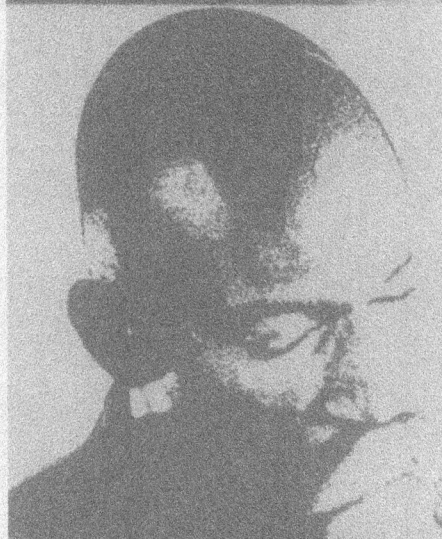

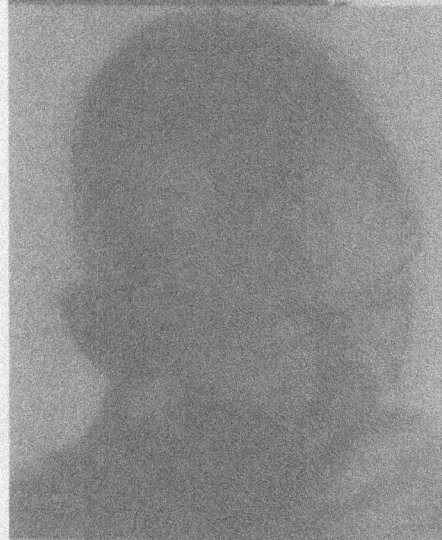

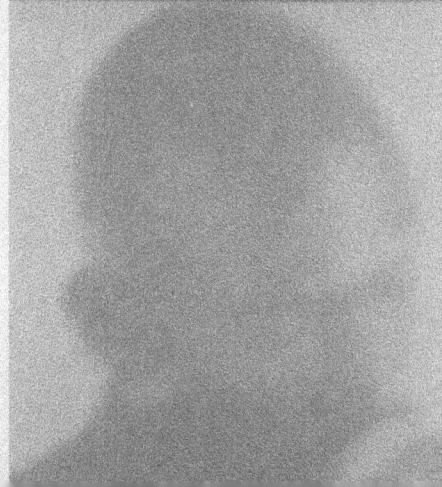

▶ Goals

- to review the format and content of the group series (already covered in the intake)
- to allow group members to meet one another and participate in warm-up exercises
- to provide a lecture/overview of mood disorders, either depression, bipolar or both, depending on the type of group.

▶ Leader's notes

This is the first of eight to 12 group sessions. This group will include introductions, including an introductory exercise for participants, and will begin to build group cohesion.

For many participants, this will be their first time meeting others who are in a similar situation, and some may express relief that there are others who understand what they have been experiencing. You will also present group format, rules and expectations at this time.

The second half of this session will be a lecture that provides an overview of the disorders, either depression or bipolar. A handout will be provided at the end.

This section is organized in three parts; Parts 1 and 2 apply to all groups, Part 3A (beginning on p. 11) is the overview for depression groups, Part 3B (beginning on p. 21) is the overview for bipolar groups.

Leaders' Introductions, Welcome and Preview of Group

Before beginning the session, ask everyone to wear a name tag with their first name printed on it to facilitate introductions.

INTRODUCTIONS

Introduce yourself to group members by providing an overview of your education and your experience with the disorder, and your role at the agency sponsoring the group.

WELCOME — THE VALUE OF A GROUP FORMAT

Groups that emphasize both support and education have been shown to be most effective in helping clients and their families cope with mood disorders. By including both information about the disorder and coping strategies, families can gain a greater sense of control.

The group setting emphasizes mutual learning and mutual support, and allows for the open expression of feelings associated with living with someone struggling with a mood disorder.

While it may not be possible to find solutions to every problem, the group will find answers to some issues. The group will also validate that much of what members are already doing is correct.

Group structure

Schedule of group meeting times and topics handed out at this time. Emphasize the importance of each topic, in order to stress the importance of participants taking good care of themselves, not just their relative.

Format: Groups meet for 90 minutes (or two hours) each week.

Format is a combination of information, exercises and group discussion. The early sessions will focus on education and later sessions will include more sharing of experiences and wisdom gained from living with the disorder. Group agendas will include practical ways of managing common situations. Participants are encouraged to ask questions and make comments throughout the series.

Handouts covering the topics will also be provided each week.

Distribute Handout 1.1, Schedule for Eight-Session Group, at this point.

Group rules

Confidentiality — Explain that group members should not divulge the names or any identifying information or personal information shared by other group members.

Punctuality — Advise that the group will always start and end on time. Reassure members that it is better to arrive late than to miss a group entirely.

Attendance — Explain that group members should call in advance if they are unable to attend.

Group interaction — Discuss the concept of respecting each member's personal level of openness. Address the fact that members will differ in their need to participate in group discussions, and different levels of openness are a natural part of the group process. Some people derive great benefit from simply listening rather than actively participating.

Group culture

Member's wisdom — Discuss the fact that although you will provide information about the disorder and coping strategies, the members themselves have a great deal of wisdom to share based on their experiences, and that members will also benefit from learning from one another.

Groups of this kind can be particularly valuable in that members can share support as they come to realize that sometimes these situations do not have solutions, but that they are doing everything possible to help their relative.

Sometimes the most valuable lessons learned will be twofold: the acceptance of a less-than-ideal situation and the coping skills to make the situation tolerable.

Differences — Explain that although group members may share many similar experiences, there may also be significant differences among their situations. Not all information will apply to all group members.

ICE-BREAKER EXERCISE

Ask group members to choose a partner whom they do not already know, and to take about five minutes each to interview one another. Advise them that they will be asked to present to the group three things about this person. It is helpful to write the three questions on a chalkboard or flipchart so that participants can refer to them.

Leaders might role-play this exercise by introducing each other, or by providing examples of possible answers to help participants get started.

The three questions

- Which member of their family has the disorder, and how long has he or she had it?
- What do they hope to take away from the group?
- What is something about them that has nothing to do with the disorder? (e.g., Mary likes mountain-climbing)

This ice-breaker exercise usually takes longer than anticipated because participants begin to talk to each other about their relative and might even begin to share what living with a mentally ill person has been like for them. Most people report that it is easier to talk to one person at first rather than the whole group.

When each person introduces his or her partner to the group, it should be within the framework of the three questions. Group leaders may then make some general comments about the common themes identified in the group introductions.

Overview of Mood Disorders

This overview provides basic information that may be expanded by the leader's own expertise. For further information, refer to the list of references on page 161.

INTRODUCTORY COMMENTS

The term depression is used both for a sad, despairing mood and for a psychiatric disorder. Everyone feels sad, down or blue at times, often following a disappointment, loss of a loved one or some other traumatic life event. Clinical depression, however, is much worse than simple unhappiness. It is one of the conditions collectively called "mood disorders." In this section we will discuss some of the factors that differentiate mood disorders from reactions commonly experienced during stress or bereavement (Bartha, C., Parker, C., Thomson, C., & Kitchen, K., 1999).

MOOD DISORDERS INCLUDE
- depression
- manic-depression or bipolar disorder
- anxiety (not covered in this series, but symptoms of anxiety can affect up to two-thirds of mood-disordered clients).

HISTORY OF MOOD DISORDERS

References to mood disorders are found throughout history. For example, the term melancholia (used to describe what we now call depression) dates back to the time of Hippocrates. Even though the descriptive terms have changed, the symptoms that are described have remained remarkably consistent over time.

Research into the causes of mood disorders, and into methods of treating them, is moving forward rapidly. Advances include a more complete understanding of the structure and biochemistry of the brain and the role of genetic factors, and the development of new medications and forms of psychotherapy for treating mood disorders.

Prevalence

Onset: Depression can occur at any point of the life cycle.

	Incidence (% of population)	
	Women	Men
Depression	15–25%	10–15%
Bipolar Disorder	1–2%	1–2%

D 11–19

Depression groups: see pages 11–19 for an overview of Depressive disorders.

B 21–29

Bipolar groups: see pages 21–29 for an overview of Bipolar disorder.

Group leaders should tell participants that, at the end of the group, they will be given handouts with this information, so they do not need to take notes.

THE DIAGNOSIS OF MAJOR DEPRESSION

Symptoms of a Major Depressive Episode

Depression can take many forms, and it often comes out of nowhere. The symptoms must last for at least two weeks, and must be present most days and last most of the day. Symptoms of depression in bipolar disorder include at least five of the following:

DEPRESSED MOOD
The mood state in depression differs substantially from normal sadness. In fact, many people with depression say they cannot feel sadness, and many people cannot cry when depressed. Being able to cry again often means the depression is improving.

MARKED LOSS OF INTEREST OR PLEASURE IN ACTIVITIES THAT USED TO BE FUN
When people have just begun to feel depressed or are mildly depressed, they can still enjoy things, and may also be distracted by pleasurable activities. When people are severely depressed, they lose these abilities.

WEIGHT LOSS OR WEIGHT GAIN
Many people lose weight when depressed, partly because they lose their appetite. However, one subgroup of patients feels hungrier, and may develop a craving for carbohydrate-rich and fatty foods. This results in weight gain. Metabolism may also increase or slow down, depending on the type of depression; such changes in metabolism can cause either weight loss or weight gain.

SLEEP PROBLEMS
Sleep disturbance is common in depression. Many people suffer from insomnia: they have trouble falling asleep, wake up often during the night or wake very early in the morning. People do not see sleep as being restful, and they may wake up feeling exhausted. Other people oversleep, especially during the day; they are said to have "hypersomnia."

APATHY OR AGITATION
Many people with depression develop slowed-down movement, speech or thinking. In severe cases, depressed people may be unable to move, speak or respond to their environment. In some people, the opposite happens, and they are very agitated. They are tormented by a severe inner restlessness — they cannot sit still, they pace, they may wring their hands. They may also show in other ways that they are agitated. Patients who feel agitated often feel very anxious, too.

LOSS OF ENERGY
Individuals with depression find it hard to complete everyday chores. It takes them longer to perform at work or at home because they lack energy and drive.

WORTHLESSNESS AND GUILT
When depressed, individuals may lack self-confidence. They may not assert themselves, and they may be overwhelmed by feelings of worthlessness. Many people cannot stop thinking about past events. They obsess about having let others down or having said the wrong things — and they feel very guilty. In severe cases, the guilt may cause delusions; that is, people feel sure that they have sinned and need to be punished for their wrongdoings. Or they may believe that God is punishing them for their past mistakes.

INABILITY TO CONCENTRATE OR DECIDE
These symptoms may be so bad that people cannot do simple tasks. They may have trouble deciding on very small matters.

SUICIDAL THOUGHTS
People with depression often think that life is not worth living or that they would be better off dead. The risk of acting upon these thoughts is high, and many people do try to commit suicide when depressed.

PSYCHOTIC SYMPTOMS
These may include false beliefs about poverty or punishment for past sins. People may believe that they have a deadly disease, such as cancer. They may also hear voices (auditory hallucinations) or may see things that do not exist (visual hallucinations).

Depressive symptoms also often include:
• severe anxiety
• worries about small matters
• complaints about physical symptoms, including pain
• many visits to the family doctor for various physical symptoms.

These symptoms are severe enough to make it difficult for the person to function. Severe depression may also include hallucinations or delusions.

Most people struggle for long periods with the symptoms before seeking mental health intervention. It is not uncommon for someone to have been depressed for many weeks, months or even years before he or she consults a family doctor or psychiatrist. Such individuals may not seek medical assistance because they fail to realize that they have a diagnosable disorder. They may have undergone several stressors, and try over time to discreetly manage their mood fluctuations. Many people seek help only when they experience serious difficulties coping at home, in the workplace or within important relationships.

A person may be diagnosed as having had a "single episode," meaning that this is the first time he or she has experienced a Major Depression, or "recurrent," meaning that the person has experienced at least one previous episode of Major Depression. Different episodes may vary in their severity — some episodes may be minor and have less impact on a person's ability to function, while others may be more severe and result in significant disruption to a person's life.

Major behavioural characteristics of depression

While it is important to understand how a diagnosis of depression is made, it is also important to understand what the disorder looks like to those living with the person wih depression.

The following are the major behavioural characteristics of depression:

NEGATIVE THINKING
People who are depressed tend to view people, events and themselves in an overwhelmingly negative manner (such as experiencing feelings of worthlessness or being a burden to family or friends; the inability to function at work or within the family; or feelings that the situation will never improve).

For people who were previously high-achievers or who had very high expectations of themselves, depression can be experienced as a tremendous failure.

DIFFICULTY IN CARRYING OUT NORMAL ACTIVITIES
Routine and straightforward tasks (such as daily child care, running errands, housekeeping, self-care and hygiene, getting to work, performing at work, paying bills, banking) are experienced as overwhelming and require excessive organization and concentration. Partners and relatives often assume these tasks while the person with depression is ill.

CHANGE IN EATING, SLEEPING AND ACTIVITY LEVELS
Changes in eating patterns directly affect weight gain or loss. People with depression may want to eat only one food type or will eat only whatever is available to avoid having to shop for food. Any physical changes experienced by people with depression can influence their self-esteem and body image.

A person who sleeps during the day may have difficulty settling and sleeping at night. The combination of a depressed mood, disrupted sleep and eating patterns can heavily influence a person's energy and activity levels.

SELF-ABSORPTION AND HEIGHTENED SENSITIVITY

Because they are experiencing such internal pain, individuals with depression may be much more sensitive to comments than when they are well. Family members may find that comments, or what is intended to be helpful advice, are met with anger, hostility and tears. Depressed people can experience feedback and suggestions as criticism, which they are not strong enough to hear.

Because their own internal pain is so overwhelming, people with depression often lack the ability to observe and be aware of other loved ones' stress and difficulties. As a result, people who are depressed may appear uncaring about others and quite demanding and controlling of family members' time and resources. These unrealistic expectations can create significant stress within a family.

INABILITY TO REACT TO FEEDBACK AND REASSURANCE

It is natural for family and friends to offer words of support and reassurance to the person with depression. Yet, the negative thinking and feelings of hopelessness of depression are very powerful. As a result, people with depression can rarely be talked out of their views, which are viewed through the "lens of depression." Offering support remains important, however, and loved ones should simply recognize that while words of support are essential, their relative may be unable to acknowledge or agree with such support.

DECREASED INTEREST IN SEX

Individuals with depression not only lose their interest in sex but also may shun other forms of physical intimacy such as hugging, kissing or touching. They may state that they no longer want the couple's relationship, which can be experienced as very rejecting by spouses and partners. However, this lack of interest in intimacy is a typical symptom of depression, and should not be viewed as a statement on the quality or nature of the partner's relationship. People who are severely depressed may view relationships in a very negative and distorted fashion, and as their mood improves, so does their ability to engage in relationships.

TYPES OF MAJOR DEPRESSIVE DISORDER

The following overview of classifications of subtypes will not apply to every group. You might briefly mention each one, but discuss only those of specific concern to group members. Or you may choose to address only specific questions from group members.

Atypical Depression

People with atypical symptoms also share the general features of Major Depression, but they tend to struggle more with overeating and oversleeping. Evening tends to be the most difficult time of the day. While a person with typical symptoms is generally unresponsive, atypical depression is characterized by "mood reactivity." This means that a person is able to respond positively to something good or a pleasurable event, such as a visit from a relative, but will quickly become depressed again when the source of this pleasure disappears.

Depression with Melancholic Features

This designation applies if, in addition to meeting the requirements for a Major Depression diagnosis, the person has the following features:

SYMPTOMS
- low mood, which the person experiences as the primary symptom, and that does not let up, even with usually pleasurable activities
- depression that is usually worse in the morning
- early-morning awakening
- significant lack of appetite, or weight loss
- excessive or inappropriate guilt
- marked psychomotor agitation or retardation.

Postpartum Depression

The onset of the Major Depressive symptoms occurs within four weeks of the birth of a child. Postpartum depression is now becoming better understood and can affect up to 13 per cent of women who have recently given birth. Situational factors can exacerbate this type of depression, such as having few supports to help care for the baby, being a single parent, poverty, and so on.

Seasonal Affective Disorder (SAD)

Depression that occurs at a particular time of year, usually during the fall and winter, with the symptoms improving during the spring and summer. While medications are effective in treating this type of depression, light therapy is also a good intervention.

Additional subtypes

Other ways in which a Major Depression may be described by the doctor include the following:

Major Depression with Psychotic Features

A depression in which delusions or hallucinations are also present.

Hallucinations — perceptual distortions where the person is seeing things or hearing voices that do not really exist.

Delusions — distortions or exaggerations of inferential thinking, where the person may develop beliefs that are not grounded in reality (paranoid delusions that the CIA is spying on the person or that the television is communicating with him or her).

OTHER DEPRESSIVE DIAGNOSES

Although most group members' relatives have likely been diagnosed as having Major Depression, it might be helpful to know about the other types of depressions.

Dysthymia

How is it different from Major Depression? Major Depression is characterized by one or more episodes of extremely low mood. Dysthymia is a more chronic condition. The person exhibits some of the more moderate symptoms of depression such as poor appetite or overeating, inability to sleep or sleeping too much, low energy or fatigue, low self-esteem, poor concentration, difficulty making decisions and feelings of helplessness, but he or she usually can maintain some of the normal life roles. However, the low mood can persist for years.

A person may have dysthymia and then suffer a major depressive episode. This is known as double depression.

Depression Secondary to Medical Illness

Symptoms of depression are present, and there is evidence that it is directly caused by a specific medical condition. For example, clients who have had cardiac intervention, been diagnosed with cancer or have a chronic, debilitating physical illness may develop a secondary depression that requires treatment.

Substance-Induced Depression

Alcohol, street drugs and some prescription medications can provide temporary relief from some of the symptoms of depression. This "self-medication" simply masks — and sometimes worsens — the symptoms of depression, which resurface when the substance abuse ends.

In other cases, depression can be triggered by the abuse of alcohol and other drugs. In both instances, ongoing abuse can lead to further health problems and disrupt a person's ability to function in some or all areas of his or her life. Usually, treatment of the substance abuse is provided first, and then if the depression persists, the mood disorder becomes the focus of intervention.

THEORIES OF WHAT CAUSES DEPRESSION (THE ETIOLOGY OF DEPRESSION)

No one cause

In general, there is no single cause of depression in all people suffering from the disorder. As a result, it is important to consider all genetic, biological, psychological and sociological factors. Some individuals may be at higher risk of developing a depression as they have several risk factors present, while others may be at substantially lower risk as only one risk factor is present.

1. GENETICS AND FAMILY HISTORY

A family history of depression does not necessarily mean that children or other relatives will develop a major depression. However, those with a family history have a slightly higher chance of becoming depressed at some stage of their lives. There are several theories to explain this phenomenon.

Genetic research suggests that depression can run in families. Studies of twins raised separately have shown that if one twin develops the disorder, the other has a 40 to 50 per cent chance of also being affected. This rate, though moderate, suggests that some people may have a genetic predisposition to developing depression.

A genetic predisposition alone, however, is unlikely to cause depression. Other factors, such as a traumatic childhood or adult life events, may act as triggers. The onset of depression may also be influenced by what we learn as children. Some people may have been raised by parents struggling with depression and learned to use these strategies to cope with their own life stressors. Growing up with one parent who has been depressed puts a child at a 10 per cent risk of developing the disorder. If both parents are depressed, this figure rises to 30 per cent. *It is important to note that these figures are actually lower than those for other types of illnesses that may be passed on from parent to child. It is also important to know that there are protective strategies that can be implemented to build resiliency in children being raised by a parent struggling with depression (see Group 4).*

2. BRAIN CHEMISTRY AND PHYSIOLOGICAL CHANGES IN THE BODY

Depression may arise following unusual physiological changes such as childbirth and viral or other infections. This has given rise to the theory that hormonal or chemical imbalances in the brain may cause depression. Studies have shown that differences exist in the levels of certain biochemicals (serotonin, norepinephrine) between subjects who are depressed and those who are not. These neurotransmitters, which are the messengers that send signals among brain cells, start the complex chemical interactions that influence behaviour, feelings and thoughts.

The fact that depression can be treated with medication and electroconvulsive therapy (ECT) tends to support this theory.

3. LIFE EVENTS

Environmental stressors, either in childhood or adulthood, can contribute to the onset of a depression. Some studies suggest that early childhood trauma and losses, such as the death or separation of parents, or adult events, such as the death of a partner or child or loss of a job, can be precursors to a depressive episode. Suffering several severe and prolonged difficult life events increases a person's chances of developing a depressive disorder.

Living with chronic family stress can also seriously affect a person's mood and lead to depressive symptoms. People living in emotionally abusive or violent relationships can feel trapped, both financially and emotionally, and feel hopeless about their future. This is particularly true of mothers with young children.

Once a person develops a serious depression, he or she may need intensive treatment before feeling able to deal with the situation or life stressors that triggered the onset of the illness.

4. PSYCHOLOGICAL CHARACTERISTICS

We all have certain personality traits and psychological vulnerabilities that are the result of inborn temperament and environmental influences. For some individuals, regardless of why they developed characteristics, the characteristics themselves may serve as protective or risk factors to developing depression later in life.

- People at greater risk of experiencing depression include those who have low self-esteem or are self-critical.
- People who tend to hide their feelings, internalize their problems and have difficulty expressing negative emotions (such as anger or distress) are at greater risk.
- People who are perfectionists, tend to be highly dependent on others and have difficulty forming relationships that can provide social support, also tend to be at greater risk.
- People who are more flexible and expressive, have a wide range of coping strategies, and have established a network of social supports, are less likely, but not entirely protected, against depression. If a person has a family history and suffers several overwhelming life events, he or she may still experience depression.

It is the combination of factors, as expressed by the stress vulnerability model, that best explains why some people facing adversity develop depression while others do not. In general, the more of the possible causes that are present, the greater the risk that a person may develop a clinical depression.

A Family History + **High** + **Few Social** = **Greater Chance of Developing**
of Depression **Stress** **Supports** **Major Depression**

CONCERNS FOR THE FAMILY

Denial

Some people with depression worry that admitting to their depressed feelings is a sign of weakness, or that they will be stigmatized for having psychiatric problems. Others try to cope on their own and do not realize until they are acutely depressed that they have a disorder that can be treated.

Discontinuing treatment

Once stabilized, the family will likely observe their relative make slow but steady improvement. Over time, he or she may want to discontinue the medication, because of the side-effects, or cease attending psychotherapy, because of the time commitment.

Resistance to lifestyle changes

Some people rush into a full schedule of activities to prove to themselves and others that they are fully recovered. This "flight into health" leaves them feeling both overwhelmed and exhausted.

Group leaders should distribute Handouts 1.2 and 1.4, Major Depression — Overview and Cause (etiology) of Major Depression, at this point.

Overview of Bipolar Disorder

➤

Group leaders should tell participants that, at the end of the group, they will be given handouts with this information, so they do not need to take notes.

WHAT IS BIPOLAR DISORDER?

Bipolar disorder is a medical condition in which people experience mood swings that are out of proportion or totally unrelated to events in their lives. These mood swings consist of both depressive (low moods) and manic (high, euphoric moods). The depressive moods resemble those of major depressive episodes.

These swings not only affect mood but also thought, behaviour and functioning. Bipolar disorder is not the individual's fault, nor is it the result of a "weak" or unstable personality. It is a medical disorder, for which there are treatments that help most people.

Onset

The first signs of bipolar disorder are typically recognized in adolescence or early adulthood. The younger the person is when he or she first develops bipolar disorder, the less typical the symptoms may be. In adolescents the symptoms may be attributed to normal teenage distress or rebellion. For this reason, bipolar disorder is often not diagnosed until adulthood.

A person may, however, have a first episode of bipolar disorder in his or her forties or fifties. Bipolar disorder affects approximately one per cent of the population.

SYMPTOMS OF BIPOLAR DISORDER

Bipolar disorder includes three major symptom groups: mania, hypomania and depression.

1. MANIA

Sometimes, a person may seem abnormally and continuously high, irritable or expansive for at least one week. If this change in mood is accompanied by other symptoms (see below) the person may be in a manic phase of the bipolar illness. Not everybody who enters a manic phase feels happy or euphoric. Instead, a person may feel very irritable, or may be terribly angry, disruptive and aggressive.

People in a manic phase do not just have mood symptoms. They must have at least three of the following symptoms to an important degree:

EXAGGERATED SELF-ESTEEM OR FEELING OF GRANDEUR

People feel invincible or all powerful; they believe they understand "how the world works" or how to save it. They may feel they have a special mission in life (that is, God has sent them or given them special powers).

LESS NEED FOR SLEEP

People feel rested after just a few hours of sleep. Sometimes they may not sleep at all for a few days or even weeks.

INCREASED TALKING

People may talk very quickly, too loudly and much more than usual. They may like to tell jokes or rhyme words and may become angry when interrupted. They may keep switching topics and cannot converse properly with others.

FLIGHT OF IDEAS OR RACING THOUGHTS

People easily lose their train of thought and have trouble interacting because they are easily distracted. They may be impatient with others who cannot follow their fast thinking and changing plans and ideas.

SPEEDED-UP ACTIVITY

People may socialize more than usual at work or school, or may be much more active, with seemingly boundless energy. In the early manic phase, they may be productive, but as symptoms worsen, people are more frantic in their activities and start but do not finish many projects.

POOR JUDGMENT

People may not be able to control or plan how they act. They may take part in unusual and risky activities without realizing harmful consequences (e.g., shopping sprees, bad business choices and bad decisions). They may feel more sexual, become more sexually active and take less care in choosing their sexual partners. This increased sexual activity may lead to unwanted pregnancies, sexually transmitted diseases, guilt and disrupted relationships.

PSYCHOTIC SYMPTOMS

People may experience delusions, or beliefs that are not based in reality. They may hallucinate — most often, they hear voices.

The symptoms of hypomania are less severe than those of mania but may still be disruptive. People may feel happy and have lots of energy but do not usually get into serious trouble. Hypomania may progress to a full-blown manic episode or a severe depression, and therefore needs treatment.

What mania looks like in an individual

People displaying symptoms of mania can present as highly irritable and impatient with those around them.

They may make impulsive, hurtful and rejecting statements or engage in impulsive, even dangerous, behaviour.

Mania causes people to be highly reactive and emotional. For people who have poor anger management skills or frustration tolerance, this can lead to violent behaviour.

2. HYPOMANIA (HYPOMANIC EPISODE)

While the symptoms of hypomania are less severe than those of mania, they can interfere with the person's ability to function in a variety of roles. Historically, hypomania was viewed as a minor condition. More recently, it has been acknowledged as having more impact on a person's life and relationships than was previously recognized.

3. DEPRESSIVE EPISODE

Depression can take many forms, and it often comes out of nowhere. The symptoms must last for at least two weeks and must be present most days and last most of the day. Symptoms of depression in bipolar disorder include at least five of the following:

Depressed mood
The mood state in depression differs substantially from normal sadness. In fact, many people with depression say they cannot feel sadness, and many people cannot cry when depressed. Being able to cry again often means the depression is improving.

Marked loss of interest or pleasure in activities that used to be fun
When people have just begun to feel depressed or are mildly depressed, they can still enjoy things and may also be distracted by pleasurable activities. When people are severely depressed, they lose these abilities.

Weight loss or weight gain

Many people lose weight when depressed, partly because they lose their appetite. However, one subgroup of patients feels hungrier and may develop a craving for carbohydrate-rich and fatty foods. This results in weight gain. Metabolism may also increase or slow down, depending on the type of depression; such changes in metabolism can cause either weight loss or weight gain.

Sleep problems

Sleep disturbance is common in depression. Many people suffer from insomnia: they have trouble falling asleep, wake up often during the night or wake very early in the morning. People with depression do not see sleep as being restful, and they may wake up feeling exhausted. Other people oversleep, especially during the day; they are said to have "hypersomnia."

Apathy or agitation

Many people with depression develop slowed-down movement, speech or thinking. In severe cases, they may be unable to move, speak or respond to their environment. In some people, the opposite happens, and they are very agitated. They are tormented by a severe inner restlessness — they cannot sit still, they pace, they may wring their hands. They may also show in other ways that they are agitated. Patients who feel agitated often feel very anxious, too.

Loss of energy

Individuals with depression find it hard to complete everyday chores. It takes them longer to perform at work or at home because they lack energy and drive.

Worthlessness and guilt

When depressed, individuals may lack self-confidence. They may not assert themselves, and they may be overwhelmed by feelings of worthlessness. Many people cannot stop thinking about past events. They obsess about having let others down or having said the wrong things — and they feel very guilty. In severe cases, the guilt may cause delusions; that is, people feel sure that they have sinned and need to be punished for their wrongdoings. Or they may believe that God is punishing them for their past mistakes.

Inability to concentrate or decide

These symptoms may be so bad that people cannot do simple tasks. They may have trouble deciding on very small matters.

Suicidal thoughts

People with depression often think that life is not worth living or that they would be better off dead. The risk of acting upon these thoughts is high, and many people do try to commit suicide when depressed.

Psychotic symptoms

These may include false beliefs about poverty or punishment for past sins. People with psychotic symptoms may believe that they have a deadly disease, such as cancer. They may also hear voices (auditory hallucinations) or may see things that do not exist (visual hallucinations).

Depressive symptoms also often include:

- severe anxiety
- worries about small matters
- complaints about physical symptoms, including pain
- many visits to the family doctor for various physical symptoms.

What depression looks like in an individual

While it is important to recognize the major symptoms of depression, it is also important to understand how the disorder appears to those living with the person with depression.

The following are the major behavioural characteristics of depression that family members and friends may observe.

Negative thinking

People who are depressed tend to view other people, events and themselves in an overwhelmingly negative manner (such as experiencing feelings of worthlessness or being a burden to family or friends; the inability to function at work or to parent effectively; and a belief that the situation will never improve).

For people who were previously high-achievers or who had very high expectations of themselves, depression can be experienced as a tremendous failure.

Inability to function in normal roles

Routine and straightforward tasks (such as daily child care, running errands, housekeeping, self-care and hygiene, getting to work, performing at work, paying bills, banking) are experienced as overwhelming and require excessive organization and concentration. Partners and relatives often assume these tasks while the depressed person is ill.

Change in eating, sleeping and activity levels

Changes in eating patterns directly affect weight gain or loss. People with depression may want to eat only one food type or will eat only whatever is available to avoid having to shop for food. Any physical changes experienced by a person with depression can influence his or her self-esteem and body image.

A person who sleeps during the day may have difficulty settling and sleeping at night. The combination of a depressed mood, disrupted sleep and eating patterns can heavily influence a person's energy and activity level.

SELF-ABSORPTION AND HEIGHTENED SENSITIVITY

Because they are experiencing such internal pain, individuals with depression may be much more sensitive to comments than when they are well. Family members may find that comments, or what is intended to be helpful advice, are met with anger, hostility and tears. Depressed people can experience feedback and suggestions as criticism, which they are not strong enough to hear.

Because their own internal pain is so overwhelming, people with depression often lack the ability to observe and be aware of other loved ones' stress and difficulties. As a result, people who are depressed may appear uncaring about others and quite demanding and controlling of family members' time and resources. These unrealistic expectations can create significant stress within a family.

INABILITY TO REACT TO REASSURANCE, SUPPORT, FEEDBACK OR SYMPATHY

It is natural for family and friends to offer words of support and reassurance to the person with depression. Yet, the negative thinking and feelings of hopelessness of depression are very powerful. As a result, people with depression can rarely be talked out of their views, which are viewed through the "lens of depression." Offering support remains important, however, and loved ones should simply recognize that, while words of support are essential, their relative may be unable to acknowledge or agree with such support.

DECREASED INTEREST IN SEX

Individuals with depression not only lose their interest in sex but also may shun other forms of physical intimacy such as hugging, kissing or touching. They may state that they no longer want the couple's relationship, which can be experienced as very rejecting by spouses and partners. However, this lack of interest in intimacy is a typical symptom of depression and should not be viewed as a statement on the quality or nature of the partner's relationship. People who are severely depressed may view relationships in a very negative and distorted fashion, and as their mood improves, so does their ability to engage in relationships.

Other symptoms that may occur during a bipolar episode

Up to 25 per cent of depressed clients with bipolar disorder and up to 28 per cent of manic clients may exhibit motor abnormalities during their episodes. These motor abnormalities are called "catatonic symptoms" and include a wide variety of symptoms such as extreme motor excitement or psychomotor retardation, bizarre movements or postures, or abnormalities in gestures and speech. Catatonic symptoms in mania are mostly restricted to mixed episodes and usually characterize particularly severe episodes. Catatonic symptoms remit completely after specific treatment.

TYPES OF BIPOLAR DISORDER

Some people experience manic or mixed, depressed and well phases during their illness. Such people are said to have "Bipolar-I" disorder. A milder form of mania is called "hypomania." People who have hypomania, depression and intervals without symptoms, but no full manic phases, are said to have "Bipolar-II" disorder.

Order and frequency of the various states

The manic/hypomanic, mixed and depressive states usually do not occur in a certain order, and their frequency cannot be predicted. For many people there are years between each episode, whereas others suffer more frequent episodes. Over a lifetime, the average person with bipolar illness experiences about 10 episodes of depression and mania/hypomania or mixed states. As the person ages, the episodes of illness come closer together. Untreated manias often last for two to three months. Untreated depressions usually last longer, between four and six months.

Rapid cycling

In about 20 per cent of cases, patients have four or more (sometimes many more) episodes a year and have short phases without symptoms. Patients with four or more episodes a year are said to be having rapid cycling, which is a subtype of bipolar disorder that needs specific treatment. We don't know for certain what causes rapid cycling. Sometimes, its course may be triggered by certain antidepressants, but how the antidepressant causes rapid cycling is not clear. Sometimes stopping the antidepressant may help the patient to return to a "normal" cycling pattern.

THEORIES OF WHAT CAUSES BIPOLAR DISORDER (THE ETIOLOGY OF BIPOLAR DISORDER)

The precise cause of bipolar disorder is not known. However, research shows that genes play a strong role.

Genes are the blueprint for all cells and their contents. Scientists thus believe that changes to genes can lead to faulty proteins being produced within brain cells. These faulty proteins may then result in bipolar disorder. Researchers today are looking at various proteins that may be affected in bipolar disorder. These include:

- proteins such as those involved in making chemicals in the brain called neurotransmitters
- proteins that use neurotransmitters to make the cell do something
- genes themselves.

We do know that too much stress or difficult family relationships do not cause the illness. However, these factors may "trigger" an episode in someone who already has the illness. Nor is bipolar illness a simple imbalance of neurotransmitters, such as serotonin or dopamine. Yet neurotransmitters may be affected during a flare-up of the illness.

What is a "trigger" for a bipolar episode?

Not all episodes can be related to any particular trigger, but many can. Triggers are situations that can provoke either mania or depression in someone who has already has a genetic vulnerability. Feeling very stressed or continually losing sleep is an example of this kind of trigger. Other triggers are chemical and include antidepressants that work "too well" and result in mania; common medications, such as steroids (for instance, prednisone used for treating asthma, arthritis, etc.); and street drugs, such as cocaine and amphetamines.

THE IMPORTANCE OF EARLY DIAGNOSIS AND TREATMENT

Early diagnosis, proper treatment and the right medication can help people avoid the following:

SUICIDE
The risk is highest in the earlier years of the illness. Suicidal thinking is a symptom of a mood disorder; it is a temporary emotional state. When properly treated, thoughts of self-harm will pass, and the person will return to more balanced thinking.

ALCOHOL/SUBSTANCE ABUSE
More than 50 per cent of those with bipolar disorder abuse alcohol or drugs during their illness.

Alcohol, street drugs and some prescription medications can provide temporary relief from some of the symptoms of depression. This "self-medication" simply masks — and sometimes worsens — the symptoms of depression, which then resurface when the substance abuse ends.

Conversely, when experiencing mania, people may engage in pleasurable activities, consume far more alcohol or experiment with street drugs in ways that are uncharacteristic for them. Such behaviour can lead to serious complications in their work and personal lives.

MARITAL OR WORK PROBLEMS
The likelihood of a person maintaining stable relationships and functioning productively at work or school is significantly higher if bipolar disorder is treated early.

TREATMENT DIFFICULTIES

There is some evidence that the more mood episodes a person has, the harder it is to treat each subsequent episode, and the more frequent the episodes may become.

Group leaders should distribute Handouts 1.3 and 1.5, Bipolar Disorder — Overview and Cause (etiology) of Bipolar Disorder, here.

OUTLINE

HANDOUTS

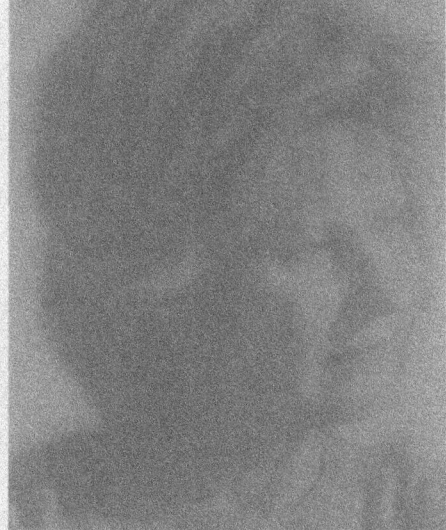

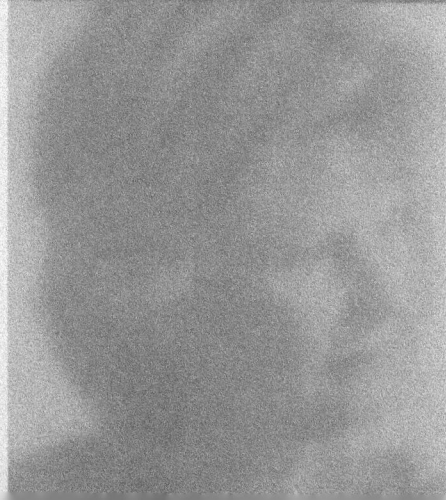

GROUP 2
Medical and Psychosocial Treatments

LEGEND:

B	Bipolar Group
D	Depression Group
◢	Handouts

▶ Goal

The goal of Group 2 is to provide information about treatments available for the disorder, including medications and psychosocial treatments.

▶ Leader's notes

The treatment information presented in this group is usually of great interest to families. It is important to emphasize that the purpose of this information is to empower family members with knowledge to support their ill relative in treatment — but not to enforce the treatment. Family members cannot be responsible for treatment compliance; this theme should be reinforced throughout the series.

This section is organized in two parts:
Section 1a (beginning on p. 35) includes the information regarding medications/treatments that should be covered in Depression groups; Section 1b (beginning on p. 41) is the medication/treatment content for Bipolar groups.
Section 2 (beginning on p. 49) covers psychosocial interventions for both disorders.

Instructions to guest lecturer

The guest lecturer should be asked to present a brief overview of the material included in this section and spend the rest of the session answering questions posed by participants. This can be a very popular session, as this will be the first opportunity for many group members to ask specific questions about medication treatment.

The overview presented below is intended to serve as a guide; material may be adapted/modified depending on the orientation and style of the speaker.

Group leaders should be mindful of time constraints and help to guide the discussion to ensure that all topic areas are covered.

Depression groups: Go to Section 1a: Medical Treatments — Depression (pp. 35–40) and then cover Section 2: Psychosocial Treatment Options (pp. 49–53)

D 35–40

Bipolar groups: Go to Section 1b: Medical Treatments — Bipolar Disorder (pp. 41–47) and then cover Section 2: Psychosocial Treatment Options (pp. 49–53)

B 41–47

Medical Treatments — Depression

Distribute Handout 2.1, The Use of Medications in the Treatment of Depression

HISTORY OF MEDICATIONS

In the 1950s, physicians discovered that Iproniazid® , a drug used to treat tuberculosis, also elevated clients' moods. Iproniazid is a member of the MAOI (monoamine oxidase inhibitors) family of antidepressants, which act by boosting neurotransmitters. Neurotransmitters are chemicals in the brain that allow cells to communicate with one another, and in some cases regulate moods.

Research has revealed that depressed clients do not have enough of the neurotransmitter serotonin, and that helping the brain to produce more serotonin seems to lessen depression. The brain, however, is a highly complex organ, and serotonin is only one of over 500 neurotransmitters. More research is needed to discover how brain chemistry contributes to depression.

On their own, or in combination with psychotherapy, medications can be highly effective. With early intervention, medications can prevent people from developing severe depression and preserve their coping skills.

Medication in the treatment of severe depression can relieve symptoms and elevate people's mood to the point where they can engage in "talk therapy" and begin to address some of the issues that may have contributed to the onset of their depression.

CATEGORIES OF MEDICATIONS (MAOIS, CYCLICS, NEWER AGENTS)

MAOIs

Monoamine oxidase inhibitors include such medications as phenelzine (Nardil®) and tranyicypromine (Parnate®).

MAOIs were the first class of antidepressants. MAOIs block the action of monoamine oxidase, an enzyme that breaks down some neurotransmitters in the brain. By blocking this enzyme breakdown, MAOIs increase the number and availability of neurotransmitters, which are helpful in the treatment of depression. MAOIs are still prescribed, often for the treatment of atypical depression.

This type of medication may not be initially prescribed because MAOIs affect a person's ability to digest and process foods that contain tyramine — foods such as aged and fermented cheeses, smoked meats and some beer. In large quantities, tyramine can be toxic and may lead to dangerous increases in blood pressure. The MAO enzyme protects us from tyramine. Because MAOI drugs inhibit the action of MAO, clients taking these drugs must avoid such foods.

CYCLICS

The second group of drugs developed were cyclics or tricyclic antidepressants. Cyclics include such medications as amitriptyline (Elavil®), maprotiline (Ludiomil®) and imipramine (Tofranil®).

Because these drugs can induce weight gain, tend to be more sedating and have more anti-cholinergic side-effects (such as dry mouth, constipation, difficulty urinating, blurry vision), they may not be used in the initial treatment of depression. Instead, physicians typically look to the newer agents that have fewer side-effects.

The newer agents

SSRIs

SSRIs are specific serotonin reuptake inhibitors such as fluoxetine (Prozac®), paroxetine (Paxil®), fluvoxemine (Luvox®) and sertraline (Zoloft®).

These drugs are often the first choice for treatment. They generally do not cause anticholinergic side-effects and are better tolerated. Initially, clients may experience some nausea, stomach upset, headaches and reduced sexual functioning. Other clients can develop long-standing sleep difficulties; however, for 70 to 80 per cent of people, these drugs significantly improve their depressed mood.

OTHER CLASSES OF NEWER DRUGS

A number of new drugs have proven effective in treating depression; however, they do not fit into any one category because they affect several different systems in the brain. These drugs include venlafaxine (Effexor®), buproprion (Wellbutrin®), moclobemide (Manerix®) and nefaxodone (Serzone®).

DRUG TRIALS

Unlike other medications, antidepressants take a long time to be effective. A drug trial generally takes six to eight weeks, and in some cases longer.

How does a physician decide which medication to use?

Interestingly, there is no difference in the efficacy of each category of drug; they all have an equally good chance of working for a client. When assessing a client for medication treatment, a physician will choose the medication with the least side-effects in order to prevent the client from prematurely discontinuing treatment. Given that a medication trial can be six to eight weeks, clients will experience side-effects first and symptom relief later. If side-effects are intolerable, clients will stop taking the drug before deriving any benefits and will likely remain depressed longer.

A second major factor is the physician's experience with certain medications. If a doctor has observed 10 clients who respond well to Prozac® or Zoloft®, he or she is likely to choose these drugs first.

A third issue may be cost. While new drugs are always coming on the market, they may be very expensive. An older medication may be just as effective and less costly to the client.

When the first medication tried does not work

For some clients, the first medication tried may result in a minimal or partial response. This means that their symptoms have improved somewhat, but they still struggle with a depressed mood. In these cases, a physician may push the prescribed dosage to the highest tolerable level to maximize its effect. This is called optimization.

In other instances, a physician may augment or boost the effects of the first medication with a second drug. The combined effect is often better than each drug alone.

Given the many different antidepressants available, there are various combinations available to physicians and clients, and it is not unusual for clients to try several different drugs or drug combinations before finding an approach that works for them.

What are the implications of the client stopping medication without consulting the doctor?

Typically, clients will discontinue their medications either because they are experiencing intolerable side-effects, they are impatient with the length of time it takes to feel better or they feel being on medication is a sign of personal weakness. It is not uncommon for family and friends who are unfamiliar with antidepressant treatment to question or criticize someone for taking prescribed medication.

Abruptly stopping antidepressant medication is unwise, because sudden stoppage can lead to unpleasant side-effects and possibly a poorer response to subsequent medications.

Consulting with the treating physician may lead to some additional strategies that can minimize the annoying side-effects, or a new treatment approach altogether.

It is also important that clients/families receive education about the nature and use of medication to overcome any negative attitudes that may compromise effective treatment. Clients should be encouraged to ask questions and read about depression and its various treatments. Self-help support groups can also help people achieve better compliance with treatment, as they feel less alone and more supported.

ELECTROCONVULSIVE THERAPY (ECT) FOR DEPRESSION

Electroconvulsive therapy (ECT) is perhaps the most controversial and misunderstood of psychiatric treatments, due in part to sensationalized and misleading depictions of the treatment in the popular media. In fact, ECT is a highly effective and safe treatment for depression and is sometimes used as a long-term "maintenance" treatment to prevent recurrence of illness after recovery.

Procedure

ECT involves administering a brief electrical stimulus through the scalp to the surface of the brain. This stimulus produces an epileptic-type convulsion, lasting typically from 15 seconds to two minutes.

During the treatment, a team of psychiatrist, anaesthetist and one or more nurses are present. The patient is given an anaesthetic intravenously to put him or her to sleep briefly during the treatment. A muscle relaxant is also given to prevent physical injury, by lessening the intensity of muscle spasms that accompany a seizure. Oxygen is administered, and heart rate and blood pressure are monitored. Although the anaesthetic lasts only a few minutes, patients feel groggy after an ECT treatment and may rest or sleep for about one hour.

Usually the treatments are administered three times a week over three to four weeks, for a total of eight to 12 treatments. For longer-term maintenance treatment, the treatments may be spread out, for example, once a month, and continued for as long as the patient and doctor feel is appropriate. ECT is usually given to hospitalized inpatients, but outpatients can receive ECT as well.

Side-effects

Patients may have a headache or jaw pain on awakening after ECT, usually requiring only a mild painkiller such as acetaminophen (Tylenol®). Some loss of recent memory or problems with concentration usually occur during treatment (for example, patients may not recall what they had for supper the night before the treatment), but these symptoms improve quickly, over a few weeks, after the course of ECT is finished. Some patients report mild memory problems persisting much longer after ECT, but this is likely due to their depression not the treatment.

ECT can be given bilaterally (the electric current is applied to both sides of the brain) or unilaterally (on only the right side of the brain). Although bilateral ECT causes more memory disruption than unilateral ECT, it is also somewhat more effective and is usually the preferred choice.

Uses of ECT in depression

ECT is the most effective, and possibly the fastest-acting treatment for severe depression, and is particularly helpful for highly agitated or suicidal patients or those with psychotic or catatonic symptoms. Some patients receive ECT early in their episode of illness because of the urgency of their situation or their particular symptoms, while others may prefer to use ECT only after various medications have failed. ECT works well for severe mania as well.

While ECT is highly effective at ending an episode of depression, the benefits may not last more than a few weeks or months following treatment. Therefore, patients usually start or continue treatment with other medications following a course of ECT. Maintenance ECT can be used in cases where medications have not prevented recurrence of illness or are intolerable due to side-effects.

RELAPSE PREVENTION

Learning about and understanding the risk factors that contribute to relapse is an important part of the treatment of depression and preserving health after recovery. Stressors that may contribute to the onset of depression, abrupt discontinuation of treatment and lack of support from family and friends may all be factors that must be managed to avert relapse.

The management of treatment-resistant or refractory depression

This is a significant challenge for clients and families and requires a multi-faceted approach:

- medications, supportive therapy and longer-term psychotherapy
- occupational therapy for activities of daily living/functional assessments/vocational issues

- family support and education
- realistic expectations — redefining goals that are still meaningful but achievable.

ALTERNATIVE THERAPIES

Many people are becoming increasingly interested in using herbal or alternative remedies to treat depression. Clinical trials in Europe have found St. John's wort to be an effective treatment of mild depression. However, research has been limited, and it is not easy to get information about the effectiveness of this and other herbal treatments. In North America, there is the additional problem that the herbal industry is unregulated. This means that over-the-counter herbal remedies vary widely in consistency among manufacturers. If you are interested in herbal remedies, it is important to talk to your doctor. It is helpful to have a doctor who is knowledgeable about alternative therapies, because these herbs can interact with other medications.

Many people also benefit from relaxation techniques and stress management strategies. Others find massage and acupuncture helpful in dealing with some of the symptoms, such as anxiety, associated with depression.

Medical Treatments — Bipolar Disorder

Distribute Handout 2.2, The Use of Medications in the Treatment of Bipolar Disorder

HISTORY OF MEDICATIONS

Lithium, a mood stabilizer, was discovered in the 1800s for general medical use and was viewed as a panacea to treat all types of ailments and disorders. It was later applied to psychiatry in the 1880s. In those pre-scientific days, physicians and doctors were unaware of the dangers of lithium toxicity, and some people became ill. Between the 1880s and 1950s, lithium was discarded as a treatment for all disorders, and other mood stabilizers were developed in the 1970s and 1980s. Interestingly, during the time of the American Civil War, a physician treating people with mood disorders noted that lithium seemed to be effective in the treatment of bipolar disorder, but he later dropped the drug's usage. In recent years, with the advent of medication trials and the recognition that drugs must be monitored in order to keep them at therapeutic levels and not toxic levels, lithium has returned as a treatment of choice in bipolar disorder.

HOW IS BIPOLAR DISORDER TREATED?

Bipolar disorder is treated in several stages:

ACUTE TREATMENT PHASE
The focus is on treating the current manic, hypomanic or mixed episode.

PREVENTIVE TREATMENT PHASE
The focus is on preventing future episodes.

What are the components of treatment?

Medication: prescribed for nearly all clients during acute and preventive phases.

Education: Psychoeducation — a specific term for health education for psychiatric illnesses — should be considered a routine treatment for all new clients and is often helpful periodically through the illness. Psychoeducation involves teaching about the causes of the illness, its treatment, how to self-manage the illness (at least to some extent) and how to prevent future episodes.

Psychotherapy: Psychotherapy is a very helpful treatment — but as an addition to medications, not a substitute. Every client should receive some supportive therapy, which involves not only medication management but also attention to the various problems that a person with bipolar disorder may experience.

CATEGORIES OF MEDICATIONS

Mood stabilizers

Mood stabilizers are medicines that help to reduce the oscillation of abnormal moods and help prevent fresh mood episodes.

1. Lithium, a naturally occurring salt, is the most studied. Lithium has been used for 50 years and still plays a major role in bipolar disorder.

2. Carbamazepine, an anticonvulsant, was also discovered to be a mood stabilizer in the 1970s, and is used occasionally.

3. Valproic acid (also including its various forms of sodium valproate and divalproex sodium) is another anticonvulsant that has become widely used in the 1990s as a mood stabilizer. It is widely used because many doctors believe that it has a broader range of activity and fewer side-effects than lithium, although it is not necessarily "better" than lithium.

Antipsychotic medications

Antipsychotic medication is commonly used in bipolar disorder, both for rapid control of mania (as a powerful sedative) and for the treatment of psychotic symptoms such as delusions of grandeur or persecution, and hallucinations. Traditional antipsychotics can also prevent new attacks of mania, but long-term use is associated with serious side-effects such as tardive dyskinesia. Newer antipsychotics such as olanzapine (Zyprexa®), risperidone (Risperdal®), quetiapine (Seroquel®), and clozapine (Clozaril®) are also proving useful in bipolar disorder, and may work to some extent like mood stabilizers, with research ongoing to determine whether these medications can treat not only mania but also depression and prevent new episodes. These newer medications have the advantage of fewer side-effects than traditional antipsychotics.

ANTI-ANXIETY MEDICATIONS OR MILD SEDATIVES

Anxiety is common in bipolar disorder, and sleep disturbance typically occurs during acute episodes. Benzodiazepines such as lorazepam (Ativan®) and clonazepam are often prescribed and may be used for short periods without risk of addiction. Clonazepam is particularly useful for treating the excessive energy and reduced sleep of hypomania. For more severe anxiety problems such as panic attacks, cognitive behaviour therapy may be very helpful, and needed, because the antidepressants used to treat anxiety disorders may provoke manic attacks.

ANTIDEPRESSANTS

At times, a mood stabilizer alone will not adequately treat the severe symptoms of bipolar depression. A specific antidepressant may be required along with a mood stabilizer. If given alone, antidepressants may cause a major problem in bipolar disorder by pushing a person's mood up too high and inducing hypomania or mania.

While the first antidepressant/mood stabilizer trial may work, it is not uncommon to go through several trials of antidepressants before finding an effective combination. While waiting for the medication to work, a person may also benefit from sedating medication to help with sleep disorders, anxiety or agitation.

Many antidepressant drugs are effective, but the following are considered preferred choices by experts in the bipolar field:

Drug Class	Generic Name	US Trade Name
SSRIs	fluoxetine	Prozac®
	fluvoxamine	Luvox®
	paroxetine	Paxil®
	sertraline	Zoloft®
MAOIs	phenelzine	Nardil®
	tranylcypromine	Parnate®
Tricyclics	amitriptyline	Elavil®
	imipramine	Tofranil®
Other Agents	buproprion	Wellbutrin®
	nefazodone	Serzone®
	venlafaxine	Effexor®
	lamotrigine	Lamictal®

How does a doctor choose the right medication?

Lithium and valproate are most commonly used for acute-phase treatment of manic episodes. Three of the criteria a doctor will use to decide which of the medications to prescribe are:

1. Has the person successfully used either of them before?

2. Has the person experienced particular side-effects that might affect his or her preference?

3. What subtype of bipolar disorder does the person have?

Lithium is usually recommended for people with euphoric (over-happy) moods, and valproate is recommended for people with a combination of manic episodes and unhappy or irritable moods or who are rapid cyclers.

How long does initial treatment of acute episodes take?

There is usually a significant improvement within a few weeks of starting treatment with lithium or valproate. If the first medication does not work, or if it results only in a partial response, the doctor may suggest trying another medication or combination of medications. Another effective medication — particularly with mixed episodes or rapid cycling — is carbamazepine.

Anti-anxiety and antipsychotic medications may be used to control severe symptoms until the mood stabilizers take effect.

Does maintenance medication mean taking a mood stabilizer for life?

Bipolar disorder is a highly recurrent disorder. Most individuals who are untreated will experience a relapse within two years. Medications not only treat symptoms but also prevent their return. The likelihood of remaining well is significantly higher if the client continues taking medications rather than discontinuing them. Recommendations for maintenance (longer-term) treatment depend on the nature of the illness. For some individuals, who have a mild single episode that is not particularly impairing, remaining on medications for one to two years may be reasonable. For most people, however, longer-term treatments are recommended and, in many cases, indefinite treatment is required.

Does preventive medication over one's lifetime really work?

YES. Mood stabilizers (lithium, valproate, carbamazepine) are the core of prevention. This type of management will allow about one-third of bipolar clients to remain symptom-free. However, most people will at least experience a great reduction in their symptoms and the number and severity of episodes.

What other strategies prevent relapse?

Self-monitoring strategies help to prevent relapse. Client and family education, and clients learning to self-monitor (identifying a person's personal warning symptoms of a developing manic or depressive episode) are a major way to prevent further acute episodes.

Early signs of a developing episode include slight changes in mood, sleep, energy, self-esteem, sexual interest and concentration. For example, some clients may have learned that a disruption in their sleep routines is a warning sign. Paying attention to such signals and reporting them immediately to the treating physician could result in a minor medication adjustment that may avert a full manic/depressive episode. In this way the physician and client work in partnership to manage the disorder.

In the beginning, self-monitoring can be an anxiety-producing exercise as clients may confuse emotions and reactions, that are not due to their illness, as being a sign of a developing illness. Initially, the fear of relapse and a focus on relapse prevention can be overwhelming.

It is possible for people with bipolar disorder to have a good day and feel joyous and not be hypomanic. Self-monitoring is a process that evolves over time and benefits from ongoing discussion and consultation with a physician and other mental health practitioners familiar with the disorder.

DISCONTINUING MEDICATION

It is natural for people who haven't experienced an episode of bipolar disorder for several years to hope that they can eventually stop taking medication. However, although mood stabilizers prevent episodes, they do not cure the disorder. Because a serious relapse may occur — sometimes as soon as a few months after medication is discontinued — any decision to stop taking medication should be made only after a thorough discussion with the treating physician.

If this decision is made, medications should be tapered slowly (over weeks to months). Abrupt cessation, in some cases, can lead to a poorer response the next time the client tries the same medication. For this reason, if one medication is working well, the decision to stop taking it should be done thoughtfully, because the next time it is tried, it might not be as effective.

ELECTROCONVULSIVE THERAPY (ECT) FOR BIPOLAR DISORDER

Electroconvulsive therapy (ECT) is perhaps the most controversial and misunderstood of psychiatric treatments, due in part to sensationalized and misleading depictions of the treatment in the popular media. In fact, ECT is a highly effective and safe treatment for both the depressive and manic phases of bipolar disorder, and is sometimes used as a long-term "maintenance" treatment to prevent recurrence of illness after recovery.

Procedure

ECT involves administering a brief electrical stimulus through the scalp to the surface of the brain. This stimulus produces an epileptic-type convulsion, lasting typically from 15 seconds to two minutes.

During the treatment, a team of psychiatrist, anaesthetist and one or more nurses are present. The patient is given an anaesthetic intravenously to put him or her to sleep briefly during the treatment. A muscle relaxant is also given to prevent physical injury, by lessening the intensity of muscle spasms that accompany a seizure. Oxygen is administered, and heart rate and blood pressure are monitored. Although the anaesthetic lasts only a few minutes, patients feel groggy after an ECT treatment and may rest or sleep for about one hour.

Usually the treatments are administered three times a week over three to four weeks, for a total of eight to 12 treatments. For longer-term maintenance treatment, the treatments may be spread out, for example, once a month, and continued for as long as the patient and doctor feel is appropriate. ECT is usually given to hospitalized inpatients, but outpatients can receive ECT as well.

Side-effects

Patients may have a headache or jaw pain on awakening after ECT, usually requiring only a mild pain killer such as acetaminophen (Tylenol®). Some loss of recent memory or problems with concentration usually occur during treatment (for example patients may not recall what they had for supper the night before the treatment), but these symptoms improve quickly, over a few weeks, after the course of ECT is finished. Some patients report mild memory problems persisting much longer after ECT, but this is likely due to their depression not the treatment.

ECT can be given bilaterally (the electric current is applied to both sides of the brain) or unilaterally (on only the right side of the brain). Although bilateral ECT causes more memory disruption than unilateral ECT, it is also somewhat more effective and is usually the preferred choice.

Uses of ECT in bipolar disorder

ECT is the most effective, and possibly the fastest-acting, treatment for severe depression, and is particularly helpful for highly agitated or suicidal patients or those with psychotic or catatonic symptoms. Some patients receive ECT early in their episode of illness because of the urgency of their situation or their particular symptoms, while others may prefer to use ECT only after various medications have failed. ECT works well for severe mania as well.

While ECT is highly effective at ending an episode of depression or mania, the benefits may not last more than a few weeks or months following treatment. Therefore, patients usually start or continue treatment with mood stabilizers and/or other medication following a course of ECT. Maintenance ECT can be used in cases where medications have not prevented recurrence of illness or are intolerable due to side-effects.

TREATMENT OF REFRACTORY BIPOLAR DISORDER ("BRITTLE" PATIENTS)

About 30 per cent of clients with bipolar disorder develop a more severe form of the illness that requires multiple medications for a long period of time. These people may not respond well to the treatments that are currently available, and it can take much longer to find a balance of medications (mood stabilizers, antidepressants, anti-anxiety medications) that are effective. This can have a profound impact on many areas of their lives, such as work, school or functioning in their families.

These people also tend to have more difficulty staying well. This is because, even after an effective mix of medications is found, mild stressors or changes in their lives can trigger relapse, resulting in the need to modify or switch medications. With this change, it may again take a long time to establish an effective balance of medications.

ALTERNATIVE THERAPIES

Natural remedies may have a role in treating bipolar disorder. These include fish oil and inosital, a type of sugar. Yet when these products are sold through health food stores, they are often unreliable. Because they have not been precisely formulated, they cannot be recommended. Furthermore, little research has been done on these products. St John's wort has been well studied in unipolar depression; however, it has not been studied in bipolar disorder.

Psychosocial Treatment Options

This section integrates content for both depression and bipolar disorder. Distribute Handout 2.3, Psychosocial Treatments — Depression/Bipolar Disorder, at this point.

INTRODUCTION: PSYCHOEDUCATION AND SUPPORTIVE PSYCHOTHERAPY

Psychotherapy and supportive psychotherapy can be either short- or long-term talk therapy. The focus is on providing a supportive environment in which the individual can learn about his or her illness and develop strategies to cope with and manage it. It can be particularly helpful for a recently diagnosed person to come to terms with the diagnosis.

Goals of talk therapy

1. Resolve past life event issues that contribute to current problems (such as major losses, childhood trauma, life changes, style of stress management).

2. Develop new ways of thinking/problem solving to promote or maintain wellness.

3. Deal with current family or relationship difficulties that contribute to stress and relapse.

Talk therapy focuses on particular issues that the person is struggling with such as:

• accepting the diagnosis of a mood disorder
• dealing with the changes/losses associated with having a serious illness (job, relationships, future goals)
• future planning
• stressful events that occur during periods when the person feels particularly unwell.

Talk therapies can be very helpful when combined with medication therapy.

Psychosocial therapies can be provided to an individual, couple, family or in a group. The treatment(s) chosen is based on the individual's needs, strengths and, on a practical level, what resources are available in a particular community.

TIPS FOR THE EFFECTIVE MANAGEMENT OF MOOD DISORDERS

- Receiving early diagnosis and seeking help early can lead to more effective intervention.
- Becoming educated about the disorder so that your relative can receive the best treatment, as well as being an effective partner in treatment with his or her clinician.
- Treatment compliance and continuing with treatment even when results are not immediate. This is often difficult because the individual must acknowledge that he or she has a disorder and must also follow through with medication long term.
- Reducing stress. Stress is a risk factor in relapse.
- Self-awareness. Acknowledging that individuals living with a mood disorder may have vulnerabilities that other people do not have. For example, someone who has a history of struggling with low self-esteem and guilt may have greater difficulty recovering from a depressive episode. These factors should be taken into account when planning a treatment plan.

COMMON FRUSTRATIONS EXPERIENCED BY FAMILY MEMBERS

- The relative denies having trouble functioning.
- The relative feels better and goes off medications or stops seeing the therapist.
- The relative refuses to alter his or her lifestyle to reduce stress and create optimum circumstances for staying well.

TYPES OF PSYCHOSOCIAL THERAPIES FOR BOTH DEPRESSION AND BIPOLAR DISORDERS

A variety of short-term and long-term models of therapy are used to treat mood disorders. It is useful to highlight the two short-term models of interpersonal therapy (IPT) and cognitive-behavioural therapy (CBT) as they are empirically based and found to be highly effective. In smaller cities and communities, however, it may not be possible to find a specialist in IPT or CBT.

Individual treatments — the talk therapies

Many clinicians practise an eclectic model that integrates elements from a number of different modalities, such as interpersonal therapy, cognitive-behavioural therapy and insight-oriented psychotherapy.

COMBINING PSYCHOTHERAPY AND DRUGS

Families and clients often ask if it is appropriate to combine psychotherapy, or talk therapy, with medication.

Severe bipolar disorder or major depression should be treated with both. When individuals are extremely ill, they may not be able to utilize psychotherapy because talking and listening are so difficult. As people improve, however, psychotherapy can be very helpful in identifying and dealing with issues that may have contributed to the illness.

Mild to moderate bipolar disorder also requires medication, but some clients may not feel that talk therapy is necessary. Their own internal resourcefulness can be enough to help them recover and maintain good health. However, even these people may find education about the illness and strategies for effective management to be very helpful. This would include gaining information about the illness, warning signs of relapse and stress management.

Mild to moderate depression can be treated with psychotherapy alone. Interpersonal therapy and cognitive-behavioural therapy can be highly effective and, over the long term, may contribute more to the prevention of relapse.

INTERPERSONAL THERAPY FOR DEPRESSION

Interpersonal therapy for depression (IPT) is a short-term (12 to 16 weeks) intervention that focuses on identifying and resolving specific problem areas in establishing and maintaining satisfying relationships. This may include dealing with loss, life changes, conflicts, and increasing ease in social situations. This model has not been researched with the bipolar population (Klerman, G., Weissman, M., Rounsaville, B. & and Chevron, E., 1997).

COGNITIVE-BEHAVIOURAL THERAPY FOR DEPRESSION

In depression, cognitive behavioural therapy (CBT), the most scientifically proven type of psychotherapy, is a **short-term** treatment that helps people become aware of how automatic thoughts, attitudes, beliefs and expectations can produce and maintain unpleasant moods. This awareness along with practising new thoughts can help establish new, more adaptive patterns of behaviour.

Cognitive behaviour therapy is now being tested to determine whether it helps treat bipolar depression and assists in relapse prevention. This type of short-term therapy (which lasts for 15 to 20 weeks) is done in combination with a mood stabilizer (Padesky, C. & Greenberger, D., 1995).

INSIGHT-ORIENTED PSYCHOTHERAPY

This form of therapy may be either **long or short term.** The focus is on understanding how traumatic life events have influenced a person's coping strategies, self-esteem and identity. The individual can make changes to his or her situation by developing insight into the causes and effects of these traumatic events, and by practising new problem-solving strategies, with the support of a trusted therapist.

VOCATIONAL COUNSELLING

This treatment involves providing assistance in returning to work, school, volunteer or leisure activities through structured counselling or a formal rehabilitation program.

CASE MANAGEMENT/COMMUNITY MENTAL HEALTH WORKERS

In situations where the course of an individual's illness is more complicated and longstanding, it may be helpful for a case manager or community mental health worker to be involved in ongoing care. Case managers co-ordinate services, such as housing or financial services, to individuals as well as link clients with day treatment, vocational or volunteer services. Case managers can also assist in day-to-day activities, such as attending appointments, budgeting and setting up a daily routine, as well as provide emotional support and counselling. Depending on the community, case managers and community mental health workers may be accessed through community mental health agencies, housing services and homecare.

Group treatments

Mental health professionals lead psychotherapy groups of eight to 12 people who support one another while practising new coping strategies. These groups are often closed (new members are not invited to drop in) and time-limited.

SELF-HELP GROUPS

Self-help groups are support and information groups, made up of people with a problem or diagnosis in common. These groups are usually open-ended (people can join or leave the groups at any time) and led by clients or family members who have experience in the mental health system. Some self-help organizations also offer services for families.

Family interventions

MARITAL AND FAMILY THERAPY

Research has shown that when there is negative emotional intensity (such as intrusiveness, criticism or conflict) in the ill person's environment, recovery time is prolonged and relapse more likely. This therapy focuses on resolving conflictual issues to reduce emotional intensity. Therapy can also assist the family in supporting the client's treatment compliance.

EDUCATION AND SUPPORT GROUPS

These groups, similar to the self-help groups for clients, offer information and support for family members who have an ill relative. They may be offered through hospitals, agencies or self-help organizations.

Promoting overall good health

While the medical and psychosocial therapies are specifically designed to treat a disorder, it is important to remember that promoting and maintaining overall good health is also important. Nutrition and exercise are important for both the person who is ill and for family members coping with a difficult life problem.

Two ways to reduce stress are:

- Minimize multiple stressors, which create a greater potential for relapse; this is especially important in bipolar disorder.
- Lower the level of emotional intensity in the family. When there is conflict, it is important to handle it without critical comments or verbal and physical aggression.

A general discussion following the presentation of this material can introduce two themes:

- the frustration of dealing with ill relatives who refuse treatment or who do not engage in treatment reliably

- what families can do to persuade a person to take treatment.

These themes will be discussed in later groups.

OUTLINE

HANDOUTS

GROUP 3
Stress Management for Family and Caregivers

LEGEND:

B	Bipolar Group
D	Depression Group
▷	Handouts

▶ Goals

- to shift the focus from the needs of the client to the needs of the family
- to provide a safe environment for family members to express their negative, conflicted feelings about the situation with the ill relative
- to provide an overview of the basic principles of stress management
- to facilitate group discussion regarding stress management strategies that can be incorporated into everyday life.

▶ Leader's notes

This section incorporates both depression and bipolar disorder.

In this group the emphasis will not be on the relative who is ill, but on the caregivers themselves. Participants will learn more about their own needs and limitations and will be introduced to the idea that there are some things that they are unable to change.

For some group members who have been dealing with their loved one's illness for a long time, this will be an opportunity to appreciate how much they have already learned about coping. For others, the idea of focusing on themselves may be new. This topic stresses the importance of taking good care of yourself.

Life is a marathon, not a sprint. Even though we would like to view our relative's illness as temporary, it is useful to learn how to keep some energy in reserve, in case of a relapse. You will be teaching and modelling this perspective during this session.

You will focus on the stressful issues that group members experience and will suggest coping strategies to deal with those stresses. During this group, members may need to vent their feelings and it may be the first time that they have been able to do so with others in a similar situation. The schedule allows time for such sharing of feelings.

The following points need to be stressed in this group and are important for participants to understand before moving on to the remaining topics:

- It is critical to recognize the effects of caring on the caregiver.
- Family members must recognize their own limitations as well as recognizing the limitations of the situation. The irony of living in this situation is that we must first recognize how limited we are in our ability to change others before we can know how to be helpful. The "Serenity Prayer" states this effectively.
- Family members must recognize and acknowledge what is stressful about the situation, in order to find ways to look after themselves.
- It is vital that family members/caregivers receive support through information, education, skill building, and emotional support and stress management.

- Given the shrinking health care resources, families are finding it increasingly difficult to access public assistance.

The teaching style for Session 3 begins with a group discussion, rather than a lecture, and a flipchart or chalkboard will be useful. It may still be helpful to still ask participants to wear nametags to assist with group participation and the development of group cohesion.

How Has Your Life Been Changed by Your Relative's Illness?

CHANGES REPORTED BY FAMILY MEMBERS

Introduce the topic with a brief discussion of how you know from talking with other family members that their lives change when a relative becomes ill, regardless of whether it is a physical or a mental illness. Also acknowledge that a diagnosis of mental illness brings some unique stresses.

Ask the group to share the ways in which their lives have been changed by their relative's illness and list these changes on the chalkboard or flipchart. If you feel that it is needed, reassure participants about the agreement of confidentiality within the group.

The following are the most common changes reported. If participants do not suggest them, offer them as suggestions to start the group process or use them to expand the discussion.

1. CHANGES IN ROLES AND EXPECTATIONS
   - assuming more responsibilities as a result of the illness
   - determining when to assume a responsibility that was previously handled by your relative, and when to trust that your relative will handle it
   - deciding whether certain responsibilities can be ignored without negative consequences

Distribute Handout 3.1, Managing Stress, at this point. Introduce the Serenity Prayer included within the handout to emphasize the importance of appreciating that one part of lowering stress will be accepting that there will be some things you will be unable to change.

2. EMOTIONAL AND SOCIAL ISOLATION AS A RESULT OF YOUR RELATIVE'S ILLNESS
   - fearing social stigma against your relative or your family

3. FEELING EMOTIONALLY AND PHYSICALLY EXHAUSTED BY THE DEMANDS OF CAREGIVING

4. QUESTIONING WHICH OF YOUR RELATIVE'S BEHAVIOURS ARE A RESULT OF THE DISORDER AND WHICH BEHAVIOURS ARE A REFLECTION OF HIS OR HER PERSONALITY

5. FINANCIAL WORRIES
   • handling the financial worries by yourself or worrying about the future

6. UNDERSTANDING YOUR RELATIVE'S TREATMENT AND TRYING TO DETERMINE WHERE YOU FIT IN
   • dealing with the health care and legal systems and the Mental Health Act

7. ENCOURAGING YOUR RELATIVE TO COMPLY WITH MEDICATION AND TREATMENT

8. FEELING THAT YOUR CARE IS MISUNDERSTOOD
   • feeling that regardless of whatever you try to do to be supportive, it's the wrong thing

9. LOSS OF COMPANIONSHIP, INTIMACY AND SEXUAL RELATIONSHIP

10. LOSS OF A PARENTING PARTNER, AND FEELING LIKE A SINGLE PARENT
    • Often, spouses will say that they could not have anticipated the enormity of the burden when they married their partner or created a family with their partner.

When generating this list, allow group members to add their own experiences to what others have reported. If the group does not raise the issues of loss, grief and fear of the future, the facilitator should introduce the following.

LOSS AND GRIEF

Grief, or a profound sense of loss, arises as the symptoms of the mood disorder affect the behaviours, thoughts and personality of the ill relative. Family members may feel as though the person they love has disappeared into his or her depression or mania, and they may fear that he or she might not re-emerge.

This "invisible" quality of mental illness isolates families from others, contributing to their sense of loss. Families are often hesitant to allow the illness to become visible by reaching out to others for fear that they or their family member will be stigmatized when others learn of the diagnosis. This often deepens their sense of isolation.

Reviewing the stages of loss and giving examples of each can help to normalize participants' feelings. It also gives participants the opportunity to reverse the isolation by sharing their experiences with other group members.

When discussing the stages of grief, remind members that grief is not necessarily experienced in the order presented and that when people grieve they often move among the stages.

STAGES OF GRIEF

SHOCK AND DISBELIEF
"This couldn't really be happening. It will go away on its own."

SADNESS
"I feel overwhelming sorrow that this is happening."

ANGER
"This shouldn't be happening. Why is it happening to us?"

BARGAINING
"Everything will go back to normal when we find the right medications. We will be okay if it just doesn't get any worse."

ACCEPTANCE
"This isn't how I would have chosen for things to be, but I will work to make sense out of them and cope, so that I can make life work."

(Adapted from Elizabeth Kübler-Ross (1997), *On Death and Dying, New York: Touchstone*)

ANXIETY AND FEAR ABOUT THE FUTURE

The other natural feeling is apprehension about the future. Once a relative becomes ill, both the relative and the family member's lives are forever changed. This is not something most people have anticipated having to cope with. Even if the relative goes into remission and the illness is well controlled by medications and other treatments, the family member is aware that it may return.

This awareness leads to thoughts about how the future of each family member and their children might be affected by the relative's illness. It is natural to wonder whether children may have inherited a predisposition to the illness, and such concern should be openly discussed within the group. Aging parents may also worry that they will not always be able to care for their ill children.

Describe and allow participants to discuss their feelings about living with anxiety about the future. Introducing fear of the future and loss as normal parts of dealing with their relative's illness allows participants to acknowledge these feelings and accept the feelings and themselves.

When you have listed most of the ways that participants feel their lives have changed, review the list so that group members can fully appreciate how much they are coping with. If it has not already come up, introduce the idea that their lives have changed in ways they never expected and that a part of adjusting to this change will be to make sense out of their new relationships with their relative. This process will involve acceptance of the fact that they will not be able to go back to the time before these changes occurred.

How Do You Recognize Stress in Yourself?

This section follows logically from the previous work. You have established that participants are coping with numerous changes, and this discussion explores the signs of stress as a result of these changes.

Again, listing these signs on a chalkboard or flipchart can help participants really "see" how much they are coping with. If you are using a flipchart, post the previous list alongside this one so that you can easily refer back and forth between the two.

You will focus on the three areas where stress shows up: physical, emotional and behavioural. Some of the signs of stress are listed below, as well as being included in Handout 3.1, Managing Stress.

SIGNS OF STRESS

PHYSICAL
- chronic fatigue
- trembling
- vague physical complaints
- weight gain or loss
- body motions indicating anxiety, such as foot tapping
- sweaty palms
- dilated pupils

EMOTIONAL
- sadness
- anger
- easy distractibility
- daydreaming
- frequent mood changes

BEHAVIOURAL
- sleep disturbance
- explosive outbursts
- impulsive actions
- complaining

- negative or resentful statements
- cynical or hostile remarks
- self-criticism
- overly critical of others
- withdrawn or difficult to communicate with
- talking about the past much more than the future
- use of drugs or alcohol
- difficulty with authority
- change in productivity on the job
- lack of attention to details
- difficulty handling usual responsibilities

As group members generate this list of symptoms, point out that although it is normal to have symptoms in response to stress, it is vital to take care of oneself when these symptoms develop.

Often, participants will feel that their stress symptoms have a lot in common with their relative's disorder, especially depression. This gives you an opportunity to begin the third topic for this session.

Coping Strategies

This session will help family members to appreciate that their energies are limited and that they must take care of themselves. Two powerful metaphors illustrating these two concepts are:

- "Life is a marathon, not a sprint."
- Emergency procedures on an aircraft require that if you are travelling with a person who requires your assistance, you put on your oxygen mask first, before helping him or her.

Participants should learn to recognize the effects of stress, and to appreciate the impact that the stress of their relative's illness has on their own lives.

Often participants tend to view the relative's illness as more like a "sprint," expecting that their lives will eventually return to normal after only a brief crisis. The realities of a long-term illness should be part of a group discussion at this point.

Before presenting the following coping strategies, distribute Handout 3.2, Your Support System, and allow participants time to complete it. Then take a few minutes to emphasize the importance of having different kinds of support and having more than one person for support. This leads to the lecture and discussion of four significant steps that participants can take to better care for themselves.

STRESS REDUCTION STRATEGIES

Listing the four strategies on chalkboard or flipchart as they are presented emphasizes their importance. Taking questions and comments during the lecture will facilitate understanding and group cohesion.

Establish a good support system for yourself.

- Avoid becoming isolated. Have a few people whom you can turn to when you are feeling overwhelmed. As you have discovered, not everyone can put themselves "in your shoes," so it will take some time and effort to determine who those chosen few are.
- Turn to self-help organizations, support groups, professionals and trusted family members and friends who are supportive, non-judgmental and good listeners. You can canvass

other group members for ideas regarding how they have found support within their communities.

Cultivate interests outside the family.

Physical — Take time for regular exercise. Join a club or gym. Take walks. Participate in sports and yoga.

Emotional — Focus on your needs. Spend time with a friend. Spend time doing something just for you, such as reading, keeping a journal or developing a hobby. Plan regular times to recharge your emotional batteries.

Spiritual — Develop and appreciate your spiritual life. Take time to breathe. Learn to meditate and practise it each day if that helps you slow down. Today's session ends with a relaxation exercise, and you will receive the script so that you can make a tape of it for yourself. Research has shown that regular use of meditation and relaxation techniques are associated with reduced physical stress reactions.

Create a low-stress environment.

- Relapse prevention is facilitated by reducing stress at home. Communicating quietly and calmly are important for you and your relative. Reminding yourself of the wisdom of the Serenity Prayer can help reduce stress.

Avoid martyrdom.

- Acknowledge that negative feelings are normal and remind yourself of this whenever you begin to feel guilty about them.
- Give yourself permission to have and set limits. Forgive yourself when you have trouble sticking to them, and start again.
- Recognize that you must develop a balance between caring for your relative and taking care of yourself.
- Get respite care when needed. No one can be on call 24 hours a day.

It is important to remember that your stress levels will lower as your coping ability improves.

Relaxation Techniques

RELAXATION EXERCISE

Get in a comfortable position. If you're sitting, uncross your legs and put your feet flat on the floor. Rest your hands on your thighs. Let your spine support your upper body in a natural position. Take a breath, let it out, and let your head fall easily forward, so that your chin rests on your chest. You might find it useful to close your eyes. Let your shoulders feel the natural gravitational pull downward.

Take another breath, in and out, slowly and deeply, all the way down to your diaphragm, and rest there for a moment. Now, take another breath, slowly, deeply, in, then out.

We will begin with your feet. Be aware of the tension in your feet and then begin to let it out. You may simply feel like the tension being replaced by relaxation, or it may feel like a comfortable heaviness, or even like the tension is actually draining out and down into the floor. However it feels and however much you are able to relax, let yourself take another deep, slow breath.

Now, begin to let that relaxation move slowly up your legs, first into your calves, then higher through your knees and thighs. If you find that you get distracted, remember that you are just practising. There's no right or wrong way to do this.

Now, take another breath before beginning to allow whatever relaxation you are able to feel to move up into your buttocks, through your low back and stomach. Just rest with this relaxation as you breathe deeply and easily.

Now, feel the relaxation begin in your hands, and then slowly spread up through your forearms and upper arms. Your arms are now becoming more relaxed as you continue to breathe as deeply and easily as possible.

Let the breath come from your diaphragm so that your stomach moves in and out with each breath, and, surprisingly, your shoulders will not move up and down, even though you might be breathing more deeply than you are used to. Now the relaxation is moving up through your chest and shoulders, letting yourself feel heavy and warm, really supported by the chair beneath you.

Now, continuing to be aware of breathing deeply and easily, becoming just as relaxed as you can at this time, let the comfortable relaxation move up through your neck and face, including your jaw, eyes, forehead and over your entire head.

Allow yourself to continue to breathe deeply and easily, feeling the comfortable heaviness, and being aware that this is something that you can do for yourself each day. And realize how important it is to let yourself have a little time each day for breathing.

When you are ready, take one more deep breath, then open your eyes and take a stretch.

Reminder. When you are practising this exercise at home, you might find that you become even more relaxed when lying down. Some people even use muscle-relaxation techniques to help them fall asleep at night. However, one of the values of continuing to practise sitting up as we did today is that you can get used to relaxing whenever and wherever you need to.

Just remember not to use any relaxation technique when you need to be alert, such as when you are driving.

(Reproduced with permission from Kate Kitchen; the use of relaxation techniques was originally developed by Edmund Jacobson. For more information, see Jacobson, E. (1974). *Progressive Relaxation*. Chicago: The University of Chicago Press, Midway Reprint.)

Group leaders should distribute Handouts 3.1, 3.2 and 3.3, Managing Stress, Your Support System and Relaxation Exercise, here.

GROUP 4
Communication Strategies

LEGEND:

B | Bipolar Group

D | Depression Group

| Handouts

▶ Goals

- to inform participants how the listening/communicating skills of individuals with mood disorders are compromised
- to teach participants the basic skills for communicating more directly and clearly
- to practise these skills in the session
- to allow members to express the level of difficulty they experience with this process and to provide support and encouragement to one another
- to build the foundation for the section on problem management.

▶ Leader's notes

This group integrates material for both depression and mania. For those groups focusing on depression only, omit the sections referring to the management of mania.

The previous discussion of stress management emphasized the importance of family members learning to take care of themselves. Most people come to these groups feeling frustrated in their interactions with their ill relatives, and learning to manage their stress is the first step in change. Feeling less stressed and overburdened is key to having more positive interactions with a relative who has a mental illness. The communication strategies presented here require thoughtfulness, patience and slowing down the process between family members. A tired, stressed person will experience great difficulty doing this.

This session helps participants to build more adaptive approaches to dealing with their ill relative's communication style.

The session concludes with a brief section that addresses how to talk to children about mood disorders. This section is optional, depending on group members' needs.

Effective Communication and Common Communication Problems

HOW EFFECTIVE COMMUNICATION CAN IMPROVE YOUR SITUATION

Brief outline to reinforce how effective communication can help

1. Research has shown that living in an environment filled with intense expressions of hostility and criticism inhibits recovery. Clear, direct communication that includes support and warmth has been shown to aid recovery.

2. For caregivers, effective communication enables you to develop and maintain better relationships not only with your relative, but also with helping professionals and the health care system.

3. Clear communication also allows you to better deal with conflict, a common dynamic in families with an ill relative. This helps to de-escalate crisis situations.

4. Better communication will make you feel more effective.

However, it is important to have realistic expectations; less conflict and improved communication will not cure your relative, but it will make the living situation less stressful.

Common communication problems: A group exercise

Using the flipchart or a chalkboard, generate a list from participants of common obstacles to communication with their ill relatives. This allows group members to share support and reduce feelings of isolation as they share similar situations.

Use the situations presented as illustrations of obstacles to communication.

OBSTACLES TO COMMUNICATION
Behavioural/cognitive obstacles arising from the ill relative's disorder include:

- self-absorption
- denial of illness
- poor concentration and distractibility

- confused thinking
- racing or grandiose thoughts
- lowered self-esteem
- poor social skills
- hypersensitivity to criticism
- unpredictability
- short-tempered, impatient, irritability
- secretive about treatment.

Obstacles arising within family members include:

- fatigue (from having assumed the roles and responsibilities of the ill person)
- fear of saying the wrong thing, so they avoid saying anything
- self-imposed pressure — feeling that if they just say the right thing, they can make him or her feel better
- anger and frustration with the situation
- an inability to choose the right time to talk
- a feeling of hopelessness — they believe that the situation is unlikely to improve.

Obstacles that both the ill relative and family member may experience include:

- feeling overwhelmed about the diagnosis
- fears about the future
- feeling isolated or stigmatized
- feeling confused about what is expected.

NEGATIVE INTERACTIONAL SEQUENCES

Negative interactional sequences simply refers to a process where an initial attempt to have a neutral or pleasant discussion shifts into a series of negative statements. The end result of this downward spiral leaves both the family member and ill person feeling discouraged, angry and frustrated.

Negative interactional sequences: Depression example

Depressed son is sitting silently at the kitchen table. Parent enters and tries to start conversation to cheer up son.

- "Looks like a nice day, why don't you go for a walk today — the doctor says you need to get outside more."
- "I don't want to go outside … I just don't feel like it."

Mother tries to encourage and cajole son to plan something for the day.

- "Well, you can't stay in all day — it'll just make you feel worse. Why don't you go buy a paper?"
- "I don't feel like it — reading the paper makes me feel worse and I can't concentrate anyway."
- "Well, why don't you take the dog for a walk?"
- (voice more terse) "I don't feel up to it."
- "How about calling your friend and asking him to come with you?"
- (voice raised) "I can't, I don't want to talk about it anymore."

Mother becomes exasperated.

- "I just can't bear to see you in all day — the doctor says you need to be more active. At least try to get out just for a few minutes."
- (loud and irritable) "No, I don't feel like it — just leave me alone."

Mother appears hurt and retreats.

- "Well, I was just trying to help."
- "Well you're not helping, you're bothering me and making me feel worse. Why can't you leave me alone?!"

Negative interactional sequences: Bipolar example

Relative with mania is exhibiting racing thoughts and grandiose ideas. Is planning to go on a lavish trip to pursue an acting career.

- "I've got this great idea. I'm going to L.A. to get an acting job in a play. I know that this time I can really get my career going."

Well relative is alarmed at the thought of what this trip will cost, as well as the ill person travelling alone without supervision. Out of a need to protect the ill person, raises her concerns.

- "Have you thought about what this will cost? And you can't go down there all alone — imagine what could happen. It's not safe."

Relative reacts with anger and hostility.

- "Why do you always put down my ideas? Spending the money is worth it — I know I can be a great actress. What's wrong with you — why don't you ever support my ideas?"

Family member tries to backtrack.

- "It's not that I don't support you, it's just that ... well ... I just don't think now is a good time for you to be travelling or spending a lot of money ... you're not yourself ..."
- "What do you mean I'm not myself? There is nothing wrong with me. I feel great. You just don't want to see me be successful. You've always wanted to hold me back, you've never supported me. I don't know why I tell you anything."

Ill person leaves room in a rage, family members feels worried and scared of what relative will do next.

Effective Communication Skills

This lecture format covers the components of good communication that can help family members improve their ability to communicate with their relatives.

Various "dos and don'ts" for effective communication are provided. As each point is presented, suggest to participants that they consider how these might apply these suggestions to their individual situations. It is not uncommon for family members to state they have tried and failed with many of the suggested strategies. It is important that they really explore whether they applied the strategy as it is being defined in the group. It is also important to state clearly that not all strategies work in all families; they may need to choose the one that works best for their situation.

Following this discussion, you will choose a scenario for the role-play based on their real situations.

List these on the chalkboard or flipchart so that members can refer to them as they go along.

THE DOS OF EFFECTIVE COMMUNICATION FOR DEPRESSION AND MANIA

1. Try to talk about one subject at a time.

2. Speak in a calm, quiet tone of voice; this contributes to a more relaxed conversation.

3. Keep your statements or requests short, simple and stated as a positive (e.g., "It would be nice to go out today").

4. Use "I" statements. This will focus on how you feel and what you need. "You" statements can be interpreted as accusations or criticism and might make your relative feel defensive. For example, say, "I really need you to tell me when you are having a bad day," rather than "You should have told me you were feeling particularly bad today."

5. Make requests direct and positive. For example, "I would really like it if you would ..."

6. Aim to be clear. Try to have your words and facial expressions and body language all communicate the same message. For example, when agreeing with a suggestion that you may not fully agree with, do not shake your head indicating your refusal while saying, "Okay, we'll give it a try."

7. Pair a positive with a negative. The positive makes up the first half of the sentence, and the negative is the second half. In this way you communicate that you have heard and understood your relative's point of view first, even though you are presenting another idea. For example, "I know you have been very tired lately, but I would really appreciate it if you could put your coffee cups in the kitchen."

8. Combine the above suggestions with "I" statements so that your relative knows that you are simply expressing your own thoughts and feelings. And offer compromises so that your relative can feel that he or she is part of the solution. For example, say, "It is disruptive for me to have you sleep in the daytime and be up in the middle of the night." Then offer a compromise, such as "Could you start to go to bed an hour earlier each night to begin to re-establish a normal sleep pattern?"

9. Repeat your statements — mood disorders affect listening and information processing. This is sometimes called the "broken record" technique.

10. Use "active listening." Nod occasionally to let your relative know that you are paying attention.

11. Offer praise for small accomplishments. We all find change difficult.

THE DON'TS OF EFFECTIVE COMMUNICATION FOR DEPRESSION AND MANIA

1. Avoid using "shoulds," which can sound critical and judgmental.

2. Avoid jumping to give reassurance. Your ill relative has a lot to figure out. Giving quick reassurances can get in the way of problem-solving and send the message that you lack confidence in your relative's ability to recover. It is entirely appropriate to say, "I don't know how and when things will work out, but I am confident they will." Listening, rather than reassuring, gives you a chance to hear your relative's thoughts, plans and worries. If it is difficult for you to refrain from jumping in, try to stay calm by reminding yourself that recovery takes time.

3. Don't try to be constantly available and positive. You can't be expected to have all the answers. Sometimes just listening can be helpful.

4. Try not to take your relative's comments personally; mood disorders can cause people to make hurtful, even rejecting, statements that they regret once they are well.

5. Don't try to discuss something of importance when you are feeling angry, tired or frustrated.

Depression groups: go directly to "Summarizing Information for Effective Communication Skills," at the bottom of this page.

D

ADDITIONAL COMMUNICATION MANAGEMENT FOR MANIA

Do

1. Reduce stimulation: people with mania are easily overstimulated. You may need to reduce the number of people who visit with the person at the same time, or minimize the noise/activity level in the house.

2. Have brief conversations.

3. Deal only with immediate issues. Do not try to reason or argue.

4. Discourage the discussion of feelings.

5. Try not to be authoritative, but be firm, practical and realistic.

6. With mania, avoid debating your relative's ideas or pointing out what the person is saying is illogical. This will inevitably lead to an argument.

Don't

1. Jump to fulfill the person's demands.

2. Get caught up with the person's euphoria or unrealistic expectations.

3. Argue with the person to convince him or her that his or her plans are unrealistic.

SUMMARIZING INFORMATION FOR EFFECTIVE COMMUNICATION SKILLS

(both groups)

After you introduce this information, family members may feel overwhelmed and unable to apply these principles. Remind them that you will role-play a scenario for them, and this will illustrate the simplicity of how these strategies can be implemented. Also remind them that it is much easier to apply these principles at certain times rather than others.

Introduce the **HALT** slogan, borrowed from AA:

Don't discuss something important when you are too

HUNGRY

ANGRY

LONELY

TIRED.

At those times, our frustration tolerance is much lower, and we accomplish very little. Select times for more important discussions when you have had time to think about how you will approach your relative.

The other acronym for HALT is

HOPE

ACCEPTANCE

LOVE

TOLERANCE.

These qualities allow us to enhance our communication with others. The great thing about communication is that you always get more than one chance to experiment and try again.

Leader's Role-Play of a Common Communication Problem

CHOOSING A TYPICAL SCENARIO

Ask the group to choose one of the situations that have been discussed that they would like the leader to role-play. The purpose is to demonstrate the communication principles that have been discussed. Participants often comment that the communication strategies are difficult to put into practice, so it is useful for participants to observe the leader tackling a problem.

It is important to model an interaction that does not solve a problem but simply demonstrates a small sample of neutral or positive communication.

Throughout the eight weeks you will help the group to develop tolerance for situations that may have no obvious solutions. In this session it is helpful for members to see just how slowly the process occurs within the leader's role-play. Even hearing a role-play end with, "We can talk more about this at another time," can be reassuring for participants.

By the time you have reached this point in the group process, a particularly problematic issue shared by several group members has usually emerged. This issue relates to their relative's social isolation, withdrawal, irritability and impulsiveness. Bipolar groups tend to focus heavily on the challenges of managing mania rather than depression. You can ask whether the group would like to see the leaders role-play this interactional sequence.

Inform the group that following the role-play, they will have the opportunity to practise the communication strategies themselves; reassure them that they will not have to role-play in front of the entire group.

The leaders then role-play the requested scenario, demonstrating:

- use of the 11 points of effective communication

- the slow pace of communication and modelling of patience

- the achievement of tiny, positive interaction, as opposed to solving a problem in one sitting.

Depression role-plays should illustrate neutral ways of generating conversation with an acutely depressed individual, as well as short, simple sentences that a depressed individual can follow. Family members benefit from seeing that silence, pauses and a slow conversation are an acceptable part of being with a depressed individual. Many family members have experienced this but feel they are doing something wrong because they cannot motivate their relative to engage in more lengthy conversations.

Mania role-plays should illustrate ways of neutralizing or de-escalating an interaction with an agitated individual. Typically, family members will try to reason with their ill relative, and this frequently becomes a heated, even violent, argument. Strategies of backing out of a discussion, or making neutral, non-committal statements, should be modelled.

Family members who feel intimidated by the role-plays benefit from the observation, as the application of these principles becomes much more practical and realistic.

PARTICIPANTS' ROLE-PLAY

It is helpful to keep the information on effective communication posted during this exercise so that participants can refer to it during their role-plays. You can structure this exercise in two ways. If you have a large group (12 to 15), ask members to get in groups of three, with two other participants whom they don't know well. In this case, one person will play their ill relative, one person will play him- or herself, and one person will act as a coach, offering suggestions and support to the person practising the new ways of communicating. Group members can switch roles after five minutes, but in this case, there will probably not be time for all three to practise all three roles.

If you have a smaller group, ask participants to do the role-play with one other person whom they don't know personally. In both cases they will stay in role for only five minutes to practise the communication skills presented, using the same problem shown in the leader's role-play.

The leaders will go around the room, sitting and listening to the dialogue of the pairs or three-somes, and offer support and suggestions.

Briefly, process observations and feelings from this experience, reinforcing that learning how to use these communication strategies takes time and practice. Encourage the group members to be aware of their communications with their relative over the next week. Suggest that they try to implement one strategy.

Communication with Your Support Network

> If you run short of time, the following part can easily be moved to the next week, so that it leads into the topic of problem solving.
>
> This is a short lecture and question-and-answer session.

Why do people need support systems outside the family?

Having good communication with significant people in our lives can increase our chances of getting what we need from them. This becomes more important as we deal with more problems. However, when we are stressed, we sometimes become so absorbed with our relative's illness that we find it difficult to communicate clearly.

Determining who to network with, and how, means that you will be better prepared when you need to solve a problem or to deal with a crisis.

Obstacles to building a support network

> Generate a list of the obstacles.

Some obstacles to note

- not knowing what we need
- not knowing how to ask for help
- being unsure if it is acceptable to ask for help with a family problem
- fear of rejection
- fear of conflict
- asking for more than another wants to give
- fear of being stigmatized if you disclose what is happening outside the family.

Ways to develop realistic expectations of understanding and support

- Educate others about the disorder.
- Be selective as to who you tell about your situation.

- Interview friends and family about how they might help.

Suggestions to improve communications with support networks so you get what you want

- Acknowledge that extended family, friends and colleagues probably know very little about the reality of mental illness. People tend to operate on dated information and myths. Offer basic information and facts.
- Although public awareness campaigns have raised awareness about mental illness, a stigma typically still exists. Be thoughtful about who you choose to confide in. Look for people who are open and receptive to the information.
- As relatives, you need the opportunity to discuss your situation with friends and at times will need them to be there just for you. It is important to maintain a balance, where your friends also experience you listening to their interests and issues.
- Finally, if you need help and support from a friend, be clear about what you need (e.g., time to talk or to go to a movie together). Friends tend to respond when clear boundaries are defined.

Talking with Children about Their Parent's Mood Disorder

Parents are often very concerned about how their partner's mood disorder is affecting their children. In explaining the situation to children, it is important to take these points into account.

TALKING WITH CHILDREN

- Explain the illness, taking into account the children's level of development, so that they can understand their parent's behaviour. You do not need to go into detail about the diagnosis. Your goal is simply making sense of their parent's actions.
- It is important for children to know that it is not their fault. They must understand that an illness is causing the problem and not that their parent is angry at them or that they are being punished for misbehaviour.
- It is not the child's responsibility to fix it or to take on adult roles to compensate for their parent's problem. They should be reassured that adults will take care of the problem.
- During a time when their ill parent is feeling better, it is useful for the parent to acknowledge the illness to the children, and to reinforce that it is not the children's fault.

You can reassure group members who have children that there are things they can do to help children cope with their parent's mental illness. These "buffers" have been shown to help kids get through the rough times.

BUFFERS FOR CHILDREN

- **The presence of a well parent in the home:** The parent who continues to function as a loving, thoughtful parent who the children can rely on provides support and a model for normal adulthood.
- **Remaining active outside the family:** Ensure that children have outside activities, so that their lives are not completely absorbed by problems at home.

Distribute Handouts 4.1, 4.2 and 4.3, Communication Skills: Depression, Communication Skills: Bipolar Disorder and Talking with Children about Their Parent's Mood Disorder, here.

GROUP **5**
Problem Management

LEGEND:

B	Bipolar Group
D	Depression Group
	Handouts

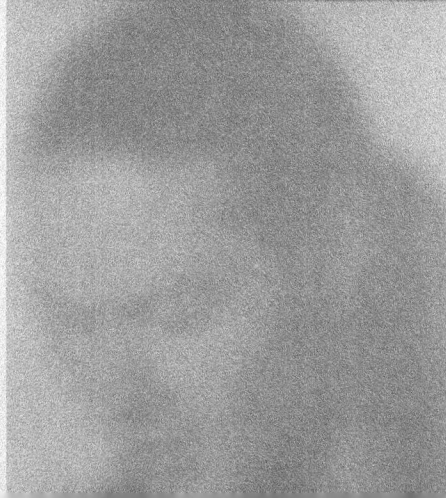

▶ Goals

- to help group members develop a new way of viewing problems and their management. Emphasis will be placed on having realistic expectations and using specific strategies. This is why this session teaches problem-solving skills but is called problem management. Problems are rarely solved all at once, but by practising specific problem-solving skills, over time group members can minimize their problems.
- to emphasize that in some cases a problem can be managed by a change in attitude toward the problem. We often feel that a problem is being managed or solved only when we observe a change in our relative's behaviour. In the case of mood disorders, however, there will be many times where no change in our relative is possible; in these situations, the solution to the problem may come from our ability to shift our internal expectations and attitudes.
- to practise the new problem management approach
- to discuss the feelings (grief, frustration) associated with accepting situations where family members have very little impact on solving their relatives' difficulties.

▶ Leader's notes

This group integrates the content for both depression and bipolar groups.

This group builds on the information and skills in Group 4, so that participants can integrate communication strategies with problem-solving principles.

This session includes a paper-and-pencil exercise, an interactive lecture, using the flipchart or chalkboard, and a brainstorming exercise. It builds on the rapport and mutual support that has developed within the group. You will need to provide paper and writing materials for participants.

Review of
Communication Strategies

Briefly review the major points to effective communication from last week. Post the flipchart page from last week so that participants can refer to the list throughout this session. Answer any questions that members have about the communication strategies.

Sometimes members have tried to implement the communication strategies through the preceding week, with differing degrees of success, and it can be helpful to briefly discuss their experiences. This provides a lead-in to the importance of this week's topic and an opportunity for group members to share support.

Introduction of
Problem Management

"PUT YOUR PROBLEM DOWN ON PAPER" EXERCISE: PART I

Provide participants with paper and pencil and ask them to write down a problem they are experiencing with their relative. Reassure them that this is not an exercise that they will have to share with others. Give them a couple of minutes and then ask them to keep it. We will return to this later.

IMPORTANCE OF PROBLEM MANAGEMENT

As a starting point, it is important to practise how to

- identify problems
- break them down into their different parts
- decide which parts we want to work on changing.

It is important to learn these steps so that we can feel less overwhelmed and more in control as we develop strategies for problem management.

How to Choose a Problem

INTRODUCTION

We all manage problems without thinking of the process as involving a "problem-solving strategy." However, when a family member is mentally ill, particularly when he or she lives with or frequently interacts with you, you are confronted with unique and multiple problems.

It then becomes important to think about defining and managing problems in a more systematic way. This will also enhance your sense of control over your life.

STEPS TO CHOOSING A PROBLEM

Why is this important?

Every day we are faced with multiple demands and problems. Without breaking things down and being organized and methodical, it is possible to be busy all day long and yet feel as though you haven't accomplished anything of significance.

For example, you are planning a large family event and you need a lot of food. You rush to the grocery store to get what you need and try to organize the menu while going up and down the aisles. You spend over $150 and arrive home to discover that you have forgotten several essential items and have nothing to make for dinner tonight.

Step 1: Defining or choosing one problem

It is important not only to slow down and focus but also to begin to break problems and issues down into smaller, more manageable parts. Problems are overwhelming when viewed in their entirety. Beginning to break the big problem down into smaller parts is a step that can lead us to possible solutions.

By choosing one part of the problem to work on, we are prioritizing, or making a conscious decision about which parts need immediate work and which ones can be put off until later.

For example, our old house needs to be fixed up. We might be most excited about the beautiful fireplace in the living room, but we know that we should concentrate on the kitchen first or we won't be able to live in the house. Only after we have a workable kitchen can we then focus on decorating the living room.

The same is true when dealing with your ill relative. Here is an example.

DEPRESSION EXAMPLE
Problem:

My husband stays in bed all day and he's up all night. He is unable to go to work and he doesn't help around the house at all. I come home from work and have to take care of everything.

Instead of seeing this as one big problem, break it down into its general parts.

1. Husband is not sleeping at night.

2. He stays in bed during the day.

3. He doesn't go to work.

4. He doesn't help with household responsibilities.

5. Wife assumes his roles and responsibilities.

6. Wife is feeling overwhelmed with the burden.

BIPOLAR EXAMPLE
Problem:

My wife is out of control. I didn't want her to, but she insisted on driving when we went out last night and she drove too fast. In fact, she was driving so fast she almost hit another car. I don't think that her medication is helping, but she refuses to discuss it.

1. Wife driving too fast.

2. She ignores husband's fears about her ability to drive carefully.

3. She resists discussing her medication.

4. Husband is afraid and frustrated.

From the example, you can see that trying to solve all the parts of the problem at once will not be possible. But, when you break the problem into smaller parts, you will be able to prioritize so that you can choose one part to work on.

Step 2: Consensus, compromise or working on your own

CONSENSUS

Where possible, it is best for you and your relative to agree on which part of the problem to focus on. Here you will need to use the communication skills already covered. Choose a good time to approach your relative and introduce the topic. For example, you could say, "I've been doing some thinking and wondered if we could talk about how you feel about how your days are going."

Don't underestimate the amount of time that will be needed to come to a point of agreement about the part of the problem to be worked on.

It is also important to remember the parts of the problem that involve safety. **Address any unsafe behaviours or situations first.** For example, you might say, "I've been doing some thinking and wondered if we could talk about my concerns about driving while on medication."

COMPROMISE

Often there will not be a consensus, and instead you can try to reach a compromise. Using the communication skills from last session, you can compromise and agree to work on the part of the problem where there is the most agreement. You could say, "I understand that you are sleeping during the day because you can't at night, but I'm finding it hard to do all the housework when I get home from work. Can we just talk about that part?"

WORKING ON YOUR OWN

If you cannot reach a compromise, and you still consider the problem to be an important one, work on the part that you feel is most important by yourself. You might say, "If I can't help us work together on the housework, maybe I need to deal with this on my own so I won't feel so frustrated all the time. Should I lower my standards or hire a cleaner?"

Often group members bring up their problems and as you deal with their questions about these situations briefly, you can begin to think about one that might be useful for the brainstorming exercise that comes next.

Step 3: Be specific.

In addition to defining the problem and breaking it down into its components, it is also necessary to define the problem in detail and explain why it is a problem from your perspective. Although this can be time-consuming, the more specifically a problem is understood, the easier it will be to tackle it.

Using our examples:

DEPRESSION

The problem of the husband's habit of staying up at night could be stated more specifically, as:

"My husband keeps me awake by playing the television loudly while I'm trying to sleep. When my sleep is disrupted, I don't cope as well with my duties at work. As long as work is going well, I feel I can cope with things at home."

BIPOLAR DISORDER

The problem of the wife's driving could be stated more specifically as:

"When my wife speeds, she could get a speeding ticket or cause a serious accident that might seriously injure or kill somebody. I am so afraid of this happening, I can't sleep at night. As a result, I am not coping well during the day."

Step 4: Sometimes we need to probe a bit deeper to find the hidden problem.

Some problems, as stated above, are straightforward. Others are more complex and contain hidden issues. Until we consciously think about it, we may not be aware of what is really bothering us.

In our **depression** example, imagine what would happen if the husband agreed to listen to the television with earphones — the wife would get more sleep and cope better with work. However, if she is actually bothered by her husband's inability to help raise their children, her sense of being overwhelmed may not improve as she had expected.

In our **bipolar** example, the wife might agree to let her husband drive the car, and his fears about safety in the car would be alleviated. However, if a further unexpressed concern is his fear that the medication and treatment plan are inadequate, he will remain anxious about safety issues.

It is important to address the emotions within a problem, or else the problem might appear to be solved on the surface, while the underlying uncomfortable feelings remain.

"PUTTING YOUR PROBLEM DOWN ON PAPER"
EXERCISE: PART II

Ask participants to revisit their individual problem. In light of the previous discussion, ask them to list three parts of their problem. Some people might list the parts by importance, but the point of this exercise is to separate the problem into its smaller components.

Using Brainstorming to Solve Problems

Brainstorming is a useful technique for developing and practising skills for effective problem solving. Encouraging participants to work together as a team on the problem presented by one group member will help them develop the skills for effective problem management. Group members will brainstorm possible solutions to the problem, with the encouragement of the leader, who also acts as a recording secretary. This helps group members to expand their ideas about what constitutes a solution and also to build group cohesion.

BRAINSTORMING

Brainstorming was first developed in the field of advertising as a way of exploring all possible solutions to a problem. It was most helpful in situations where people could remove the limitations of preconceived ideas to their problems. When people were allowed to stimulate another's creativity within a group, a chain reaction of new ideas could emerge (de Bono, 1992, p. 40).

Brainstorming includes having a leader who helps the group define the problem and review solutions already tried; keeps the group on course and acts as recording secretary so that no ideas are lost in the process. The leader will be the "process champion" (de Bono, 1992, p. 311), bringing the group back to the question at hand, if they stray from the topic, begin to criticize ideas or narrow the solutions suggested.

Some group members will find it useful to learn that they can explore and then choose options, so it is important to stress this point throughout the group exercise. One way to do this is to use Mae West's famous quotation: "Whenever I have to decide between two evils, I always like to choose the one I haven't tried yet."

Putting Brainstorming to Work

GROUP EXERCISE

This exercise gives the group an opportunity to work together, using the tool of brainstorming. Leaders should remind members that no ideas presented will be left off the list of alternatives. For many it will be their first chance to generate ideas without discarding them before they've even been considered.

Most groups will be able to identify a member with a problem that needs attention. Participants often share a problem that is pressing and, when asked, appreciate the fact that the group is willing to help them identify possible solutions. A problem might even have emerged from last week's group session; a leader might ask that participant for permission to use it in this exercise.

If this has not already happened, leaders can explain the exercise and ask whether someone has a problem that he or she would like help from the group with. If neither is a possibility, leaders can use the example problem, either depression or bipolar, from earlier in this session.

After reminding participants of the importance of confidentiality, the volunteer is asked to describe the problem fully. The rest of the group will have the opportunity to provide support and creative ideas to someone who is in a difficult situation, similar to their own.

A leader will act as recording secretary, listing all the alternatives presented by group members. Everything suggested will be listed, and the leader asks questions only to ensure that she or he understands the suggestion. As flipchart pages are filled, they will be taped up so that the group can observe their progress.

BRAINSTORMING EXERCISE

Brainstorming is effective because it generates many novel solutions to a problem. But for it to be useful, several guidelines will need to be followed.

1. Define the problem.

Why is this a problem for the family member?

Ask the family member to break down the problem into its components, then choose one to focus on. The exercise will be more successful if the problem is broken down into workable parts. You will work only on one of those parts. Previous practice on narrowing one's focus for effective coping will be helpful here.

2. Review what has already been tried.

▶

The group shouldn't have to "reinvent the wheel." List the solutions that have already been tried.

3. Put brainstorming to work.

The value of brainstorming is that one idea inspires another. Ideas build on other ideas. Ideas will not be evaluated or criticized during the brainstorming exercise.

▶

- Set a time limit so that the group will know the length of the exercise.
- Ask group members to jump in "popcorn style" with any suggestions.
- Remind group members not to censor their suggestions.
- List all suggestions on the flipchart. When one flipchart page is filled, tape it to the wall so that it remains visible and the ideas aren't overlooked during the process.
- The leader will ask only questions of clarification. If two people talk at the same time, the leader will ask them to take turns so that no ideas are lost.

4. Review the ideas listed on the flipchart sheets.

▶

- Stop the exercise at the end of the stated time.
- The leader ensures that all ideas are stated correctly.
- Group the suggestions according to three or four major themes. This serves two purposes. It helps to organize the work of the group and reinforces the cohesiveness and caring that have emerged as everyone has worked together to benefit one of the members. In addition, other members will also benefit from the review of possible solutions to their problems.

5. The participant with the presenting problem chooses his or her favourite solution.

You are trying to continue the attitude of curiosity and optimism that developed during the brainstorming exercise. Ask him or her to choose one that might be of interest to try as an experiment. Then, suggesting that — like Mae West — it can be helpful to have additional ideas on hand should one not work, ask for second and third choices. Remind the member that it is possible to abandon ideas that don't work.

Even as you are moving the participants from the openness of brainstorming to prioritizing and choosing specific ideas to try out, you are still modelling that there is likely more than one approach to managing a problem.

End by offering the flipchart paper of suggestions to the participant who presented the problem. This does two things. It says for the group that their efforts are valued and reinforces the confidentiality of the group.

Thank the group for their suggestions and for working together as a team. Thank the group member who allowed his or her problem to be used for the exercise, and express respect for his or her willingness to share the problem with the group.

Ask whether anyone has any questions. Suggest to participants that they consider experimenting with using brainstorming when they encounter a problem during the week. Discuss that it might feel awkward and slow at first and that this is a normal part of learning something new. Offer to discuss any questions that emerge from their experiment next week.

Distribute Handout 5.1, Problem Management — Brainstorming.

GROUP 6
Crisis Management

LEGEND:	
B	Bipolar Group
D	Depression Group
	Handouts

▶ Goals

- to present the basic principles of how to deal with a crisis (this will be an integration of the skills and strategies covered in the communication and problem-management groups)
- to specifically address the management of suicidal ideation and violence
- to process the feelings of distress/grief that are triggered when family members must deal directly with these issues.

▶ Leader's notes

This session integrates content for both depression and bipolar groups.

During the Communication Skills and Problem Management Groups, participants often raise examples of crisis situations that they have faced. This session applies the skills from previous sessions to the serious situations that family members have described. This topic is the reason that many of the participants were drawn to the group in the first place.

The main message is that group members need knowledge, self-care, patience and good planning to be prepared to handle the crises presented by their relative's situation.

At the beginning of this group, take a few minutes to check in with members about last week's group. It is especially important to check in with the volunteer who allowed the group to brainstorm his or her problem.

This session includes an interactive lecture with some specific information on how to handle crisis situations. Members often disclose difficult crises (such as suicide attempts and violence) that they have had to deal with, and the rapport and mutual support that has developed within the group should provide an atmosphere of safety for them to do so.

In preparation for the conclusion of the series, it is useful to remind members that this is the sixth group of the eight-week series.

Issues of concern that have not been covered should be identified and scheduled into the remaining weeks. There is usually time during the final session to discuss these topics.

Check in with participants, especially the volunteer who provided the sample problem last week. Group members often report having given a great deal of thought to that person's situation and frequently express hope that the pressure of the situation lessened over the past week.

Beginning the group with this "checking-in" process can support group cohesion and promote experimentation with new coping strategies.

Ask specifically whether other group members used any of the strategies discussed in the previous week. If so, what it was like to try something new? Leaders can provide encouragement or reassurance about the difficulty as well as the value of adopting and practising new behaviours.

Introduction to Crisis Management

Managing a crisis uses the same communication and problem-solving skills that you have been practising, but, as you know all too well, even when you do your best, there are times when a problem can quickly become a crisis.

WHAT IS A CRISIS?

If your relative is depressed, his or her mood can deteriorate, and he or she may experience severe despair and suicidal thoughts or behaviour. A crisis can also occur due to a manic phase when the person behaves in a reckless or aggressive manner, which can endanger him- or herself or others. Situations involving housing, financial losses or child welfare can also become crises.

WHEN A PROBLEM BECOMES A CRISIS

Emphasize individual differences and recognize that something that is a problem for one person may be a crisis for another. Or that a problem that is not adequately dealt with can become a crisis.

"What Crisis Have You Had to Deal With?"

AN EXERCISE

This is an exercise that encourages participants to air feelings about crisis situations they have dealt with in the past and at present. It focuses on strategies to use when their relative is distressed; the development of a concrete emergency action plan will be addressed in Group 7.

You will likely be familiar with the types of crises raised by group members, as aspects of these crises will have been discussed in previous groups. The value is in sharing with others who have also been through similar experiences. The leader will set a tone of acceptance and appreciation for what members have lived through. For many participants, it will be the first time they have felt that their feelings of anger, frustration or fear are not minimized or judged. As a leader, you will also be looking for examples to illustrate the importance of planning ahead. The crises shared by group members will lead into the next topic.

Ask the group for examples of crises they have dealt with. Pay attention to whether the group has primarily dealt with suicide or violence since this will influence how you emphasize the content and example portions of this group.

To encourage discussion, ask members to share what experiences were the most difficult for them. What was it about that particular situation that made it a crisis rather than a problem?

Strategies for Handling a Crisis

INTRODUCTION

> This is an interactive lecture that makes use of the flipchart or chalkboard. Emphasize that in handling a crisis, group members will use the same skills they learned in the Communication and Problem Management sessions. Reassure them that what they have already learned will be put to use here.
>
> This section will include general guidelines, as well as ways of handling specific situations. Practical application to examples of situations provided by the group members is an excellent way to make this information seem user-friendly and relevant.

GENERAL GUIDELINES

Tips for managing a crisis

These tips will seem familiar to group members because they come directly from the Communication Session.

However, just because they are familiar does not mean that they are easy to put into practice when your relative is upset and you see a potential crisis looming. The more you can practise good communication skills when the situation is calm, the better prepared you will be to use the skills when it appears as though things could get out of control.

1. Remain as calm as possible. The calmer you are, the more likely you will be able to develop a good plan.

2. Slow down. Everyone involved needs to speak quietly and one at a time. This will help to calm things down. Examples are: "Let's sit down and talk." or "I need to proceed a little more slowly."

3. Speak with a quiet, normal tone. You will communicate confidence and care by speaking carefully and thoughtfully.

4. Decrease other distractions. By decreasing distractions, you will reduce stimulation and have a better chance of keeping the situation from escalating.

5. If necessary, ask others to leave the room. Not only do you need to be calm, but others around you must also be calm.

6. Allow your relative to have personal space in the room. Try not to crowd your relative.

7. Recognize that too much emotion on your part can further upset your relative and allow the situation to escalate. A situation that could easily turn into a crisis brings out strong emotions, but expressing your feelings now is likely to worsen the situation.

8. Use validating and neutral statements about what you observe. Examples are: "I can see that you seem afraid and confused." "I can see that you are angry. Can you tell me what is wrong?"

9. Repeat questions or statements when necessary, using the same words each time. When people are upset, they lose their powers of concentration. Repeating what you want your relative to understand gives you a better chance of getting through.

10. Speak positively, without judgment. Do not lose your temper or belabour your point. If you do, both of you will lose control. Even if you feel that your relative is behaving like a child, this is not the time to point it out.

11. Remind yourself not to take your relative's behaviour personally.

This is a long list. It might be helpful for some group members to remember four things to avoid when they are in the midst of an escalating situation.

Four things to avoid

- shouting
- criticizing
- maintaining continuous eye contact
- arguing with other people about what to do

WHAT TO DO IN SPECIFIC SITUATIONS

Participants have already dealt with a number of difficult and specific situations, and they know that there are others that they might have to prepare for. This part of the group will provide some tips for how to handle common crisis situations.

Dealing with suicidal episodes

One of the most terrifying aspects of a serious mood disorder is when your loved one talks about suicide. While it is difficult to discuss, it is helpful to be knowledgeable about suicide and how to deal with it.

Depressive states and suicidal thinking

It is important to remember that suicidal thinking and statements are symptomatic of depression and are usually a temporary emotional state. **Most people do not want to end their lives.** Suicidal thinking or attempts typically occur during a major depressive episode when the person feels helpless, hopeless and in a state of despair. Depressed people do not believe that these intense feelings will pass. It is often helpful for you to provide a concrete reminder that these thoughts are part of the "lens of depression" and influence the way the ill person sees the world and his or her future. You can say, "I know this is very hard to hear because this feels so real to you, but this is the depression talking."

Dealing with suicidal thoughts and statements is a difficult balancing act. We can help people deal with these thoughts and feelings; however, it is also important to recognize your own limitations. Family members must realize that they do not have absolute control to change things and cannot be responsible for all of their relative's actions.

Prevention of an escalation in suicidal thinking by seeking professional intervention is more likely if you are informed and aware of the following:

WARNING SIGNS

1. Your relative discusses suicide and what it would be like to have things end. He or she may make comments such as, "When I'm gone..."

2. Your relative is concerned with having a will providing for children or pets, if he or she is not around. Your relative is preoccupied with the distribution of his or her possessions.

3. Your relative expresses feelings of worthlessness, such as, "I'm no good to anybody."

4. Your relative shows signs of feelings of hopelessness about the future, reflected in comments such as, "What's the use?"

5. Your relative has distorted beliefs, such as his or her partner is having an affair, or that money that he or she is entitled to is being withheld.

Any discussion of suicide must be taken seriously. If your relative speaks of suicide or inflicts wounds on him- or herself, contact the doctor immediately or take your relative to the emergency department of your local hospital.

Passive suicidal thinking

Long-term sufferers of depression can experience passive suicidal thinking. Thoughts of self-harm become a chronic feature of the depression, and it is difficult to differentiate between statements that reflect an immediate risk of self-harm and those that reflect the client's fatigue with feeling depressed. In these cases you will need to discuss the situation with the doctor in order to establish a management plan.

If you discover your relative after a suicide attempt

- Phone 911 immediately.
- If you know first aid, administer it immediately.
- Phone someone to accompany you to the hospital or to stay with you at home.
- Do not try to handle the crisis alone; contact a support group to help you with your immediate reactions and long-term feelings.

Where violence is an issue

It is not uncommon for partners and family members to have tolerated both verbal and physical aggression, but to feel that they had no choice because it was due to their relative/partner's disorder. When violence has been or is a real possibility, it is essential to have a well-thought-out plan.

Here, the process of brainstorming is useful. Many group members will have tried some strategies that did not work; they will need to review their options and develop a different plan should an aggressive or violent incident occur again.

Although it is difficult to acknowledge, particularly with mania, violence can be a very real threat. The first step in dealing with violence is to acknowledge that it exists and to state that mental illness is not an appropriate excuse or justification for violence in the home.

When dealing with violent behaviour, there may not be time to talk calmly or call for assistance; you may need to have an exit plan. The following points should be considered:

1. If your relative threatens to harm him- or herself or you, or to seriously damage property, you must do whatever is necessary to protect yourself and others (including your relative) from harm.

2. You may need to:

- leave the premises to call for help
- call a friend or family member and alert him or her to the situation that requires help
- secure your relative in a room while you go for help. This is advisable only under extreme circumstances.

3. You may need to evaluate whether it is safe for you to drive alone with your relative to the hospital.

4. You may need to call the police.

Understandably, many families are reluctant to call the police; however, extreme circumstances may require their involvement. There are some important things to know when there is a need to call the police for help.

- Sometimes, just telling your relative that you are calling the police will cause him or her to calm down.
- When you call 911, tell the emergency operator that your relative requires emergency medical assistance and your relative's diagnosis. State that you need assistance getting him or her to the hospital.
- Be prepared for a variety of responses from the police, depending on their knowledge of mental illnesses.
- Record the names of the officers, their badge numbers and their response time.
- While the police are present, you may have time to call the doctor. The police may recommend taking your relative to the hospital.

When going to the hospital

There are some important things to know when you must go to the hospital (in response to suicidal or violent episodes):

- If possible, it is best to have your relative go to the hospital voluntarily. (The next session will cover the issue of involuntary hospitalizations as a part of the discussion about the legal system).
- If your relative will not listen to you, ask someone else whom he or she trusts to convince him or her to go to the hospital. Ideally, this will be arranged in the action plan, which we will discuss next.
- Try to offer your relative a choice, such as "Will you go to the hospital with me, or would you prefer to go with John?" This gives your relative more of a sense of being a part of the plan.
- At the emergency department, speak directly with the doctor, social worker or nurse.
- Find out whether your relative will be admitted. If not, find out what follow-up treatment is recommended.

- If the hospital decides to discharge your relative, and you feel that your relative must be admitted for his or her safety, you can tell the medical person in charge that you do not feel that it is safe to take the person home. You can ask him or her to explain to you why he or she feels that the decision is a safe one.

Behaviours That Should Not Be Tolerated

In addition to dealing with these potential crisis situations, it is also important to help group members with limit-setting. Some group members may present situations in which they have questions about the appropriateness of their relative's behaviours, and this often includes questions of safety for all involved. It is important to support them in setting limits on unsafe, abusive or destructive behaviours.

The following behaviours are unacceptable:

- physical aggression such as pushing, grabbing or pinching
- clear emotional abuse, such as yelling profanity or verbally aggressive threats
- sexual abuse
- property damage, such as damaging furniture or cars
- setting fires or creating fire hazards, such as smoking in bed
- stealing from family, friends or others
- using non-prescribed drugs or alcohol, which complicate the psychiatric disorder
- financial mismanagement, such as engaging in spending sprees
- severely disruptive or tyrannical behaviours, such as insisting that all family members eat only certain foods, refusing to let anyone use the phone or barricading the doors.

Group leaders should emphasize the following:

- **It is not helpful to their relative to allow them to do things that are dangerous to themselves or others.**

To do so out of feelings of intimidation or concern about hurting their relative's feelings will only delay dealing with a difficult or dangerous situation.

- **Abusive or dangerous situations will not go away on their own.**

You can encourage participants to use the skills they have learned in dealing with these situations. When you take questions, you can help members in making plans for dealing with their individual situations using the skills they have been learning, while always emphasizing the importance of safety.

Although you have helped members to deal with these issues throughout this series, this exercise gives you the chance to reiterate their importance, and the handout will help reinforce this once the series has ended.

At this point, members often discuss the importance of the group in their lives and that it is easier to make these changes while attending the group. You can begin the process of helping them to gain confidence in their newly learned skills by reviewing and reminding them that they can refer to the handouts after the group ends.

When we have held follow-up groups several months later, members often state that they were able to remember what they had learned and used the handouts as reminders.

Distribute Handout 6.1, Crisis Management.

GROUP 7
Working with the
Medical and Legal Systems

LEGEND:

| B | Bipolar Group |

| D | Depression Group |

| | Handouts |

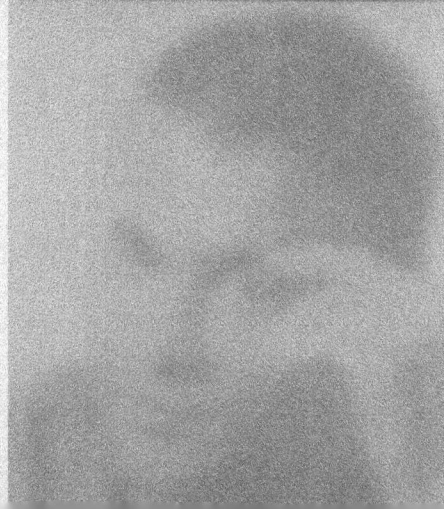

▶ A note about Handout 7.3

Because the medical and legal systems vary from country to country — and even between provinces in Canada and between states in the United States — this handout must be individualized based on the laws of your community. The following handout contains information that is specific to Ontario. It can, however, serve as a template for developing a handout that is appropriate for your groups.

To customize the handout, you will need to research the applicable laws in your province or state concerning:
- criteria for allowing voluntary hospitalization
- the procedure for obtaining involuntary hospitalization
- if there are criteria for allowing involuntary treatment, and if so, what they are
- if the law permits involuntary treatment, and if so, will it automatically take place or must someone request it
- which authorities can obtain involuntary hospitalization and/or treatment
- the minimum period before an involuntary patient can leave the hospital
- the procedure for keeping the patient in the hospital after the mandated period has elapsed
- the mandated length of time for involuntary treatment
- Community Treatment Orders: have they been enacted? If so, how does this affect the criteria and procedures for involuntary hospitalizations?

▶ Goals

- to present the emergency action plan — an exercise that incorporates material from the previous three groups
- to provide a brief, historical overview of the political influences that have shaped our current mental health legislation in North America
- to discuss strategies that can be helpful when interacting with the police, emergency services, and hospital staff.

▶ Leader's notes

This section incorporates information for both depression and bipolar groups.

This session provides practical information. Building on the information from last session, this week begins with the development of an emergency action plan. Until now, all efforts have focused on reducing the chance that a crisis will occur or defusing one that has already begun. This week begins with the recognition that it is not always possible to keep the situation under control. You are sending the message that, despite their best efforts, group members will sometimes have to handle things without their relative's help. A person who is suicidally depressed or has full-blown mania will need someone who cares about him or her to take the situation in hand.

Developing a plan for such emergencies can be a great relief for group members, and involving their relatives in the development of an emergency action plan (when that is possible) can help them to begin the process of talking with their relative about their disorder.

You will also provide group members with other resources in this meeting. Reminding them that next week will be the last time you will meet is also important for their planning.

Handouts 7.1 and 7.2, Developing an Emergency Action Plan and Your Emergency Action Plan, will be distributed early in the group (see Leader's Notes), while Handout 7.3, Working with the Medical and Legal Systems, will be handed out at the end.

As a follow-up to the last session, group leaders should check in with the group member who volunteered his or her problem with the group exercise. In some cases, the group member may have tried some of the strategies generated by the group process, and an exploration of his or her success or frustration can be helpful. Before moving on to the Emergency Action Plan, it is also helpful to ask the group if they feel that the process of brainstorming and implementing small strategies seems "do-able."

This can be a helpful introduction to the discussion of the emergency action plan, which builds on the skills of the problem-management and communication sessions. These strategies, combined, allow people to plan ahead and develop concrete plans for handling difficult situations that may quickly arise when a family member has a mental illness.

Present and list the parts of an emergency plan. Giving participants permission to plan how to cope with a serious problem is often reassuring. It may be the first time that someone has suggested that they don't have to just react. It can be useful to suggest that they will be helpful to themselves, their relatives and their families by becoming proactive. The emergency plan that you present is a "Cadillac" Plan. Participants may be unable to accomplish all of the goals included, but even beginning to plan for hard times will give them much more stability than having no plan at all.

Emphasize that making and maintaining an emergency plan is a process — an ongoing process. Encourage members to include their relative's input during times when the relative is stable.

Sometimes participants worry that planning for an emergency means that one is more likely to occur or that even discussing the possibility may trigger a deterioration in their relative. Remind them that they have car insurance, and that it gives them security even if they don't have an accident. It is understandable that when our relatives are stable, we would hope that they will remain that way, but planning ahead for a possible emergency gives us added peace of mind.

An emergency action plan should be updated periodically so that it appropriately reflects the situation that both you and your relative are facing. For example, the person you would call for support today may not be the same person you would call five years from now.

ELEMENTS OF AN EMERGENCY PLAN

1. Establish a list of phone numbers for the following:

    • doctor(s)
    • police
    • emergency department.

2. Ask the doctor, ahead of time, which hospital you should bring your relative to, should the need arise.

3. If possible, with your relative's consent, try to establish a strong relationship with the doctor.

4. Consider consulting with the police in advance. It can be helpful to know how your call will be received and helpful for them to know what they can expect should you need to call in an emergency.

5. Establish who you can call, day or night, for support.

6. If you are the parent of young children, arrange for emergency child care in case you must go to the hospital.

7. Know which relatives or friends your relative trusts in the event of an emergency.

8. Develop an emergency plan at a time when your relative is well and can participate and consent to the plan. Consider a power of attorney (to be discussed in Section 3 of this group).

Developing an Emergency Action Plan

This exercise is designed to help participants who have never developed an emergency plan before as well as those who would like to review their current plan.

Distribute Handouts 7.1 and 7.2, Developing an Emergency Action Plan and Your Emergency Action Plan.

Allow time for group members to complete Handout 7.2. At the end, review what was helpful and ask whether there are any parts participants would like to develop further. This will be a group discussion; reassure them that sharing information about their situation will be strictly voluntary and will be kept confidential by group members.

YOUR EMERGENCY ACTION PLAN

This form is designed to help you begin to develop an emergency action plan for your unique situation.

Ask yourself the following questions:

1. Do I know the phone numbers for the following people?

    My relative's doctor(s)?   It is _____ .

    Police?   It is _____ .

2. Do I know which hospital my relative's doctor uses?

    It is _____ .

    Hospital emergency department phone number _____

3. Do I know my relative's medication(s)?

    _____

4. Who could I call day or night for support?

    Name _____   Phone Number(s) _____

    _____

    _____

5. Who are the relatives or friends whom my relative trusts in the event of an emergency?

Name _____ Phone Number(s) _____

Name _____ Phone Number(s) _____

Name _____ Phone Number(s) _____

6. For parents of small children: What child care could I use in case I had to accompany my relative to the hospital?

_____

_____

Contact Name_____ Phone Number(s) _____

Contact Name_____ Phone Number(s) _____

7. Have I discussed an emergency action plan with my relative during a stable time? If so, what are my relative's requests?

_____

_____

_____

8. Are there additional steps that I could take to improve my emergency action plan? If so, list the steps here:

1. _____

_____

2. _____

_____

3. _____

9. Crisis Centre phone numbers: _____

_____

10. Do I need to revisit my plan? If so, how often?

_____

How to Work with the
Medical and Legal Systems

It is important for participants to understand when and how their relative can be admitted to a hospital and what their relative's legal rights are at various times in his or her illness and treatment. The following is a brief overview of the key points that are useful to family members. This section may trigger group members' frustrations with

a. the limitations of the system

b. negative experiences with professionals.

This is an excellent process opportunity to integrate good communication skills with how to work with the system. Family members benefit from the facilitators modelling assertive communication rather than aggressive communication.

HISTORICAL BACKGROUND

It is useful to understand the historical background of mental health legislation in order to put it into perspective. The same process occurred in both the United States and Canada; however, Canada's revised legislation occurred about 10 years after the United States embarked on a revision of its legislation, which is sharply in favour of clients' rights to refuse or accept treatment independent of their families and the state.

The roots of the mental health legislation come from the monarchy's Parens Patriae Doctrine, which named the King as the Supreme Parent. Intervention occurred only when the family was unable or unavailable to provide care and protection for children of the mentally ill.

In Canada, from the 1870s until about the 1960s, the state had the power to involuntarily hospitalize clients for treatment. Early on, people were committed to asylums and poor houses due to poverty, developmental delays or mental illness. Gradually, the mentally ill were separated out and hospitalized, even though no real treatments were available. In order to be released, clients had to undergo treatment and demonstrate improvement. As treatments were not available, many people were committed to institutions with little or no chance of improving or ever being released. Many individuals' civil rights were seriously compromised as a result.

In the 1960s in Canada, the increased use of antipsychotic medications led to more effective treatments of the mentally ill. At the same time, the civil rights movement challenged the historical approach to treating the mentally ill. These combined trends led to increased rights for clients and the introduction of deinstitutionalization, where clients were discharged to the community in cases where it was assumed that community-based resources (such as housing and case management) would ensure that they were adequately cared for. This was also viewed as a less expensive way of caring for people with mental illnesses.

In the 1960s, judicial review of the mental health system led to new approaches for the involuntary committal of the mentally ill. The courts ruled that there were only two ways for the state to deprive a person of his or her liberty:

1. If someone broke the law, the state/police could arrest him or her and, if found guilty, the person would receive punishment.

2. The state could intervene if a parent failed to provide appropriate care of a child.

Treatment for a mental disorder was no longer viewed as a justifiable reason to deprive someone of his or her liberty unless the person was a threat to him- or herself or others. This is the system we have today.

While there is no doubt that changes were needed and were enacted with the best of intentions, our current system has created complex problems for families. As a result of these reforms, it is difficult for families to obtain care for relatives who refuse it because they will not acknowledge their illness. Only extreme events allow involuntary intervention.

The following is a description of the ways in which a person suffering from a mental illness can obtain psychiatric inpatient care.

COMMUNITY TREATMENT ORDERS

A community treatment order (CTO) is a legal tool or mechanism, issued by a medical practitioner, that defines the conditions under which a person with a mental illness may live in the community (CMHA/Ontario Division). If the individual fails to follow the order, he or she is returned to a psychiatric facility for assessment, but not hospitalization.

Public concern about the apparent increase in the number of mentally ill in the community who are not engaged in treatment raises important questions about alternative mechanisms such as CTOs, which may be used to aid clients in becoming more treatment compliant. This group of people actually represents two distinct groups:

- individuals who come into contact with the mental health system and for various reasons do not engage in the treatment offered
- individuals with virtually no contact with the mental health system who are living in the community and who are visibly mentally ill, many of whom are homeless.

CTOs have traditionally been designed to meet the needs of the first group. Proponents of CTOs assume that the orders are a viable mechanism for linking this group of individuals with the treatment system. Opponents, however, argue that there are better approaches to the problem of how to engage clients who are difficult to treat, and the evidence is thin regarding the effectiveness of CTOs.

While CTOs have existed in some form or other for decades, their effectiveness remains a contentious issue, with no research to date to support their effectiveness. In a survey of the 35 states in the United States with legislation, only 12 reported its use as "common" or "very common." CTOs have, however, existed in Saskatchewan for several years and have been introduced in Ontario with the passing of Bill 68 in June 2000. It is likely that the other provinces will follow suit.

Given the newness of the legislation, there are more questions than answers. It is important for families to be aware of this legislation and to ask questions as to what it will mean to them and their relative. A group discussion focused on the following questions may be facilitated and group members could be encouraged to voice their concerns to their elected provincial or state representatives.

Families must consider the following important questions:

- Will this legislation benefit my family member?
- How does the government define liability and responsibility? In other words, who is legally responsible for a person under a CTO?
- Are there appropriate community supports and monitoring?
- How long does it apply for?
- How does one get off a CTO?
- What is the review process?
- Will my relative have access to an inpatient bed in the presence of this legislation?
- Will families, clients and service providers receive education on the legislation?
- Will the government be evaluating the effectiveness of the legislation?

(Centre for Addiction and Mental Health, February 2000.)

CRITERIA FOR INPATIENT ADMISSION TO PSYCHIATRIC HOSPITAL

This section applies to the legislation of Ontario. The history of the development of the legislation for involuntary committal of the mentally ill is similar throughout Canada and the United States, so you will be able to use much of the information contained in the historical background section throughout the states and provinces.

Because of the similarity in history, there will also be similarities in the laws for involuntary committal. However, there will be some differences in language and protocol. For this reason, it will be important to use the Criteria for Inpatient Admission to Psychiatric Hospital section as a guide for how to present the criteria. You will need to review the law for involuntary committal for your state or province to ensure that you are providing accurate information for group members. You can do this by researching in a law library or consulting a lawyer who specializes in this field.

A person can be admitted to a general or psychiatric hospital in one of two ways: voluntarily or involuntarily.

Voluntary patients

With the recommendation of a physician and the consent of the client, a person can be admitted voluntarily to a psychiatric hospital. Criteria for admission is that the person is in need of the observation, care and treatment provided by an inpatient psychiatric facility. This is the preferred situation, since the person is usually more likely to engage in a treatment plan with staff, and the family do not feel that they are acting against their relative's wishes.

The person wishing to go into hospital can contact his or her doctor or mental health worker, if he or she has one, or go to an emergency department of a community hospital that has an inpatient psychiatric department, to a psychiatric hospital directly, or to a local distress centre.

Involuntary patients

This is a much more difficult situation for all concerned. The law identifies three ways in which a person can be admitted as an involuntary, or certified, patient.

1. The person must be seen to be a danger to him- or herself, is suicidal or self-harming.

2. The person is seen as being a danger to others or is homicidal.

3. The person is unable to care for him- or herself and is in imminent risk as a result, such as refusing to eat or drink.

HOW CAN A PERSON BE HOSPITALIZED ON AN INVOLUNTARY BASIS?
(Ontario, Canada only)

A **form 1** is used by a physician who has seen your relative within the last seven days and has found the person to meet one or more of the three criteria listed above. Then the person can be brought into the psychiatric hospital and detained, restrained, examined and observed for up to 72 hours. At that time the person may be found to be sufficiently well as to no longer meet any of the three criteria and will be given voluntary status. The person then can choose to stay in hospital or leave without medical approval.

A **form 2** is obtained when the family member goes to the Justice of the Peace and provides information about the relative's mental state. This information is included in an affidavit containing enough detail to satisfy the Justice of the Peace that the committal criteria of

- danger to self and others
- inability to care for self; **and**
- suffering from a mental illness

are met. Again, the individual may be detained up to 72 hours at which time the patient must be re-evaluated for certifiability.

You or the police may then take your relative to the hospital.

A **form 3** is issued when a form 1 or a form 2 expires and the patient still meets conditions for certifiability. This lasts two weeks. If the patient is still deemed to be certifiable, a **form 4** can be issued that will last for four weeks.

When someone is admitted involuntarily, he or she will be visited by a Patient's Rights Adviser. The adviser will ask the patient if he or she wishes to appeal the form, and the adviser will assist with the appeal process. Families are usually invited to the hearing by the patient or by the doctor to give information about the patient's condition.

COMMON PROBLEMS FOR FAMILIES

Members often have had experiences where they found it difficult to be heard by their relative's doctor or hospital. The group will benefit from the opportunity to express their negative experiences and discuss the systemic problems they have encountered.

Commonly asked questions should be covered at this point. During this process, group members should be encouraged to share successes and failures and support one another. This is also a good time to problem solve around systemic issues they have all experienced. (For example, the patient is discharged from hospital without notice to the family; change in treatment is implemented and family is not told even where patient consents; emergency-room staff will not listen to the family's input.)

Here are some commonly asked questions:

My relative's doctor won't talk to me. How can I give the doctor information that I think is necessary for my relative's care and safety?

Because the law does not allow a doctor to communicate with family members without the patient's permission (except in the cases listed where there is a risk of immediate harm), the best way to be able to talk with your relative's doctor is for your relative to sign a Form 14 (Ontario), or an equivalent release-of-information form in the person's jurisdiction.

What if my relative won't sign a release-of-information form?

This makes your situation more difficult. Here are some options:

1. Ask your relative to allow you to accompany him or her to an appointment with the doctor. Discuss with your relative what you want to cover in the session, so that he or she does not feel that you are trying to take away control of his or her life.

   It may take some time to convince your relative of the importance of this and of your good intentions. Remember to use the communication skills learned in Session 4.

2. If your relative does not agree to this plan, you can call or write to the doctor on your own. Because of the laws of confidentiality, the doctor will not be able to give you information about your relative, and usually will not even be able to acknowledge that your relative is a patient. It can be helpful to acknowledge to your relative's doctor that you are aware of this right at the beginning of the conversation.

   You are not under the same confidentiality constraints as the doctor, so you can explain that you have information that you think is important for the doctor to know for your relative's care and safety. You can provide information to the doctor without jeopardizing the doctor's confidentiality.

   Remember, the doctor needs to maintain a good, trusting relationship with your relative and will likely feel the need to inform your relative that this communication has taken place. It is better to inform your relative yourself that you will be communicating one way with the doctor rather than having it come as a surprise to the patient from the doctor.

   If I need to take my relative to the emergency department of the hospital, how can I ensure that I have the chance to communicate the necessary information to the staff so that they understand the seriousness of the situation?

   When you accompany your relative to the emergency department, the staff should interview you as well as your relative. You have information that they need to make an informed decision about your relative's treatment.

   When you bring your relative in, inform the staff that you would also like to talk with them. Try to provide an organized account of the events leading up to the hospital visit. If safety is an issue, make sure you state this clearly and emphatically.

   What if I take my relative to the emergency department and they want to release him or her, and I don't think that he or she is safe to go home?

If you fear that your relative will be released and that is not safe decision, you can ask to speak with the doctor who has seen your relative. You can ask him or her for the decisions that your relative is safe to be released.

Inform the doctor that you would like assurance that your relative and family will be safe before you agree to take your relative home. **If there are children in the home, inform the doctor of this.**

TREATMENT

We have just outlined the process and criteria to have someone admitted to hospital as either a voluntary or involuntary patient. However, giving treatment requires a different set of consent requirements.

No patient, either voluntary or involuntary, may receive treatment without the consent of the patient, or other authorized person, except in emergencies when life, limb or vital organ is endangered.

In order for a consent to be valid, the consenting individual must

1. be competent to give the consent

2. have the intellectual capacity to make the decision

3. give the consent voluntarily

4. be given enough information to make an informed decision, including information relating to potential risks or side-effects.

Both voluntary and involuntary patients must be competent to consent to treatment. If a patient is involuntary and found to be mentally incompetent, the Mental Health Act (Ontario) outlines how the consent of the nearest relative must be obtained, starting with spouse, children at the age of majority, siblings and next of kin. If the nearest relative does not consent to the treatment, a Review Board (made up of several different professionals) order for treatment must be obtained.

Beyond this, the patient has access to an appeals board if he or she objects to ongoing treatment. However, once a patient is stabilized, he or she no longer meets the criteria to remain an involuntary patient and, upon becoming voluntary, can once again refuse treatment if he or she chooses. Unfortunately, in some cases, this leads to discontinuation of medication/treatment and another relapse and involuntary admission to hospital.

Other types of intervention for involuntary patients are as follows:

PUBLIC TRUSTEE (ONTARIO)

This is a government official who acts in the best interests of an individual. The individual may voluntarily appoint a trustee to administer his or her assets. If the person is incompetent, a physician may issue a Certificate of Incompetence and refer the person to a Public Trustee who will act for the person or determine whether any family members can do so in a competent and just manner.

POWER OF ATTORNEY

This is a legal document and must be signed by an individual when he or she is mentally competent. This gives the person who is acting as power of attorney the right to act on behalf of the individual during any subsequent legal incapacity on the individual's part.

WILLS

Parents or relatives may wish to leave a portion of their estate to a person who has a mental disability. In some cases, it is advisable to appoint a trustee to handle the assets for the disabled relative.

This is intended as a brief overview of some legal issues pertaining to families and mental health issues. Since legal issues can be complex, family members should seek professional advice for certain problems.

Discussion. Ask participants for their questions and comments. It is important for them to have the opportunity to express feelings about what they have dealt with in either trying to get help for their relative or trying to convince their relative to accept help. Direct the dialogue to focus on adaptive ways to work with mental health professionals. This will overlap with good communication strategies already discussed in Group 4.

Be assertive and persistent rather than aggressive and hostile.

Prioritize your issues and focus on one topic at a time.

After your best efforts, if you cannot get a response from the doctors/mental health workers, contact a more senior administrator for help.

Distribute Handout 7.3 Working with the Medical and Legal Systems.

Preparation for Group 8

Section 3 of Group 8 is a group discussion, the goal of which is to encourage the group members to talk about their hopes for the future. We have found that an article that deals with the impact of mental illness on families will often act as a catalyst to discussion. "Out of the Ashes," reproduced in Appendix 6, is included as an example. In the course of your own reading, you will most likely come across other material that will be appropriate for the groups you work with.

Note: Most publishers require that you request permission to make multiple copies of their material. You can get information directly from the publisher, or from Cancopy at www.cancopy.com (Canada) or the Copyright Clearance Centre at www.copyright.com (U.S.).

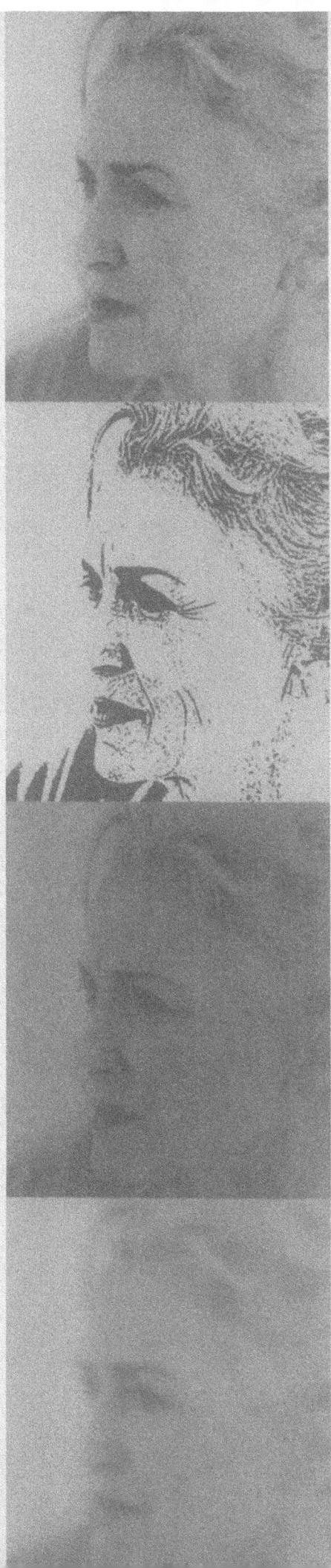

OUTLINE

PART I
SECTION 1 (10 MIN.): Review of Groups 1 to 7 (p. 151)
SECTION 2 (20 MIN.): Community Resources (p. 153)

PART II
SECTION 3 (30 MIN.): Looking to the Future (p. 155)
Discussion
SECTION 4 (30 MIN.): Sharing Observations and Feelings
(p. 157)

HANDOUTS

HANDOUT 8.1: Client and Family Resource List
HANDOUT 8.2: Client and Family Reading List
HANDOUT 8.3: Online Resources — Depression
HANDOUT 8.4: Online Resources — Bipolar Disorder

GROUP 8
Summary and Planning for the Future

LEGEND:

B — Bipolar Group

D — Depression Group

Handouts

A note about Handout 8.1

Handout 8.1 (Client and Family Resource List) contains a list of associations and agencies that would be easily accessible to people living in the Greater Toronto Area. This handout can be used as a template to build a resource list that is customized for your community.

The following is a list of some of the types of organizations you could include in your Resource List. Many organizations and agencies have Web sites that, in addition to providing information about their services, also provide links to other mental health, healthcare and social service organizations.

National: Canada
Canadian Mental Health Association — National Office
www.CMHA.CA (the Web site has links to local CMHA offices as well as to other organizations)

National: US
National Institute of Mental Health
www.nimh.nih.gov/
National Alliance for the Mentally Ill
www.nami.org

Provincial
provincial ministry of health
advocacy groups such as the Mood Disorders Association of Ontario

Local
distress centres
crisis centres
referral services
agencies providing advocacy and education (may include local chapters of national groups)
agencies providing self-help groups for relatives and friends
women's organizations providing resources specifically to women
family service agencies
home care agencies
case management organizations

▶ Goals

- to provide a summary of the overall program content
- to highlight the most salient areas from the series (for example, in one group, violence and limit-setting may have been emphasized, in another group, accepting the limitations of what family members can do may have been particularly important)
- to process the feelings associated by being part of the group
- to allow the leader and group members to process the feelings associated with ending the group.

▶ Leader's notes

This group integrates content both for depression and bipolar groups.

This will be the final group in the series.

This group will include wrapping up, in terms of responding to any outstanding questions or concerns. Because groups differ in their pacing, it is not unusual to have leftover material that must be covered in this final group. For this reason, this session is less structured than the previous seven. It is designed to allow for some catch-up in content, and to cover additional issues that need closure prior to ending the group.

This session will provide members with additional written resources and an article written to help families find meaning through this difficult and unexpected journey with their ill relatives.

At this point, distribute all the Group 8 handouts, (Handout 8.1, Client and Family Resource List; Handout 8.2, Client and Family Reading List; Handout 8.3, Online Resources — Depression; Handout 8.4, Online Resources — Bipolar Disorder). In the resource lists, include both professional and self-help organizations. It is important that participants leave the group knowing the resources that are available in their community.

For many participants this has been a unique experience. For some, it was the first time they could talk openly with others who live in situations similar to their own. For that reason it is important that members have the opportunity to process the impact of the group on their views and to say goodbye.

Finally, group members may wish to stay in touch. With the group's permission, a phone list can be distributed or mailed out to participants. This can facilitate the development of a more informal self-help group, with or without support from the facilitators.

COMPLETE PREVIOUS TOPICS

At this time you can finish up any outstanding content from the previous seven weeks. This session is designed to be flexible enough that you can shorten the included topics in order to complete anything that has been left unfinished.

REVIEW

If you have completed all previous weeks' content, immediately begin the review. This gives participants an opportunity to focus on what they have learned and to clarify areas where they have questions.

The review should include the first two groups, which focused on the client and his or her needs:

1. Causes of the illness — an overview of what mood disorders are, how they are diagnosed and that they have multiple causes. It was important to dispel some of the myths and misconceptions about mood disorders.

2. Medications — overview of medications, ECT and how they are used.

    Psychosocial treatments — introduction to therapy, support groups, case management.

The remaining six groups focused on the family and their needs:

3. Stress Management Strategies

4. Communication Skills

5. Problem Management

6. Crisis Management

7. Developing an Emergency Action Plan.

With each area, ask for questions or comments.

Provide a brief survey of the material in each group. Highlight themes that were relevant to your group. Much of what you present to the group in this section will be based on your notes as you and the group members worked through the first seven sessions.

Distribute Handouts 8.1, 8.2, 8.3 and 8.4, Client and Family Resource List, Client and Family Reading List, Online Resources — Depression and Online Resources — Bipolar Disorder, here.

Provide members with a chance to review and comment on the contents of the handouts. Some participants will have read books or searched the Internet a great deal, and they will likely have additional suggestions, or comments on the resources listed.

The same will be true for Community Resources. Give group members the opportunity to share information and views on resources that will be helpful to the entire group.

Do not rush this process. Group members are aware that this is their last meeting, and this is an opportunity to share information.

Looking to the Future

Group discussion

The purpose of this section is to stimulate discussion among group members about their hopes for the future.

The following are examples of the types of questions, based on the article you distributed to the group at the end of group 7, that can be used to stimulate discussion:

This article addresses both the positives and negatives about the issues that families must deal with.

• What were your feelings as you read this article?

• Was there anything new in it for you?

• What do you think your relative could learn from this article?

• When you think about this article, was there anything in it that can help you in dealing with your relative's illness?

• Who else do you think might benefit from reading an article of this kind? In what ways?

This does not have to be a long discussion. In fact, as previously discussed, you may not have time for a long discussion. The goal is to provide the group with a positive message about the potential for human growth, and that they are doing their part by participating in this group. Finally, we hope that their relatives are also able to participate.

Sharing Observations and Feelings

REVIEW OF GROUP

> You might find that you move into this last part of the group naturally from the previous section, but it is important to spend some time on this final part of the group.

WHEN YOU THINK ABOUT THE GROUP, WHAT PARTS WERE MOST HELPFUL FOR YOU?

> Allow participants time for discussion. You will be surprised at the variety of answers here. As leaders, we see the big picture, and our goals are for participants to be able to develop better stress management strategies and to communicate more clearly. But group members who are dealing with very specific situations will often say things like,

"It was really helpful for me to find out that I could have a 'Plan B' if the first plan didn't work out."

"I'll always remember that HALT slogan — that I shouldn't try to talk to my relative if I'm too hungry, angry, lonely or tired."

"I didn't fully understand the importance of my relative taking the medications everyday, even if he was feeling better, until the doctor explained how they work."

> As a leader, you will gain a greater appreciation of the positive impact of a group of this kind every time you receive this feedback. We think that we know why we lead these groups, but it isn't until we hear these responses that we really know the significance of them in group members' lives.

SAMPLE PROMPTS FOR FEEDBACK
• In order to help us prepare for future groups, can you tell us what you would have liked us to cover in more depth?

• Were there things that we covered that you did not find helpful?

Let participants take their time in discussing the significance of the group in their lives. It is also important for them to be able to make suggestions for possible improvements for future groups.

Finally, before you close, remind group members of your appreciation of the time and energy they have taken to participate in this group.

Options

Sometimes, group members may exchange phone numbers. You may or may not decide to be a part of that. Also, if you will be holding a follow-up session in three months, this is the time to set the date for that. Some leaders provide light refreshments at the end of the last group to help participants make the transition to the group's ending.

Afterword

The Family Group closes very differently from the way from it began. It started with family members struggling on their own to try to make sense of their relative's illness and attempting to do the right thing to support the relative in making progress toward health. These people, who were strangers to each other, came together and, over the weeks, they were changed by the experience of sharing their struggles with others who could understand. They were no longer alone in making their way along a complicated path.

As Stearns has pointed out, life can never be the same for families caring for a relative with mental illness, but happiness is possible. We can, she says, learn from our pain in such a way that our learning becomes useful to ourselves and others (Hatfield p. 64). The group has provided family members with a safe and supportive place to make this important transition. They have gained knowledge about the disorder and coping skills for how to deal with it. Equally important is that the group also focused on them and their needs in their own right, and not only as caregivers.

Not only it is important to give group members an opportunity to talk about the importance of the group in their lives and about their hopes for the future, but it is equally important for you to appreciate the significant role you have played in this growth. The authors of this book have had the opportunity to participate in many groups and hope that you will find the satisfaction that we have in getting to know and work with these courageous families.

References

Bartha, C., Parker, C., Thomson, C., & Kitchen, K. (1999). *Depressive Illness: An Information Guide.* Toronto: Centre for Addiction and Mental Health

Bipolar Clinic Staff, Centre for Addiction and Mental Health. (2000). *Bipolar Disorder: An Information Guide.* Toronto: Centre for Addiction and Mental Health

Centre for Addiction and Mental Health, February 2000. *Best Advice: Community Treatment Orders: Overview and Recommendations.* Toronto: Centre for Addiction and Mental Health

De Bono, E. (1992). *Serious Creativity.* Toronto: HarperCollins.

Hatfield, A. (1996). Out of the ashes of mental illness ... a new life. In B. Abosh and A. Collins (Eds.) *Mental Illness in the Family, Issues and Trends.* (58-66). Toronto: University of Toronto Press

Khan, D., Ross, R., Rush, J. & Panico, S. (2000). *Expert Consensus Treatment Guidelines for Bipolar Disorder: A Guide for Patients and Families.* A Postgraduate Medicine Special Report. The McGraw-Hill Companies, Inc.

Klerman, G., Weissman, M., Rounsaville, B. & Chevron, E. (1997). *Interpersonal Psychotherapy of Depression.* New Jersey: Jason Aronson Inc.

Kübler-Ross, E. (1997). *On Death and Dying.* New York: Touchstone

Padesky, C. & Greenberger, D. (1995). *Clinician's Guide to Mind over Mood.* New York: Guilford Press

Woolis, R. (1992). *When Someone You Love Has a Mental Illness: A Handbook for Family, Friends and Caregivers.* New York: Tarcher/Putnam (Penguin/Putnam)

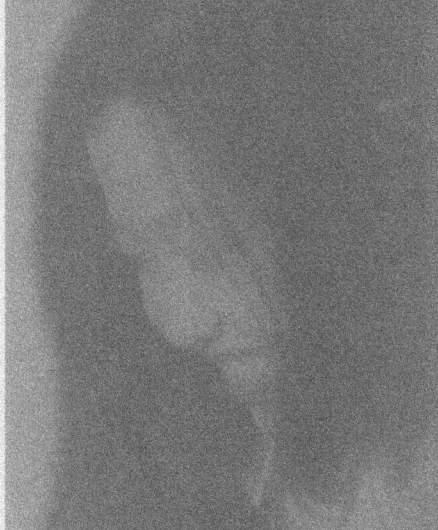

APPENDICES

Building Our Knowledge in Helping Families

This program evaluates the effectiveness of the group model in meeting the special needs of families who have a relative with a mood disorder.

To do this, group members may be asked to complete several questionnaires before and after the program. Your feedback will help us design better and more effective services for families.

How Can I Find Out More About the Group Program?

If you are interested in attending the group, call our Inquiry Line at (416) 979-4747, extension 2580.

Interested participants are required to attend an individual appointment prior to registering for the next group series.

Centre for Addiction and
Mental Health
Clarke Site
250 College Street
Toronto, Ontario M5T 1R8

Aussi disponible en français

Mood Disorders Clinics

Help for Partners & Relatives of Adults with Depression or Bipolar Disorders

Education & Support Group

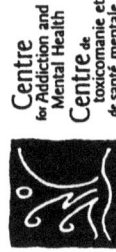

Centre for Addiction and Mental Health
Centre de toxicomanie et de santé mentale

Addiction Research Foundation
Clarke Institute of Psychiatry
Donwood Institute
Queen Street Mental Health Centre

Living with Depression or Bipolar Disorder

Families of people diagnosed with depression or bipolar disorder (also known as manic depression) face unique challenges and situations.

Partners, parents and siblings struggle with providing emotional and practical support to their loved one, in addition to dealing with their own daily stresses.

Support and Education Group for Partners and Relatives

In order to support the special role of partners and relatives, the Mood Disorders Clinics at the Centre for Addiction and Mental Health offer an eight-week support and education group.

The groups are run several times per year and alternate between bipolar disorder and depression. For example, one series will serve families of depressed patients, while another series will serve families with bipolar relatives.

As these groups are designed to meet the unique needs of relatives and caregivers, the diagnosed relative does not attend.

About the Program

Each group series runs for eight consecutive weeks at the Centre's Clarke site. The sessions are 90 minutes in length and the time of the series varies. Sessions cover topics such as:

- understanding mood disorders
- medication and treatments
- stress management for caregivers
- crisis intervention
- problem management
- legal issues
- navigating the mental health system
- community resources

Mood Disorders Screening Form

SCID

Relative Screening Scale for Mood Disorder
(Clinician complete at intake interview)

Subject No. _____   Date _____   Initials_____

Rating Scale

1 = almost never
2 = somewhat
3 = very much

Major Depression

Has your relative ever experienced the following symptoms for two or more consecutive weeks?

Part A	PAST			CURRENT		
1. Depressed mood most of the day, nearly every day (feels sad or empty).	1	2	3	1	2	3
2. Markedly diminished interest or pleasure in all, or almost all, activities, most of the day, nearly every day.	1	2	3	1	2	3

Part B						
3. Significant weight loss, when not dieting, or weight gain.	1	2	3	1	2	3
4. Insomnia or hypersomnia nearly every day.	1	2	3	1	2	3
5. Psychomotor agitation, or retardation, nearly every day.	1	2	3	1	2	3

	PAST			CURRENT		
6. Fatigue or loss of energy nearly every day.	1	2	3	1	2	3
7. Feelings of worthlessness or excessive or inappropriate guilt nearly every day.	1	2	3	1	2	3
8. Diminished ability to think or concentrate, or indecisiveness, nearly every day.	1	2	3	1	2	3
9. Recurrent thoughts of death (not just fear of dying), recurrent suicidal ideation without a plan, or with a plan.	1	2	3	1	2	3
10 The symptoms caused clinically significant distress or impairment in social, occupational, or other important areas of functioning.	1	2	3	1	2	3
11. Symptoms not better accounted for by bereavement, substance abuse or GMC.	No	Yes		No	Yes	

Number of symptoms present Part A _____
(At least one must be rated 3)

Number of symptoms present Part B_____
(At least 3 must be rated)

MANIA

Rating Scale

1 = almost never
2 = somewhat
3 = very much

Part A

Has your relative ever experienced:

	PAST			CURRENT		
1. A distinct period of abnormally or persistently elevated, expansive or irritable mood?	1	2	3	1	2	3
2. Did it persist for at least one week or result in hospitalization?	Yes	No		Yes	No	

Part B

During that time were any of the following present?

	PAST			CURRENT		
3. Inflated self-esteem.	1	2	3	1	2	3
4. More talkative than usual, or pressure to keep talking.	1	2	3	1	2	3
5. Flight of ideas or subjective experience that thoughts are racing.	1	2	3	1	2	3
6. Increase in goal-directed activity (either socially, at work or school, or sexually) or psychomotor agitation.	1	2	3	1	2	3
7. Excessive involvement in pleasurable activities that have a high potential for painful consequences (buying sprees, sexual indiscretions, foolish business investments).	1	2	3	1	2	3
8. Disturbance sufficiently severe to cause marked impairment in occupational, social or relationship functioning.	1	2	3	1	2	3
9. Not due to substance abuse or GMC.	Yes	No		Yes	No	

Meets criteria for Part A Yes No
(At least one is rated 3)

Number of items from Part B _____
(At least three are rated 3)

Family Support Group Intake Form

Part I: Information about Yourself (The Patient's Family Member)

Name   _____

Gender   1 = Male

            2 = Female

Age   _____years

Ethnicity   _____

Current relationship status?   1 = Married or living with someone for 1 year or more

            2 = Divorce / left partner "for good"

            3 = Living apart from partner with chance of returning

            4 = Single / Never Married

            5 = Widowed

            6 = Involved in a significant relationship but not living together

How far did you get in school?   1 = Grade 6 or less (<7th Grade)

            2 = Grade 7–9 (Junior HS)

            3 = Grade 10–11

            4 = Grade 12–13 (HS graduate)

            5 = Part College

            6 = Graduated 2-year college

            7 = Part University

            8 = Graduated _____ Year University

            9 = Part Graduate / Professional School

            10 = Completed Graduate / Professional School

Current employment

1 = Yes

2 = No

If No: are you retired?

1 = Yes

2 = No

If Employed:

Number of hours a week working

_____Hours per week

Current or usual/previous occupation

_____

Do you have history of a mood disorder?

0 = No

1 = Major Depression

2 = Bipolar

If Yes, how may episodes over how many years?

_____over _____years

Relationship to your relative

_____

On average, how much **telephone contact** do you have with your relative?

1 = Lives with patient/relative

2 = Daily

3 = 3–6 times a week

4 = 2–3 times a week

5 = weekly

6 = every two weeks

7 = monthly

On average, how often do you **visit** with your relative?

1 = lives with patient/relative

2 = daily

3 = 3–6 times a week

4 = 2–3 times a week

5 = weekly

6 = every two weeks

7 = monthly

How much have you read
about mood disorders?

1 = I have never read anything

2 = I have read a few pamphlets, possibly a magazine
or newspaper article

3 = I have read at least one book dealing with depression or bipolar disorder

4 = I have read between 2 and 4 books

5 = I have read more than 5 books

6 = I have reviewed some of the information available
on the Internet

7 = I have seen a TV or heard a radio program

Have you attended any other
support group in the past
two years?

1 = Yes
2 = No

If Yes, please specify

_____

Please describe briefly your
reasons for attending the
psycho-education group

_____

How did you learn of the
psycho-education group?

1. Referral from psychiatrist

2. Referral from family doctor

3. Flyer/newsletter

4. Self-help group

5. Family friend/other group participant

6. Other (please specify)

_____

Part II. Information about Your Relative (The Client)

Name _____

Date of Birth _____

Gender   1 = Male

                 2 = Female

Age   _____years

Ethnicity _____

Current relationship status?   1 = Married or living with someone for 1 year or more

                 2 = Divorce / left partner "for good"

                 3 = Living apart from partner with chance of returning

                 4 = Single / Never Married

                 5 = Widowed

                 6 = Involved in a significant relationship but not living together

How far did your relative get in school?   1 = Grade 6 or less (<7th Grade)

                 2 = Grade 7–9 (Junior HS)

                 3 = Grade 10–11

                 4 = Grade 12–13 (HS graduate)

                 5 = Part College

                 6 = Graduated 2-year college

                 7 = Part University

                 8 = Graduated _____ Year University

                 9 = Part Graduate / Professional School

              10 = Completed Graduate / Professional School

Sources of relative's income   1 = Wages / salaries

                 2 = Income from self-employment

                 3 = Welfare / Mother's allowance

4 = Unemployment insurance / strike pay

5 = Workers' compensation / disability

6 = Old age securities/ pensions, etc.

7 = Savings

8 = Alimony / Child Support

9 = Other (Specify)

_____

If employed:

Number of hours a
week working   _____ hours per week

Current or usual / previous
occupation
(Please be specific)   _____

What is your relative's living
situation?   1 = Alone

2 = With relative participating in group

3 = With other family member

4 = With partner

5 = Group home

6 = Shared apartment / house

7 = other

Number of children of
ill relative   _____

Ages of children   _____, _____, _____, _____

Diagnosis of your relative   1 = Unipolar

2 = Bipolar

Additional Diagnosis   _____

Age of onset of illness _____

Age at which mood
disorder diagnosis
was made _____

Number of
depressive episodes
since diagnosis _____ episodes

Number of
manic episodes
since diagnosis _____ episodes

Is your relative in treatment? 1= Yes

2= No

Where does your relative
receive treatment?
(name of hospital/mental
health services) _____

Number of hospitalizations 1 = None
since diagnosis

2 = One

3 = Two or four

4 = Five to six

5 = Seven or more

Average / approximate length
of admissions _____

Has your relative ever left
hospital AMA? 1 = Yes
(against medical advice) 2 = No

If yes, how many times? _____

Has your relative ever done 1 = Spent large amounts of money
any of the following (circle all 2 = Engaged in sexual indiscretions
that apply): 3 = Displayed verbal aggression toward you (arguing,
shouting)
4 = Threatened physical aggression toward you
5 = Been physically aggressive toward you
6 = Destroyed personal property
7 = Used alcohol to self-medicate
8 = Other (please specify)

_____

| Have the police been called to assist with your relative? | 1 = Yes |
| | 2 = No |

| Has your relative ever expressed thoughts of suicide? | 1 = Yes |
| | 2 = No |

| Has your relative ever made a suicide attempt? | 1 = Yes |
| | 2 = No |

If Yes, how many times? _____

At the time of completing form, how stable is your relative?

1= Stable (compliant with treatment, not acutely depressed or manic)

2= Partially stable (compliant with treatment most of the time, returning to previous activities/roles)

3= Unstable (may be compliant/noncompliant with treatment but symptoms are not well controlled/not able to participate in activities/roles)

Of weeks stable/unstable: _____

Please indicate your relative's present level of compliance with treatment

1 = Follows plan reliably / regularly

2 = Irregular compliance (e.g., stops medication/therapy some of the time)

3 = Non-compliant (e.g., will not take medication/ therapy most of the time)

Satisfaction Form

Mood Disorders Support and Education Family Group

SERVICE EVALUATION

Please rate the helpfulness of the content of the following groups by circling the number:

	Very Helpful	Somewhat Helpful	Not at All Helpful
1. Overview/education about Bipolar Disorder	1	2	3
2. Discussion with psychiatrist about medications	1	2	3
3. Stress management	1	2	3
4. Communicating with your relative	1	2	3
5. Problem-management	1	2	3
6. Crisis management	1	2	3
7. Navigating the mental health, legal systems	1	2	3
8. Wrap-up	1	2	3
9. Printed material provided at each group	1	2	3

Please rate the helpfulness of the following processes:

1. Hearing about the problems and experiences of other family members.	1	2	3
2. Hearing the coping strategies used by other family members.	1	2	3
3. Receiving support from other family members.	1	2	3
4. Experimenting with the role-play in the communication group.	1	2	3

The three things I will most remember from the group experience are:

1. _____

2. _____

3. _____

Please write down any further opinion/comments you have about our service.

Thank you for completing these forms.

Adjunct medication — medicine that complements a main medication.

Agitation — a severe inner restlessness that is often accompanied by anxiety. Patients typically cannot sit still; they may pace and wring their hands.

"Alternative" medicines — for bipolar disorder, these include "natural remedies," such as fish oil and inosital (a kind of sugar). Little research has been done on these products.

Anti-anxiety medication — a type of adjunct medication used to treat anxiety. Examples include benzodiazepines, such as lorazepam (Ativan®) or clonazepam (Rivotril®), and some antidepressants.

Antidepressant medication — medication used to treat the symptoms of depression.

Antipsychotic medication — formerly called neuroleptic medication. These agents quickly control mania and treat psychotic symptoms. Antipsychotics can also prevent new attacks of mania.

Anxiety — excessive worry, fear and uncertainty that are hard to control. Anxiety is common in bipolar disorder.

Benzodiazepines — a group of anti-anxiety medications that share a similar chemical structure. Some common benzodiazepines are diazepam (Valium®) and lorazepam (Ativan®).

Bipolar disorder — also known as manic-depressive illness. A disorder characterized by mood swings from depression to mania.

Bipolar-I disorder — a type of bipolar disorder in which people experience full manic or mixed episodes.

Bipolar-II disorder — a type of bipolar disorder in which people experience only hypomania and depression.

Catatonic symptoms — Patients who become catatonic have trouble with movement — they may experience extreme physical agitation or slowness and odd movements or postures.

Cognitive behavioural therapy (CBT) — a type of talk therapy where patients learn to recognize their own negative or disruptive thought patterns. Patients then try to change the behaviours that result from these thoughts. CBT is beginning to be tested in the treatment of bipolar disorder, with promising early results.

Comorbid disorder — a medical condition that often accompanies, or co-occurs with, another disorder; for example, drug or alcohol abuse, panic disorder, obsessive-compulsive disorder or binge eating disorder can co-occur with bipolar disorder.

Compliance — a patient's full participation in the treatment prescribed by the physician; for example, taking medication as directed and attending therapy sessions.

Cycle — the time from the start of one episode until the start of the next.

Delusion — a false, fixed belief not shared by other people in the same culture; for example, a person may believe that his or her thoughts are controlled by outside forces. There are various types of delusions, such as paranoid (with feelings of suspicion) and grandiose (with feelings of excessive self-importance).

Depression — an episode characterized by a loss of energy, feelings of worthlessness and loss of interest in things that usually bring pleasure (food, sex, work, friends and entertainment). Patients may think often about death or suicide. Physicians diagnose depression when at least five of a group of symptoms have lasted for at least two weeks.

Dopamine — a type of neurotransmitter, or brain chemical, thought to be affected in a person with mental illness. Making dopamine more available is one way to treat depression; blocking dopamine helps treat psychosis.

Electroconvulsive therapy (ECT) — a treatment procedure for severe depression and severe mania. ECT involves passing a controlled electric current between two metal discs applied on the surface of the scalp.

Episode — a period of illness. This can include depression, hypomania, mania or a mixed state.

Group therapy — therapy for a number of patients together. Group therapy has been used successfully to give patients support and psychoeducation.

Hallucination — a false experience involving the senses, such as seeing, hearing, tasting, smelling or feeling something that does not really exist.

Hypersomnia — the condition of sleeping too much, especially during the day. Hypersomnia can be a symptom of bipolar disorder.

Hypomania — a state characterized by a high mood and overactivity. It is not as extreme as mania.

Insomnia — the condition of not being able to fall asleep, or of waking too soon or repeatedly. Insomnia can be a symptom of bipolar disorder.

Light therapy — Light therapy is a form of treatment involving exposure to a specific type of light for 30 minutes to one hour daily, for several weeks. This light is usually provided by a special light box and is useful for the treatment of seasonal depressions and occasionally for other types of depression.

Monoamine Oxidase Inhibitor (MAOI) — a class of antidepressants that work by reducing the effects of the enzyme monoamine oxidase. This causes neurotransmitter levels to rise, often providing powerful relief to depression. However, these drugs have many side-effects and require a special diet.

Maintenance treatment — treatment intended to prevent a new episode (including depression, mania, hypomania).

Mania — a state characterized by an unusually high mood, irritability, overactivity, excessive talking, racing thoughts, inflated ideas of self, lack of insight, poor judgment, impulsiveness and financial extravagance.

Manic-depressive illness — see bipolar disorder above.

Mixed episode — an episode in which patients show both manic and depressive symptoms. The symptoms either occur at the same time or alternate quickly.

Mood disorder — a pattern of illness defined by disturbance of mood. Bipolar disorder is one type of mood disorder.

Mood stabilizers — medicines, such as lithium, that help reduce swings in abnormal moods. They can also help prevent fresh mood episodes.

"Natural remedies" — see "alternative" medicines above.

Neuroleptics — see antipsychotic medications above.

Neurotransmitters — chemicals that carry signals between neurons (nerve cells) in the brain. Neurotransmitters include norepinephrine, serotonin, dopamine and acetylcholine.

Obsessive-compulsive disorder (OCD) — patients with this disorder have intrusive thoughts (obsessions) or the urge to perform irresistible repetitive acts (rituals). The performance of these neutral acts/behaviours may reduce anxiety.

Panic disorder — an anxiety disorder characterized by attacks of severe anxiety, terror or fear.

Psychoeducation — a process that allows people to recognize and learn how to manage their psychiatric illness.

Psychosis — a term once used for any mental disorder. Psychosis now refers only to disturbances that cause the personality to disintegrate and the person to lose contact with reality.

Psychotherapy — a general term used to describe a form of treatment based on talking with a therapist. Psychotherapy aims to relieve distress by discussing and expressing feelings. The goal is to help the patient change attitudes, behaviour and habits, and develop better ways of coping.

Rapid cycling — Individuals are said to be rapid cycling if they experience more than four episodes a year. Only 20 per cent of patients experience rapid cycling.

Recovery/recovery phase — the period when a person is getting over an episode of illness. The patient often feels fragile, dependent and at risk of other episodes.

Relapse — return of the symptoms of an illness after the patient has seemingly responded to treatment but before the symptoms have fully gone.

Selective serotonin reuptake inhibitors (SSRIs) — a class of drugs used to treat depression and related disorders. SSRIs inhibit the reuptake of serotonin (a neurotransmitter). SSRIs have revolutionized the treatment of depression since the late 1980s because they are very effective and have fewer side-effects than do older antidepressants.

Side-effects — the extra effects of a drug treatment that come with the desired effects. Usually side-effects are unwanted and can include nausea, headaches, constipation and problems with sexual function.

Stressors — situations that cause stress.

Support group — a group of people who have a common interest or situation, such as a diagnosis of bipolar disorder, who meet regularly to share ideas, feelings and community resources information.

Tardive dyskinesia — a brain disorder in which the patient experiences involuntary, or unintended, movement of the face and jaw. Tardive dyskinesia can be a side-effect of long use of traditional antipsychotic medications.

Transcranial magnetic stimulation (TMS) — a treatment involving magnetic pulses to the brain. TMS is being tested, but its effects on bipolar disorder are not proven.

Tricyclic antidepressants (TCAs) — a class of older drugs used to treat depression and other disorders.

Trigger — a situation that can cause either mania or depression in a person who has already had an episode of illness. Stress, sleep loss, steroids and street drugs are some of the triggers for bipolar disorder.

Unipolar depression — one or more major depressive episodes but without mania or hypomania.

Out of the Ashes of Mental Illness...A New Life
Agnes B. Hatfield

Considerable attention has been given in the past decade to helping professionals in the field of mental health care to better understand the family dilemma that emerges when illness strikes a loved one (Hatfield & Lefley, 1987 & Lefley & Johnson, 1990; Marsh, 1992; Walsh, 1985; Wasow, 1982; Vine, 1982). Numerous programs have been developed to help families cope with a great array of daily problems (see, for example, Anderson, Reiss, & Hogarty, 1986; Bernheim & Lehman, 1985; Falloon, Boyd, & McGill, 1984; Hatfield, 1990, Woolis, 1992).

Educational programs for families are now widespread across the country, and most families have access to information about the nature of mental illness and an opportunity to learn management skills. The National Alliance for the Mentally Ill (NAMI) has been a powerful voice for families in making their needs known. While some families continue to suffer serious disruptions in their lives, many manage to achieve some degree of family stability. But achieving stability does not mean the end of painful issues and problems. New needs emerge when the chaos and confusion die down and family members begin to reflect upon the tragedy of their lives, the damage done to relationships, and the need to make some kind of meaning from it all.

The family faces a double tragedy if a healing process does not occur, and family relationships continue to be strained and no sense of family unity survives. The focus of family education programs is usually on survival in the here and now, but attention must also be given to the longer range issues of healing and coming to terms with the devastation.

THE DESTRUCTIVE FORCES IN MENTAL ILLNESS

The destructive forces in mental illness are legion and it is surprising that families manage to survive them. Whether the onset of illness was sudden or insidious, the consequences for other members can be disastrous. My purpose here is to identify some of these potentially negative effects of mental illness and suggest ways that damage might be minimized so that growth and affirmation of life are still possible.

SENSE OF LOSS
Mentally ill people lose temporarily, or permanently, many of the personality characteristics by which their relatives identify them. The changes in the person can be profound. It is as

though the family has lost the person they once knew and now have stranger in their midst. Their grief may be profound, but mourning is never complete, as it is in the case of a death, because the person continues to live, but significantly changed.

Families remember the dreams they once had, now shattered, for their relative's roles and accomplishments. Terkelsen (1987) notes that, unlike professionals who have known these individuals only in their disabled state, families knew them as well as persons full of hope and promise, and the contrast between then and now is deeply distressing. One mother wrote: 'It came as an utter and unbelievable surprise. We are all grieving now. We have watched a young life that was eager, healthy, attractive, with intelligence, humour, and incisive sensitivity into human relationships, waste away, without friends (when there were so many in the first twenty years), unable to stand any stress, being self conscious and terrified and almost never free from voices assailing him and sounds that he cannot bear' (Terkelsen, 1987, p. 137).

Emotional states aroused by the loss of a loved one include pain, yearning, sorrow, anguish, dejection, sadness, fear, anxiety, nervousness, agitation, panic, disbelief, denial, shock, emptiness, and lack of feeling (Schoenberg et al., 1970). Profound loss is an assault on our sense of fairness. Families who lose a relative to mental illness ask: Why did this happen to my son or daughter? What did we do to deserve this punishment? How could a just God let this happen to us? (Sterns, 1984).

Families may feel angry with those who do not understand their pain and seem so secure, safe, and distant. There is risk of bitterness, resentment, or envy towards those with healthy offspring able to lead successful lives. There may be a relentless search to find meaning in what seems to be so inexplicable, and this may lead to questions of etiology and self-blame. Family members may begin to feel extremely vulnerable. If something so disastrous can happen so suddenly and without warning, who knows what will happen next? Are any of their loved ones safe?

While we have culturally provided customs and rituals for easing the pain of those who have lost someone through deaths, there is little institutionalized support or practice that eases the pain of those suffering loss through mental illness (Hatfield & Lefley, 1987). Psychological theory has not been particularly relevant to supporting people faced with such existential questions of loss and deprivation (Schoenberg et.al., 1970). Practitioners are on their own and, in order to be helpful, must call upon whatever personal resources and life experiences they have. Schulman (1976) says it is important not to pathologize the stressful emotions that people are undergoing and not to expect that there is an explanation for everything.

Perhaps one of the most useful books on the subject of personal loss is one written by Ann Kaiser Stearns, called *Living through Personal Crisis* (1984). In it she says, "Our losses change us and change the course of our lives. It is not that one can never be happy following an experience of loss. The reality is simply that one can never again be the same" (p. 26).

Terrible events can precipitate growth, Schulman (1976) wrote in his book on coping with tragedy. People may develop a true vision of what counts, a more mature re-evaluation of their lives. They can develop a resolution of their loss so as to avoid feelings of jealousy and resentment. Joy and happiness are possible again as one realizes that going on with life does not mean abandoning the relative with mental illness. Resolution of feelings of guilt leads to inner calm.

In his discussion of chronic illness, Schulman (1976) says it is important not to view the struggle as a senseless tragedy leading to inexorable defeat, but to explore it as a creative challenge for those involved in it. Somehow out of the ashes of pain and despair may come new meaning and a way of life that can encompass the new reality. Professionals must find ways to help this process along.

THE PATIENT AS VICTIM

Because mental illness is so devastating to the individual, families may come to view their relatives as helpless victims who can do little to influence the course of their lives. They may expect little, and tolerate all misbehaviours as symptoms of the illness, while becoming increasingly resentful of the need to accommodate their lives constantly to the demands of the ill member.

It is not surprising that many people with mental illnesses assume a victim mentality, which prevents them from taking any responsibility for their own lives. Undergoing severe psychotic disturbance often means feeling oneself to be at the mercy of terrifying forces over which one has no control. As Estroff (1989) has noted, schizophrenia, in particular, seems to be an 'I am' phenomenon. Volition, self-control, and will power seem to disappear, and patients begin to feel that they are their illnesses. They feel that they have lost control over their lives and are inexorably at the mercy of strange internal and external forces.

Long periods of being a patient depending on the ministrations of others may reinforce the sense of helplessness and the feeling of control by others. Other family members sympathize with the pain and struggle, and avoid expecting too much or demanding accountability. As a consequence, patients may tend to go through life expecting the rest of the world to adapt to their needs, never realizing they have obligations to others as well.

While parents often have considerable reserves of tolerance of their offspring's self-centredness, siblings and children of mentally ill parents may expect more, and may feel resentful and rejecting when those expectations are not met. In order that family life be harmonious, attention must be given to helping the ill member learn to become a contributing member.

While classes and workshops train families to understand and care for their ill relative, similar efforts to teach the relative to understand how his behaviours affect the rest of the family are lacking. There is little evidence in the psychosocial rehabilitation literature that this matter has been considered. While attention is given to helping these individuals get along with peers, public servants, and employers, little training is offered on ways to get along with and be a contributing member of a family. This is unfortunate, when the family is recognized as a most important part of the support system. Support systems may be tenuous when obligations are totally unidirectional. Whereas parents may continue their support without reciprocity, siblings are unlikely to do so.

Parents face a creative challenge in finding ways in which a son or daughter who is mentally ill can be a contributing member. People with mental illnesses need to learn how their behaviours affect others and how to modify those behaviours to ensure the comfort of others. They need to learn ways to meet needs of other members of the family and ways of participating in family rituals, gift giving, and the like. To do less is to let the person with mental illness succumb to a perpetual-patient role.

VOLATILE BEHAVIOUR

Repeated acts of violence resulting in verbal attacks, assaultiveness, and destruction of property take a terrible toll on the family's ability to pull itself together. Relatives with mental illness may direct their hostility towards others because of jealousy, hypersensitivity to criticism, or perceived obstruction to their desires (Lefley, 1987).

The frequency with which family members suffer assault by their ill members has not been widely studied. However, Swan and Levitt (1986) studied 1,156 members of the National Alliance for the Mentally Ill (NAMI) and found that more than one-third of their respondents reported that their relative was assaultive or destructive in the home, either sometimes or often. Many families, though never assaulted, lived in fear of their relative and took self-protective measures to avoid injury.

Other family members may also be anxious about their own possible loss of control. Some mentally ill individuals can be so manipulative, hostile, argumentative, and provocative that even the most controlled persons feel that they could strike in fear or anger (Hatfield, 1990). Under highly chaotic conditions it is likely that most members have said or done things that they have later regretted. It is a major challenge for many families to heal the wounds that might have occurred in very troubling times.

The focus must be on prevention of violence whenever possible. Families need considerable help with this, and practitioners must be ready to offer practical steps. They must understand that managing volatile behaviour in the home is much more difficult than in institutional settings. Since situational factors play a crucial role, it is important that families understand the kinds of situations that give rise to violence (Hatfield, 1990).

Even though families become adept at preventive measures, acts of aggression might occur. No violent act should be ignored, denied, or excused on the basis of mental illness. All forms of violence must be considered serious, and attention must be given to helping the perpetrator control his or her impulses. Attention must also be given to the aftermath of an attack and the devastating consequences on family feelings and relationships. The hurt is likely to continue until some kind of healing process sets in. Former NAMI president Don Richardson (1990) shares this experience of dealing with his feelings when his son assaults and seriously injures another family member: 'Without forgiveness, life is an endless cycle of rancor, hatred, and anger. I don't want to spend the rest of my life governed by resentment and retaliation, especially toward my youngest son. I am reaching the point where I can acknowledge that this tragedy has wounded everyone in the family and now the healing process includes forgiveness and understanding that our son's action was caused by serious mental illness, and not because he is "evil" or "bad"' (p. 41).

THE RISK OF FAMILY BURN-OUT

Even though the majority of families never experience the trauma of a serious assault from a family member, the day-to-day managing of stressful events can take its toll when a family member serves as caregiver over time. Some family members may choose to opt out of further involvement because they are discouraged and exhausted. Practitioners often ask why some consumers seem to have no interested family support system. There may be many reasons, but sheer exhaustion is often one of them.

Since there is no adequate substitute for the family as a support system, and people with mental illness have great difficulty developing support systems of their own, protecting the family from burn-out should be given high priority. It is all too easy when resources are scarce to leave as much responsibility for care to the family as long as possible, with little concern for potential burn-out and damage to relationships over time. This is shortsighted, for it is the consumer who suffers when families disengage to avoid further burn-out.

REINTEGRATION OF THE FAMILY AND ROLE ADJUSTMENT

If the family is to survive as a unit, many adjustments must be made over time, in various family members' role, in apportioning responsibility in the household, in altering social and leisure-time activities, and in finding new ways to meet the diverse needs of all family members. Families face difficult moral and ethical choices as they search for the right balance between the imperatives of their ill member's care and treatment, and the needs of other children in the family, elderly parents, and the like. It is important that providers understand that many other demands and stressors must be dealt with in addition to a family member's mental illness (Hatfield, 1990).

There is no single best way for families to reorganize and adapt to meet the demands imposed by mental illness. Professionals who have strong preconceived conceptions of how all families should function may do more harm than good. The words of Kazak and Marvin (1988) in regard to parents of handicapped children may be instructive here. They say that 'successful adaptive functioning in families with handicapped children has not received sufficient attention. In their well-intentioned efforts to document areas of difficulty in families with handicapped children, researchers have sometimes neglected to describe ways in which differences may indicate successful family functioning within a different but not deviant family structure' (pp. 667-668). In the past, many family interventions were narrowly conceived without regard for the wide range of cultural differences in this country, and were laden with personal values as to how 'normal' families should behave (Hatfield, 1990). Many families labelled 'dysfunctional' may be merely different, and not deviant in any pathological sense.

CONCLUSIONS

Stearns (1984) calls the last chapter of her book 'From Out of the Ashes .... New Life'. These words best express the hope for families. As Sterns has pointed out, life can never be the same again for families caring for a relative with mental illness, but happiness is possible. We can, she says, learn from our pain in such a way that our learning becomes useful to ourselves and others.

As Kushner (1981) says in his book *When Bad Things Happen to Good People*, it becomes necessary to put the past behind and cease asking the futile question 'Why did this happen to me? Stearns (1984) sees a new kind of wisdom emerging when families can accept life as it is. 'Life as it actually is,' she says, 'though imperfect and vastly complicated with sorrow, is richer than life that is idealized' (p. 32).

Achieving this kind of wisdom is a starting-point. What must follow is the creation of a new structure and pattern to life that permits the greatest possible growth for all members of the family. As I have pointed out, the challenges are many: grieving the keen sense of loss of a loved one; healing the hurts of destructive behaviours; overcoming the identity of victimization; and just generally surviving the daily hassles that destroy morale and lead to burn-out among caregivers, to name a few.

If professionals are dedicated to preserving the family both for its own sake and because the family is vital as a support system for its ill relative, they must take a longer view of the decisions that are made and consider how they may affect the survival of the family as a supportive unit. Many family interventions at this time have a single-minded goal of helping families to create environments that are good for the ill person, with little regard for the well-being of the total family. Professionals need to take a more holistic view and be prepared to help families with the practical aspects of coping and the deeply troubling existential questions.

REFERENCES

Anderson, D. Reiss, D. & Hogarty, G. (1986). *Schizophrenia and the family*. New York: Guilford.

Bernheim, K. & Lehman, A. (1985). *Working with families of the mentally ill*. New York: W.W. Norton.

Estroff, S. (1989). Self, identity, and subjective experiences of schizophrenia: In search of the subject. *Schizophrenia Bulletin*, 15, 189-196.

Fallon, I., Boyd, J. & McGill, C. (1984) *Family care of schizophrenia*. New York: Guilford.

Hatfield, A. (1990). *Family education in mental illness*. New York: Guilford.

Hatfield, A. & Lefley, H. (Eds). (1987). *Families of the mentally ill: Coping and adaptation*. New York: Guilford.

Kazak, A. & Marvin, R. (1988). Differences, difficulties, and adaptation: Stress and social network in families with a handicapped child. *Family Relations*, 33, 67-78.

Kushner, H. (1981). *When bad things happen to good people*. New York: Schocken Books.

Lefley, H. (1987). Behavioral manifestations of mental illness. In A. Hatfield & H. Lefley (Eds), *Families of the mentally ill: Coping and adaptation* (pp.107-127). New York: Guilford.

Lefley, H. & Johnson, D. (1990). *Families as allies in treatment of the mentally ill*. Washington, DC: American Psychiatric Press.

Marsh, D. (1992). *Families and mental illness*. New York: Praeger.

Richardson, D. (1990). Dangerousness and forgiveness. *Journal of the California Alliance for the Mentally Ill*, 2, 4-5.

Schoenberg, D. Carr, A., Peretz, D. & Kutschner, A. (1970). *Loss and grief*. New York: Columbia University Press.

Schulman, J. (1976). *Coping with tragedy: Successfully facing the problem of a seriously ill child*. Chicago: Follett.

Stearns, A. (1984). *Living through personal crisis*. Chicago: Thomas Moore.

Swan, R. & Levitt, M. (1986). *Patterns of adjustment to violence to families of the mentally ill*. New Orleans: Elizabeth Wisna Research Center, Tulane School of Social Work.

Terkelsen, K. (1987). The meaning of mental illness to the family. In A. Hatfield & H. Lefley (Eds), *Families of the mentally ill: Coping and adaptation* (pp.151-166). New York: Guilford.

Vine, P. (1982). *Families in pain: Children, spouses, and parents speak out.* Westminster, MD: Pantheon.

Walsh, M. (1985). *Schizophrenia: Straight talk for families.* New York: Morrow.

Wasow, M. (1982). *Coping with schizophrenia: A survival manual.* Palo Alto, CA: Science & Behavior.

Woolis, R. (1992). *When someone you love has a mental illness: A handbook for families, friends and caregivers.* New York: Putnam.

Handouts — English

Schedule for Eight-Session Group

	DATE OF MEETING	TOPIC
Group 1		introductions and overview of disorders
Group 2		medications and psychosocial treatments
Group 3		stress management
Group 4		communication strategies
Group 5		problem management
Group 6		crisis management
Group 7		the medical and legal systems
Group 8		summary and planning for the future

Prevalence

Major depression can occur in 10 to 25 per cent of women and five to 12 per cent of men.

SYMPTOMS OF DEPRESSION

Depression is diagnosed if a person experiences five or more of the following symptoms during a two-week period:
- depressed mood most of the day
- decreased pleasure in activities
- significant weight gain or loss
- difficulty sleeping most of the time (either not sleeping or sleeping excessively)
- presence of slower physical movement or a feeling of restlessness
- fatigue or loss of energy
- difficulty making decisions and/or concentrating
- feelings of worthlessness or excessive guilt
- frequent thoughts of suicide or death.

The above symptoms interfere with a person's ability to function in all or most areas of life. Other symptoms may include:
- oversensitivity and preoccupation with oneself
- negative thinking
- unresponsiveness to reassurance, support, feedback or sympathy
- less awareness of others' feelings because of one's own internal pain
- feeling the need to control relationships
- inability to function in normal role.

Subtypes of Depression

DYSTHYMIA

An chronic low mood, which persists for at least two years. Unlike a person with depression, a person with dysthymia is not severely functionally impaired and does not exhibit changes in physical movement, feelings of worthlessness or suicidal thoughts.

POSTPARTUM

Depression that occurs following childbirth.

ATYPICAL
Mood reactivity is present — the person may brighten in response to positive events; heavy feeling in arms or legs; longstanding sensitivity to rejection.

MELANCHOLIC
Low mood that does not let up, even with usually pleasurable activities; depression is usually worse in the morning; early-morning awakening.

SECONDARY TO MEDICAL ILLNESS
Depression is caused by a medical condition.

SUBSTANCE INDUCED
Depression is caused by drug use.

SEASONAL AFFECTIVE DISORDER
Depression occurs at a particular time of year, usually during the fall and winter, and clears during the spring and summer.

WITH PSYCHOTIC FEATURES
Delusions or hallucinations are also present.

Causes of Depression — The Multi-dimensional Model

No one theory explains why people develop depressive disorders. Research points to five areas that may place a person at risk of developing a depression:
1. biological predisposition
2. genetic predisposition
3. life events
4. personality style
5. lack of social support.

People who suffer from depression struggle with the following common reactions:
• fear
• embarrassment about seeking help
• a concern that taking medication is a sign of weakness
• difficulty reducing stress and altering their lifestyles
• experiencing a positive change in their mood as a sign that they should stop treatment.

Bipolar Disorder — Overview

Prevalence

About one per cent of adults suffer from bipolar disorder. Men and women are affected equally by the disorder.

Symptoms of Bipolar Disorder

There are three major symptom groups to become familiar with: mania, hypomania and depression.

1. Mania

SYMPTOMS OF MANIA

If someone's mood is abnormally and persistently high, irritable or expansive for at least one week, he or she may be in a manic phase of the illness. However, not everyone who enters the manic phase feels euphoric. Instead, individuals may feel extremely irritable, or behave belligerently or are terribly angry, disruptive and aggressive and have no sense of euphoria at all.

In addition to their mood symptoms, people must exhibit at least three of the following symptoms to an important degree:
• exaggerated self-esteem or grandiosity
• reduced need for sleep
• increased talkativeness
• flight of ideas or racing thoughts
• speeded-up activity
• poor judgment
• psychotic symptoms — delusions (beliefs without a realistic base) and in some cases hallucinations (mainly hearing voices) are also common symptoms of mania.

WHAT MANIA LOOKS LIKE

People displaying symptoms of mania can present as highly irritable and impatient with those around them. They may make impulsive, hurtful and rejecting statements or engage in impulsive or even dangerous behaviour.

Mania causes people to be highly reactive and emotional. For people with poor anger management skills or frustration tolerance, this can lead to violent behaviour.

2. Hypomania (hypomanic episode)

While the symptoms of hypomania are less severe than those of mania, they can interfere with the person's ability to function in a variety of roles. Historically, hypomania was viewed as a minor condition. More recently, it has been acknowledged as having more impact on a person's life and relationships than was previously recognized.

3. Depressive episode

Remember that depression can take on many faces and that it frequently comes out of the blue. Symptoms of depression in bipolar disorder include at least five of the following, which must be present for at least two weeks and must be present most days all day:
• depressed mood most of the day
• decreased pleasure in activities
• significant weight gain or loss
• difficulty sleeping most of the time (either not sleeping or sleeping excessively)
• presence of slower physical movement or a feeling of restlessness
• fatigue or loss of energy
• difficulty making decisions and/or concentrating
• feelings of worthlessness or excessive guilt
• frequent thoughts of suicide or death.

The above symptoms interfere with a person's ability to function in all or most areas of life. Other symptoms may include:
• oversensitivity and preoccupation with oneself
• negative thinking
• unresponsiveness to reassurance, support, feedback or sympathy
• less awareness of others' feelings because of one's own internal pain
• feeling the need to control relationships
• inability to function in normal role.

Psychotic symptoms — These may include false beliefs about persecution, being punished for past sins, being affected with a deadly disease such as cancer, or in severe cases, denying one's own existence.

It is important to recognize that depressive symptoms often include severe anxiety, worries about minor matters, complaints about physical symptoms including pain and frequent visits to the family doctor for imagined physical disorders.

Types of Bipolar Disorder

Some people experience manic or mixed, depressed and well phases during their illness. Such people are said to have "Bipolar-I" disorder. A milder form of mania is called "hypomania." People who have hypomania, depression and intervals without symptoms, but no full manic phases, are said to have "Bipolar-II" disorder.

ORDER AND FREQUENCY OF THE VARIOUS STATES

The manic/hypomanic, mixed and depressive states usually do not occur in a certain order, and their frequency cannot be predicted. For many people there are years between each episode, whereas others suffer more frequent episodes. Over a lifetime, the average person with bipolar illness experiences about 10 episodes of depression and mania/hypomania or mixed states. As the person ages, the episodes of illness come closer together. Untreated manias often last for two to three months. Untreated depressions usually last longer, between four and six months.

RAPID CYCLING

In about 20 per cent of cases, patients have four or more (sometimes many more) episodes a year and have short phases without symptoms. Patients with four or more episodes a year are said to be having rapid cycling, which is a subtype of bipolar disorder that needs specific treatment. We don't know for certain what causes rapid cycling. Sometimes, its course may be triggered by certain antidepressants, but how the antidepressant causes rapid cycling is not clear. Sometimes stopping the antidepressant may help the patient to return to a "normal" cycling pattern.

Cause (etiology) of Major Depression

GENETICS
Depression seems to run in families, which suggests a hereditary component.

BIOLOGY
Depression is believed to be influenced by imbalances in brain chemistry and in the endocrine/immune systems. It also may be the result of a major physical illness or event.

LIFE EVENTS
Childhood trauma, such as the loss of a parent, can contribute to depression, as can major stressors in adulthood, such as the loss of a spouse or job, or serious trauma, such as domestic violence or social upheaval.

PERSONALITY STYLE
People who tend to be more introverted, dependent, greater worriers, less trusting, or less flexible have a greater likelihood of developing depression.

SOCIAL SUPPORTS
The absence of social supports leads to greater isolation, which can contribute to depression.

The stress vulnerability model suggests that depression can develop because of various causes, and that the more of the five factors that are present, the more likely someone is to develop a major depression.

Cause (etiology) of Bipolar Disorder

The precise cause of bipolar disorder is not known. However, research shows that genes play a strong role. This does not mean a person has to inherit the genes; the genes involved may be altered when a person is conceived.

Genes are the blueprint for all cells and their contents. Scientists thus believe that changes to genes can lead to faulty proteins being produced within brain cells. These faulty proteins may then result in bipolar disorder. Researchers today are looking at various proteins that may be affected in bipolar disorder. These include:
• proteins such as those involved in making chemicals in the brain called neurotransmitters
• proteins that use neurotransmitters to make the cell do something
• genes themselves.

We do know that too much stress or difficult family relationships do not cause the illness. However, these factors may "trigger" an episode in someone who already has the illness. Nor is bipolar illness a simple imbalance of neurotransmitters, such as serotonin or dopamine. Yet neurotransmitters may be affected during a flare-up of the illness.

WHAT IS A "TRIGGER" FOR A BIPOLAR EPISODE?

Not all episodes can be related to any particular trigger, but many can. Triggers are situations that can provoke either mania or depression in someone who a genetic vulnerability. Feeling very stressed or continually losing sleep is an example of this kind of trigger. Other triggers are chemical and include antidepressants that work "too well" and result in mania; common medication, such as steroids (for instance, prednisone used for treating asthma, arthritis, etc.); and street drugs, such as cocaine and amphetamines.

The Use of Medications in the Treatment of Depression

History of medications

In the 1950s, physicians discovered that Iproniazid, a drug used to treat tuberculosis, also elevated patients' moods. It was later discovered that Iproniazid acts by boosting neurotransmitters. Neurotransmitters are the chemicals in the brain that allow cells to communicate with one another and in some cases regulate our moods. Further research has revealed that people with depression do not have enough of the neurotransmitter serotonin and that helping the brain to produce more serotonin seems to lessen depression. However, the brain is a very complex organ, and serotonin is only one of over 500 neurotransmitters. More research is needed to discover how brain chemistry contributes to depression.

Even though many questions remain to be answered, antidepressant medications are used often and successfully to treat depression, either on their own or in combination with psychotherapy. With early intervention, medication can prevent people from developing a severe depressive episode and preserve their current coping skills. Medication also allows people to make better use of talking therapies than would be possible when they are acutely withdrawn and depressed. With more severe depressions, medication offers symptom relief and restores patients' moods to a more normal level, enabling them to return to regular routines and activities.

Common worries about antidepressants

Common worries about antidepressants include the fear that one will become addicted to or dependent on medication. Antidepressants are not addictive and serve an important role in the treatment of depression.

Many people hesitate to take medication, because they view reliance on medication as a sign of weakness. This suggests that these people view depression as a weakness in character, rather than as a legitimate medical disorder. Depression is an illness that, without treatment, can worsen significantly and even become life-threatening.

Even those patients who accept that medication is useful may find it hard to keep taking their medication because of unpleasant side-effects. Common side-effects from older antidepressants include dry mouth, constipation, difficulty urinating, and blurry vision. These side-effects are called **anticholinergic**. Although older antidepressants work as well as newer ones at lessening depressive symptoms, patients often stop using them because of these side-effects.

For this reason, a group of newer agents has been developed. These drugs have fewer, and more tolerable, side-effects. Although these side-effects are mild, they still may include headaches, insomnia, increased anxiety, sedation and sexual problems. An important part of the assessment and treatment process is for the physician to determine the medication that is best suited to the patient. Very few people will follow through with treatment if they experience intolerable side-effects. *If your relative is struggling with side-effects it is important that he or she consult his or her doctor, rather than abruptly stopping the medication. Although antidepressants are not addictive, sudden termination can lead to unpleasant reactions and possibly a poorer response to subsequent medications.*

Dosage

To get the best effect from a medication, a physician will gradually increase the dosage of the medication to the highest level at which it will have a therapeutic effect. This is called **optimization**.

Unlike other medications that relieve symptoms very quickly, antidepressants generally take two weeks or more to take effect. Usually, patients will experience side-effects first and symptom relief later, which may cause them to feel discouraged or disheartened. Side-effects can be offset by other medications, changes in the dosage of the drug, or if necessary, a change in medication. Although they may be annoying, side-effects are a sign that the drug is being absorbed by the body and is starting to work.

In addition to maximizing the dosage, a doctor may **augment** a medication, or boost its effect, by adding another medication. For example, the drug lithium may be chosen to augment the primary antidepressant.

Research suggests that patients will respond equally well to all classes of antidepressants but may tolerate certain drugs better than others. It is common for individual patients to try two or more different medications before finding one that has a good effect and is well tolerated. For patients who are very **dose sensitive** (meaning that they react to even small fluctuations in the amount of medication in their system), it is important to take the medication at the same time every day. Once medication has relieved the symptoms of depression, it is often recommended that patients continue to take medication for up to one year or more, in order to avoid relapse.

Different classes of antidepressants

This section is a general overview of medications, listing examples of the generic names of drugs, as well as the Canadian trade name. Trade names will vary among countries. Further information can be found in David Healy's book, *Psychiatric Drugs Explained* (London: Mosby, 1993) or Jack Gorman's *The Essential Guide to Psychiatric Drugs* (New York: St. Martin's Griffin, 1997).

The older drugs

MAOIs — MONOAMINE OXIDASE INHIBITORS

Monoamine oxidase inhibitors (MAOIs), such as Nardil® (phenelzine) and Parnate® (tranylcypromine) were the first class of antidepressants. MAOIs block the action of monoamine oxidase, an enzyme that breaks down some neurotransmitters in the brain. By blocking this enzyme breakdown, MAOIs increase the number and availability of neurotransmitters, which are helpful in the treatment of depression. MAOIs are still prescribed — often for the treatment of atypical depression.

It is important to know that MAOIs also affect a person's ability to digest and process foods that contain tyramine, foods such as aged and fermented cheeses, smoked meats and some beer. In large quantities, tyramine can be toxic and may lead to dangerous increases in blood pressure. The MAO enzyme protects us from tyramine. Because MAOI drugs inhibit the action of MAO, patients taking these drugs must avoid these foods. This restriction means that patients usually take MAOIs only when other medications have been ineffective.

CYCLICS

The second group of drugs developed for the treatment of depression were cyclic or tricyclic anti-depressants, a group that includes Elavil® (amitriptyline), Ludiomil® (maprotiline) and Tofranil® (imipramine). Because this group also tends to have more side-effects than newer, more refined drugs, they are not often a first choice for treatment. However, some patients find that these drugs are well tolerated and very effective. Tricyclic medications tend to be more sedating and are associated with anticholinergic side-effects. Weight gain and dizziness may also be experienced with these medications.

The newer agents

SSRIs — SPECIFIC SEROTONIN REUPTAKE INHIBITORS

This newer group of drugs, including Prozac® (fluoxetine), Paxil® (paroxetine), Luvox® (fluvoxamine) and Zoloft® (sertraline), is usually the first choice for treatment of depression. These drugs generally do not cause the anticholinergic side-effects of the tricyclics. Although these drugs are very effective, patients may experience initial side-effects, including nausea, stomach upset, headaches and reduced sexual functioning. Other patients may develop long-standing sleep difficulties, such as problems falling asleep or awakening throughout the night.

Other classes of newer drugs

Several newer medications have proven effective in treating depression. These drugs do not fit into any one category as they affect several different systems in the brain. They include Effexor® (venlafaxine), Wellbutrin® (buproprion), Manerix® (moclobemide) and Serzone® (nefazodone) and may prove to have fewer side-effects than the MAOIs and tricyclics.

The Use of Medications in the Treatment of Bipolar Disorder

History of medications

Lithium, a mood stabilizer, was discovered in the 1800s for general medical use. It was viewed as a panacea to treat all types of ailments and disorders. It was later applied to psychiatry in the 1880s. During these pre-scientific days, physicians and doctors were unaware of the dangers of lithium toxicity and, as people became ill, it began to be discarded generally. From the 1880s to the 1950s, lithium was discarded as a treatment for all disorders, and other mood stabilizers were developed in the 1970s and 1980s. Interestingly, during the time of the American Civil War, a physician who was treating people with mood disorders noted that lithium seemed to be effective in the treatment of bipolar disorder, but he later dropped the drug's usage. In recent years, with the advent of medication trials and the recognition that drugs need to be monitored in order to keep them at therapeutic levels and not toxic levels, lithium has again returned as one treatment of choice in bipolar disorder.

HOW IS BIPOLAR DISORDER TREATED?

Bipolar disorder is treated in phases:

• Acute Treatment Phase, where the focus is on treating the current manic, hypomanic or mixed episode
• Preventative Treatment Phase, where the focus is on preventing future episodes.

Mood stabilizers

Mood stabilizers are medicines that help reduce the oscillation of abnormal moods and help prevent fresh mood episodes.

Lithium, a naturally occurring salt, is the most studied. Lithium has been used for 50 years and still has a major role in treating bipolar disorder.

Carbamazepine, an anticonvulsant, was also discovered to be a mood stabilizer in the 1970s and is used occasionally.

Valproic acid (also including its various forms of sodium valproate and divalproex sodium) is another anticonvulsant, which became widely used in the 1990s as a mood stabilizer. It is widely used because many doctors believe that it has a broader range of activity and fewer side-effects than lithium, although it is not necessarily "better" than lithium.

How does a doctor choose the right medication?

Lithium and valproate are most commonly used for acute-phase treatment of manic episodes. Three of the criteria that a doctor will use to decide which of the medications to prescribe are:
• whether the patient has successfully used either of them before
• whether the patient has experienced particular side-effects, which might affect his or her preference
• the subtype of bipolar disorder that the patient has. Lithium is usually recommended for people with euphoric (over-happy) moods, and valproic acid is recommended for people with a combination of manic episodes and unhappy or irritable moods or who are rapid cyclers.

HOW LONG DOES INITIAL TREATMENT OF ACUTE EPISODES TAKE?

There is usually a significant improvement within a few weeks of starting treatment with lithium or valproic acid. If the first medication does not work, or if it results only in a partial response, the doctor may suggest trying another medication or combination of medications. Carbamazepine can also be effective, particularly with mixed episodes or rapid cycling.

Anti-anxiety and antipsychotic medications may be used to control severe symptoms until the mood stabilizers take effect.

Antipsychotic medications

Antipsychotic medication is commonly used in bipolar disorder, both for rapid control of mania (as a powerful sedative) and for the treatment of psychotic symptoms such as delusions of grandeur or persecution, and hallucinations. Traditional antipsychotics can also prevent new attacks of mania, but long-term use is associated with serious side-effects such as tardive dyskinesia, a movement disorder.

Newer antipsychotics such as olanzapine (Zyprexa®), risperidone (Risperdal®), quetiapine (Seroquel®) and clozapine (Clozaril®) are also proving useful in bipolar disorder and may work to some extent like mood stabilizers. Research is ongoing to determine whether these medications can treat not only mania but also depression, and prevent new episodes. These newer medications have the advantage of fewer side-effects than the old antipsychotics.

Anti-anxiety medications or mild sedatives

Anxiety is common in bipolar disorder, and sleep disturbance is very frequent during acute episodes. Benzodiazepines such as lorazepam (Ativan®) and clonazepam are often prescribed and may be used for short periods without risk of addiction. Clonazepam is particularly useful for treating the excessive energy and reduced sleep of hypomania. For more severe anxiety problems such as panic attacks, cognitive behaviour therapy may be very helpful, and needed, because the antidepressants used to treat anxiety disorders may provoke manic attacks.

Antidepressant medications

With bipolar depression, at times, a mood stabilizer alone will not adequately treat the severe symptoms of depression. A specific antidepressant may be required along with a mood stabilizer. If given alone, antidepressants can sometimes cause a major problem in bipolar disorder by pushing a person's mood up too high and inducing hypomania or mania.

While the first antidepressant/mood stabilizer trial may work, it is not uncommon to go through several trials of antidepressants before finding an effective combination. While waiting for the medication to work, a person may also benefit from sedating medication to help with sleep, anxiety or agitation.

Many antidepressant drugs are effective, but the following are considered preferred choices by experts in the bipolar field:
• Lamotrigine® (one of the most effective)
• Buproprion®
• SSRIs (such as fluoxetine, fluvoxamine, paroxetine and sertraline)
• MAOIs (such as phenelzine and tranylcypromine)
• Nefaxodone
• Tricyclics (such as amitriptyline and imipramine)
• Venlafaxine

Maintenance medication

Bipolar disorder is a highly recurrent disorder. Most people who are untreated will experience a relapse within a couple of years. Medications not only treat symptoms but also prevent their return. The likelihood of remaining well is significantly higher if a person remains on medications as opposed to discontinuing them.

DOES MAINTENANCE MEDICATION MEAN I MUST TAKE A MOOD STABILIZER FOR LIFE?
Recommendations for maintenance (longer-term) treatment depend on the nature of your illness. For some people, who experience a mild single episode that is not particularly impairing, remaining on medications for one to two years may be reasonable. For most other people, longer-term treatments are recommended and in many cases indefinite treatment is necessary.

DOES PREVENTIVE MEDICATION OVER A PERSON'S LIFETIME REALLY WORK?
Yes. Mood stabilizers (such as lithium, valproate and carbamazepine) are the core of prevention. This type of management will allow about one-third of bipolar patients to remain symptom-free. However, most people who do not remain symptom-free will experience a significant reduction in their symptoms and the number and severity of episodes.

Discontinuing medication

It is natural for people who haven't experienced an episode of bipolar disorder in several years to hope that they can stop taking medication. However, although mood stabilizers prevent episodes, they do not cure the disorder. Because a serious relapse may occur — sometimes as soon as a few months after medication is discontinued — any decision to stop taking medication should be made only after a thorough discussion with the treating physician.

If this decision is made, medications should be tapered slowly (over several weeks to months). Abrupt cessation, in some cases, can lead to a poorer response the next time the patient tries the same medication. This is why, if one medication is working well, stopping it should be done thoughtfully, because the next time it is tried, it might not be as effective.

Electroconvulsive therapy (ECT) for bipolar disorder

Electroconvulsive therapy (ECT) is perhaps the most controversial and misunderstood of psychiatric treatments, due in part to sensationalized and misleading depictions of the treatment in the popular media. In fact, ECT is a highly effective and safe treatment for both the depressive and manic phases of bipolar disorder and is sometimes used as a long-term "maintenance" treatment to prevent recurrence of illness after recovery.

PROCEDURE

ECT involves administering a brief electrical stimulus through the scalp to the surface of the brain. This stimulus produces an epileptic-type convulsion, lasting typically from 15 seconds to two minutes.

During the treatment, a team of psychiatrist, anaesthetist and one or more nurses are present. The patient is given an anaesthetic intravenously to put him or her to sleep briefly during the treatment. A muscle relaxant is also given to prevent physical injury, by lessening the intensity of muscle spasms that accompany a seizure. Oxygen is administered, and heart rate and blood pressure are monitored. Although the anaesthetic lasts only a few minutes, patients feel groggy after an ECT treatment and may rest or sleep for about one hour.

Usually the treatments are administered three times a week over three to four weeks, for a total of nine to 12 treatments. For longer-term maintenance treatment, the treatments may be spread out, for example, once a month, and continued for as long as the patient and doctor feel is appropriate. ECT is usually given to hospitalized inpatients, but outpatients can receive ECT as well.

SIDE-EFFECTS

Patients may have a headache or jaw pain on awakening after ECT, usually requiring only a mild painkiller such as acetaminophen (Tylenol®). Some loss of recent memory or problems with concentration usually occur during treatment (for example, patients may not recall what they had for supper the night before the treatment), but these symptoms improve quickly after the course of ECT is finished, over a few weeks. Some patients report mild memory problems persisting much longer after ECT, but this is likely due to their depression not to the treatment.

ECT can be given bilaterally (the electric current is applied to both sides of the brain) or unilaterally (on only the right side of the brain). Although bilateral ECT causes more memory disruption than unilateral ECT, it is also somewhat more effective and is usually the preferred choice.

USES OF ECT IN BIPOLAR DISORDER

ECT is the most effective, and possibly the fastest-acting, treatment for severe depression and is particularly helpful for highly agitated or suicidal patients or those with psychotic or catatonic symptoms. Some patients receive ECT early in their episode of illness because of the urgency of their situation or their particular symptoms, while others may prefer to use ECT only after various medications have failed. ECT works well for severe mania as well.

While ECT is highly effective at ending an episode of depression or mania, the benefits may not last more than a few weeks or months following treatment. Therefore, patients usually start or continue treatment with mood stabilizers and/or other medication following a course of ECT. Maintenance ECT can be used in cases where medications have not prevented recurrence of illness or are intolerable due to side-effects.

Alternative therapies

Natural remedies may have a role. These include fish oil and inosital, a type of sugar. Yet when these products are sold through health food stores, they are often unreliable. Because they have not been precisely formulated, they cannot be recommended. Furthermore, little research has been done on these products. St John's wort has been well studied in unipolar depression; however, it has not been studied in bipolar disorder.

Treatment of refractory bipolar disorder ("brittle" patients)

About 30 per cent of patients have a more severe form of the illness that requires multiple medications for a long period of time. These individuals may not respond well to the treatments that are currently available, and it can take much longer to find a balance of medications (mood stabilizers, antidepressants, anxiety medications) that are effective. This can have a profound impact on many areas of their lives, such as work, school or functioning in their families.

These individuals also tend to have more difficulty staying well. This is because even after an effective mix of medications is found, mild stressors or changes in their lives can trigger relapse, resulting in the need to modify or switch medications whose efficacy may take a long time to establish.

Psychosocial Treatments — Depression/Bipolar Disorder

Psychoeducation and supportive psychotherapy

Psychoeducation and supportive psychotherapy can be either short- or long-term talk therapy. The focus is on providing a supportive environment in which the individual can learn about his or her illness and develop strategies to cope with and manage it. It can be particularly helpful for a recently diagnosed person to come to terms with the diagnosis.

Goals of talk therapy

1. Resolve past life event issues that contribute to current problems (such as major losses, childhood trauma, life changes, style of stress management).
2. Develop new ways of thinking/problem solving to promote or maintain wellness.
3. Deal with current family or relationship difficulties that contribute to stress and relapse.

Talk therapy focuses on particular issues that the person is struggling with such as:
• accepting the diagnosis of a mood disorder
• dealing with the changes/losses associated with having a serious illness (job, relationships, future goals)
• future planning
• stressful events that occur during periods when the person feels particularly unwell.

Talk therapies can be very helpful when combined with medication therapy. Psychosocial therapies can be provided to an individual, couple, family or in a group. The treatment(s) chosen is based on the individual's needs, strengths and, on a practical level, what resources are available in a particular community.

Individual treatments — the talk therapies

Many clinicians practise an eclectic model that integrates elements from a number of different modalities, such as interpersonal therapy, cognitive-behavioural therapy and insight-oriented psychotherapy.

Combining psychotherapy and drugs

Families and clients often ask if it is appropriate to combine psychotherapy, or talk therapy, with medication.

Severe bipolar disorder or major depression should be treated with both. When individuals are extremely ill, they may not be able to utilize psychotherapy because talking and listening is so difficult. As they improve, however, psychotherapy can be very helpful in identifying and dealing with issues that may have contributed to the illness.

Mild to moderate bipolar disorder also requires medication, but some clients may not feel that talk therapy is necessary. Their own internal resourcefulness can be enough to help them recover and maintain good health. However, even these people may find education about the illness and strategies for effective management to be very helpful. This would include gaining information about the illness, warning signs of relapse and stress management.

Mild to moderate depression can be treated with psychotherapy alone. Interpersonal therapy and cognitive-behavioural therapy can be highly effective and, over the long term, may contribute more to the prevention of relapse.

Interpersonal therapy for depression

Interpersonal therapy for depression (IPT) is a short-term (12 to 16 weeks) intervention that focuses on identifying and resolving specific problem areas in establishing and maintaining satisfying relationships. This may include dealing with loss, life changes, conflicts, and increasing ease in social situations. This model has not been researched with the bipolar population (Klerman, G., Weissman, M., Rounsaville, B. & and Chevron, E., 1997).

Cognitive-behavioural therapy for depression

In depression, cognitive behavioural therapy (CBT), the most scientifically proven type of psychotherapy, is a short-term treatment that helps people become aware of how automatic thoughts, attitudes, beliefs and expectations can produce and maintain unpleasant moods. This awareness, along with practising new thoughts, can help establish new, more adaptive patterns of behaviour.

Cognitive behaviour therapy is now being tested to determine whether it helps treat bipolar depression and assists in relapse prevention. This type of short-term therapy (which lasts for 15 to 20 weeks) is done in combination with a mood stabilizer (Padesky, C. & Greenberger, D., 1995).

Insight-oriented psychotherapy

This form of therapy may be either long or short term. The focus is on understanding how traumatic life events have influenced a person's coping strategies, self-esteem and identity. The individual can make changes to his or her situation by developing insight into the causes and effects of these traumatic events and by practising new problem-solving strategies, with the support of a trusted therapist.

VOCATIONAL COUNSELLING
This treatment involves providing assistance in returning to work, school, volunteer or leisure activities through structured counselling or a formal rehabilitation program.

CASE MANAGEMENT/COMMUNITY MENTAL HEALTH WORKERS
In situations where the course of an individual's illness is more complicated and longstanding, it may be helpful for a case manager or community mental health worker to be involved in ongoing care. Case managers co-ordinate services, such as housing or financial services, to individuals as well as link clients with day treatment, vocational or volunteer services. Case managers can also assist in day-to-day activities, such as attending appointments, budgeting and setting up a daily routine, as well as provide emotional support and counselling. Depending on the community, case managers and community mental health workers may be accessed through community mental health agencies, housing services and homecare.

Group treatments

Mental health professionals lead psychotherapy groups of eight to 12 people who support one another while practising new coping strategies. These groups are often closed (new members are not invited to drop in) and time-limited.

SELF-HELP GROUPS
Self-help groups are support and information groups, made up of people with a problem or diagnosis in common. These groups are usually open-ended (people can join or leave the groups at any time) and led by clients or family members who have experience in the mental health system. Some self-help organizations also offer services for families.

Family interventions

MARITAL AND FAMILY THERAPY
Research has shown that when there is negative emotional intensity (such as intrusiveness, criticism or conflict) in the ill person's environment, recovery time is prolonged and relapse more likely. This therapy focuses on resolving conflictual issues to reduce emotional intensity. Therapy can also assist the family in supporting the client's treatment compliance.

EDUCATION AND SUPPORT GROUPS
These groups, similar to the self-help groups for clients, offer information and support for family members who have an ill relative. They may be offered through hospitals, agencies or self-help organizations.

PROMOTING OVERALL GOOD HEALTH
While the medical and psychosocial therapies are specifically designed to treat your relative's disorder, it is important to remember that promoting and maintaining overall good health is also

important. Nutrition and exercise are important for both the ill person and for family members coping with a difficult life problem.

Two ways to reduce stress are:
• Minimize multiple stressors, which create a greater potential for relapse; this is especially important in bipolar disorder.
• Lower the level of emotional intensity in the family. When there is conflict, it is important to handle it without critical comments or verbal and physical aggression.

Tips to remember

Your relative is someone with a disorder. The disorder does not define him or her as a person. When they are stable, individuals with a mood disorder must take responsibility for their actions, make their own decisions and develop skills for independence.

Life is a marathon, not a sprint. Learning to recognize and manage your stress will help you avoid the burnout that can arise from coping with a family member with a mood disorder.

How to recognize stress

Learn to recognize the signs of stress within yourself. By noticing when you experience stress symptoms, you can practise the coping strategies from the stress management group. Here are some cues that indicate when your stress level is increasing:

PHYSICAL
- chronic fatigue
- trembling
- vague physical complaints
- weight gain or loss
- body motions indicating anxiety, such as foot tapping
- sweaty palms
- dilated pupils

EMOTIONAL
- sadness
- anger
- easy distractibility
- daydreaming
- frequent mood changes

BEHAVIOURAL
- sleep disturbances
- explosive outbursts
- impulsive actions
- complaining
- negative or resentful statements
- cynical or hostile remarks
- self-criticism
- being overly critical of others
- withdrawal or being difficult to communicate with

- focusing on the past much more than the future
- use of drugs or alcohol
- difficulty with authority
- change in productivity on the job
- lack of attention to details
- difficulty handling usual responsibilities

Stress-reduction strategies

These strategies can help to reduce or prevent stress from taking over your life:

1. ESTABLISH A GOOD SUPPORT SYSTEM FOR YOURSELF.

Avoid becoming isolated. Have a few people whom you can turn to when you are in danger of becoming stressed. As you have discovered, not everyone can put themselves "in your shoes," so it will take some time and effort to determine who can best support you.

Look to self-help organizations, support groups, professionals and trusted family members and friends who are supportive, non-judgmental and good listeners.

2. CULTIVATE INTERESTS OUTSIDE THE FAMILY.

- Physical — Take time for exercise. Join a club or gym. Take walks. Participate in sports.

- Emotional — Focus on your needs. Spend time with a friend. Do something just for you, such as reading, keeping a journal or developing a new hobby. Plan regular times to recharge your emotional batteries.

- Spiritual — Develop and appreciate your spiritual life. Take time to breathe. Use a guided relaxation tape or learn to meditate. Research has shown that regular use of meditation and relaxation techniques are associated with reduced physical stress reactions.

3. CULTIVATE A LOW-STRESS ENVIRONMENT.

Communicating quietly and calmly will help to reduce your stress. Research has also shown that it will help to prevent relapse for your relative.

The wisdom of the **Serenity Prayer** can be a helpful reminder of this:

God, grant me
the serenity to accept the things
I cannot change;
the courage to change the things I can; and
the wisdom to know the difference.

4. AVOID MARTYRDOM.

- Acknowledge that negative feelings are normal.
- Give yourself permission to set limits. Forgive yourself when you have trouble sticking to them and start again.
- Develop a balance between caring for your relative and taking care of yourself.
- Get respite care when needed. No one can be on call 24 hours a day.

Remember: stress levels lower as coping ability improves.

Your Support System

Where do you get support?

List the people in your life who give you support in the following areas:

EMOTIONAL SUPPORT
Who understands of the difficulty of living with a mentally ill person?

_____

_____

PROBLEM SOLVING
Who can help you make a useful plan for managing a difficult situation?

_____

_____

ENCOURAGEMENT
Who cheers you on and cheers you up when you are feeling overwhelmed?

_____

_____

PHYSICAL SUPPORT
Who can you call to run an errand or take your relative to the doctor?

_____

_____

SPIRITUAL SUPPORT
Who provides inspiration to help you through difficult times?

_____

_____

Get in a comfortable position. If you're sitting, uncross your legs and put your feet flat on the floor. Rest your hands on your thighs. Let your spine support your upper body in a natural position. Take a breath, let it out, and let your head fall easily forward, so that your chin rests on your chest. You might find it useful to close your eyes. Let your shoulders feel the natural gravitational pull downward.

Take another breath, in and out, slowly and deeply, all the way down to your diaphragm, and rest there for a moment. Now, take another breath, slowly, deeply, in, then out.

We will begin with your feet. Be aware of the tension in your feet and then begin to let it out. You may simply feel like the tension being replaced by relaxation, or it may feel like a comfortable heaviness, or even like the tension is actually draining out and down into the floor. However it feels and however much you are able to relax, let yourself take another deep, slow breath.

Now, begin to let that relaxation move slowly up your legs, first into your calves, then higher through your knees and thighs. If you find that you get distracted, remember that you are just practising. There's no right or wrong way to do this.

Now, take another breath before beginning to allow whatever relaxation you are able to feel to move up into your buttocks, through your low back and stomach. Just rest with this relaxation as you breathe deeply and easily.

Now, feel the relaxation begin in your hands, and then slowly spread up through your forearms and upper arms. Your arms are now becoming more relaxed as you continue to breathe as deeply and easily as possible.

Let the breath come from your diaphragm so that your stomach moves in and out with each breath, and, surprisingly, your shoulders will not move up and down, even though you might be breathing more deeply than you are used to. Now the relaxation is moving up through your chest and shoulders, letting yourself feel heavy and warm, really supported by the chair beneath you.

Now, continuing to be aware of breathing deeply and easily, becoming just as relaxed as you can at this time, let the comfortable relaxation move up through your neck and face, including your jaw, eyes, forehead, over your entire head.

Allow yourself to continue to breathe deeply and easily, feeling the comfortable heaviness, and being aware that this is something that you can do for yourself each day. And realize how important it is to let yourself have a little time each day for breathing.

When you are ready, take one more deep breath, then open your eyes and take a stretch.

Reminder. When you are practising this exercise at home, you might find that you become even more relaxed when lying down. Some people even use muscle-relaxation techniques to help them fall asleep at night. However, one of the values of continuing to practise sitting up as we did today is that you can get used to relaxing whenever and wherever you need to.

Just remember not to use any relaxation technique when you need to be alert, such as when you are driving.

(Reproduced with permission from Kate Kitchen; the use of relaxation techniques was originally developed by Edmund Jacobson. For more information, see: Jacobson, E. (1974). *Progressive Relaxation*. Chicago: The University of Chicago Press, Midway Reprint).

Communication Skills: Depression

The DOs of effective communication for depression

1. Try to talk about one subject at a time.

2. Speak in a calm, quiet tone of voice; this contributes to a more relaxed conversation.

3. Keep your statements or requests short, simple and stated as a positive. For example, "It would be nice to go out today."

4. Use "I" statements; this will focus on how you feel and what you need. "You" statements can be experienced as an accusation or criticism, making your relative feel defensive. For example, "I really need you to tell me when you are having a bad day," rather than "You should have told me you were feeling particularly bad today."

5. When you make requests, be direct and positive. For example, "I would really like it if you would..."

6. Aim to be clear. Try to have your words, facial expressions and body language all communicate the same message. For example, when agreeing with a suggestion that you have mixed feelings about, do not shake your head indicating "No" while saying "Okay, we'll give it a try."

7. Pair a positive with a negative. The positive makes up the first half of the sentence and the negative is the second half. In this way you are communicating that you have heard and understood your relative's point of view first, even though you are presenting another idea. For example, "I know you have been very tired lately, but I would really appreciate it if you could put your coffee cups in the kitchen."

8. Combine the above suggestions with "I" statements so that your relative knows that you are simply expressing your own thoughts and feelings. And offer compromises, so that your relative can feel that he or she is part of the solution.

   For example, "It is disruptive for me to have you sleep in the daytime and be up in the middle of the night." Then offer the compromise, such as "Could you start to go to bed an hour earlier each night to begin to re-establish a normal sleep pattern?"

9. Repeat your statements — mood disorders affect your relative's listening and information processing. This is sometimes called the "broken record" technique.

10. Use "active listening." Nod every so often to let your relative know that you are paying attention.

11. Offer praise for small accomplishments. We all find change difficult.

DON'Ts that get in the way of effective communication for depression and mania

1. Avoid using "shoulds," which can sound critical and judgmental.

2. Avoid jumping to give reassurance. Your ill relative has a lot to figure out. Giving quick reassurances can get in the way of problem solving and send the message that you lack confidence in his or her ability to recover. It is entirely appropriate to say, "I don't know how and when things will work out, but I am confident they will." Listening, rather than reassuring, gives you a chance to hear your relative's thoughts, plans and worries. If it is difficult for you to refrain from jumping in, try to stay calm by reminding yourself that recovery takes time.

3. Don't try to be constantly available and positive. It's okay not to have all the answers. Sometimes just listening is the most helpful thing a person can do.

4. Try not to take your relative's comments personally; mood disorders can cause people to make hurtful, even rejecting, statements that they regret once they are well.

5. Don't try to discuss something important when you are feeling angry, tired or frustrated.

The HALT slogan from AA says it best:
Don't try to discuss anything of importance when you are too:
H - Hungry
A - Angry
L - Lonely
T - Tired

Suggestions to improve communications with support networks

1. Acknowledge that extended family, friends and colleagues probably know very little about the reality of mental illness. People tend to operate on dated information and myths. Offer basic information and facts.

2. Although public awareness campaigns have raised awareness about mental illness, there is still a stigma attached. Be thoughtful about who you choose to confide in. Look for people who are open and receptive to the information.

3. As relatives, you need the opportunity to discuss your situation with friends and at times will need them to be there just for you. Friendships need to take care of both people in order to be sustained. Therefore, it is important to try to maintain a balance where your friends also experience you listening to their interests and issues.

4. Finally, if you need help and support from a friend, be clear about what you need. (such as time to talk or go to a movie together). Friends tend to respond when clear boundaries are defined.

Communication Skills: Bipolar Disorder

The DOs of effective communication for depression and mania

1. Try to talk about one subject at a time.

2. Speak in a calm, quiet tone of voice; this contributes to a more relaxed conversation.

3. Keep your statements or requests short, simple and stated as a positive. For example, "It would be nice to go out today."

4. Use "I" statements; this will focus on how you feel and what you need. "You" statements can be experienced as an accusation or criticism, making your relative feel defensive. For example, "I really need you to tell me when you are having a bad day," rather than "You should have told me you were feeling particularly bad today."

5. When you make requests, be direct and positive. For example, "I would really like it if you would..."

6. Aim to be clear. Try to have your words, facial expressions and body language all communicate the same message. For example, when agreeing with a suggestion that you have mixed feelings about, do not shake your head indicating "No" while saying "Okay, we'll give it a try."

7. Pair a positive with a negative. The positive makes up the first half of the sentence and the negative is the second half. In this way you are communicating that you have heard and understood your relative's point of view first, even though you are presenting another idea. For example, "I know you have been very tired lately, but I would appreciate if you could put your coffee cups in the kitchen."

8. Combine the above suggestions with "I" statements so that your relative knows that you are simply expressing your own thoughts and feelings. And offer compromises, so that your relative can feel that he or she is part of the solution.

    For example, "It is disruptive for me to have you sleep in the daytime and be up in the middle of the night." Then offer the compromise, such as "Could you start to go to bed an hour earlier each night to begin to re-establish a normal sleep pattern?"

9. Repeat your statements — mood disorders affect your relative's listening and information processing. This is sometimes called the "broken record" technique.

10. Use "active listening." Nod every so often to let your relative know that you are paying attention.

11. Offer praise for small accomplishments. We all find change difficult. Remember, Rome wasn't built in a day.

DON'Ts that get in the way of effective communication for depression and mania

1. Avoid using "shoulds," which can sound critical and judgmental.

2. Avoid jumping to give reassurance. Your ill relative has a lot to figure out. Giving quick reassurances can get in the way of problem solving and send the message that you lack confidence in your relative's ability to recover. It is entirely appropriate to say, "I don't know how and when things will work out, but I am confident they will."

   Listening, rather than reassuring, gives you a chance to hear your relative's thoughts, plans and worries.

   If it is difficult for you to refrain from jumping in, try to stay calm by reminding yourself that recovery takes time.

3. Don't try to be constantly available and positive. It's okay not to have all the answers. Sometimes just listening is the most helpful thing a person can do.

4. Try not to take your relative's comments personally; mood disorders can cause people to make hurtful, even rejecting, statements that they regret once they are well.

5. Don't try to discuss something important when you are feeling angry, tired or frustrated.

   The HALT slogan from AA says it best:
   Don't try to discuss anything of importance when you are too:
   H - Hungry
   A - Angry
   L - Lonely
   T - Tired

Communication Management for Mania

Do

1. Reduce stimulation; people with mania are easily overstimulated. You may need to reduce the number of people who visit with the person at the same time or ensure that the noise and activity level in the house is minimized.

2. Have brief conversations.

3. Deal only with immediate issues. Do not try to reason or argue.

4. Discourage the discussion of feelings.

5. Try not to be authoritative, but be firm, practical and realistic.

6. Avoid debating your relative's ideas or pointing out where they are illogical. This will inevitably lead to an argument.

DON'T

1. Jump to the person's demands.

2. Get caught up with the person's euphoria or unrealistic expectations.

3. Argue with the person to convince him or her that his or her plans are unrealistic. At the same time, take steps to ensure his or her safety (e.g., removal of car keys or credit cards).

Suggestions to improve communications with support networks

1. Acknowledge that extended family, friends and colleagues probably know very little about the reality of mental illness. People tend to operate on dated information and myths. Offer basic information and facts.

2. Although public awareness campaigns have raised awareness about mental illness, there is still a stigma attached. Be thoughtful about who you choose to confide in. Look for people who are open and receptive to the information.

3. As relatives, you need the opportunity to discuss your situation with friends and at times will need them to be there just for you. Friendships need to take care of both people in order to be sustained. Therefore, it is important to try to maintain a balance where your friends also experience you listening to their interests and issues.

4. Finally, if you need help and support from a friend, be clear about what you need (such as time to talk or to go to a movie together). Friends tend to respond when clear boundaries are defined.

Talking with Children about Their Parent's Mood Disorder

Parents are often very concerned about how their partner's mood disorder is affecting their children. In explaining the situation to children, it is important to consider the following points:

Talking with children

1. Explain the illness, taking into account the children's level of development, so that they can understand their parent's behaviour. It is not necessary to provide details about the diagnosis. Your goal is simply to help them make sense of their parent's actions.

2. Children need to know that it is not their fault. They must understand that there is an illness causing the problem, and not think that their parent is mad at them or that the illness is a punishment for their misbehaviour.

3. It is not the child's responsibility to fix the problem or to take on grown-up roles to compensate for their parent's problem. They should be reassured that the adults will take care of the problem.

4. During a time when their ill parent is feeling better, it is useful for that parent to acknowledge the illness to the children, and to reinforce that it is not the children's fault.

   There are things parents can do to help children cope with another parent's mental illness. These "buffers" have been shown to help kids get through the rough times.

Buffers for children

1. **The presence of a well parent in the home** — The parent who continues to function as a loving, thoughtful parent whom the children can rely on, provides support and a model for normal adulthood.

2. **Remaining active outside the family** — Ensuring that children have outside activities, so that their lives are not completely absorbed by problems at home, also acts as a buffer for children.

Problem Management — Brainstorming

Tips for problem management

• Focus on one part of the problem at a time.
• State the problem as precisely as possible
• Express how it is a problem for you

Once you have selected one specific problem, use **brainstorming** to explore possible solutions.

Elements of brainstorming

1. State the problem.
Why is this a problem? What is the part of the problem you would like to work on at this time? (Remember that you can choose another part of the problem to work on in the future.)

2. Think over the things you have already done to try to manage this problem.
You don't want to have to "reinvent the wheel." It is frustrating to keep trying the same things that have not worked in the past. Remember what Mae West had to say on this subject: "Whenever I have to decide between two evils, I always like to choose the one I haven't tried yet."

3. Make a list of new ideas you haven't tried yet.
Include anything you can imagine that might have an impact on your problem, no matter how small or unlikely it seems. Don't censor yourself. You are just thinking of possibilities. You won't act on all of your ideas and you don't have to act on any of them.

The value of brainstorming is that one idea inspires another. Ideas build on other ideas. Ideas will not be evaluated or criticized during the brainstorming exercise. Give yourself plenty of time to make your list. Don't rush it.

4. Take a break after making your possibilities list.
Then choose the plan that you would like to try first. Don't stop there. Choose a second option and then a third. Managing a problem is a marathon, not a sprint. Over time, you are likely to use many of your ideas.

Equally important is to remember that when trying a new idea, you can always abandon it if it does not work. Problem management is a process of trying many different ideas.

5. Return to your list when you get stuck.
Add new ideas that emerge and delete the ones that have not been helpful.

It can be very difficult to think and cope effectively when faced with a sudden unexpected crisis. It is useful to plan some emergency strategies when your relative is well and to practise the communication strategies presented in earlier groups.

Tips for managing a crisis

Do

1. Remain as calm as possible and decrease other distractions.

2. If necessary, ask others to leave the room or house.

3. Take turns talking, slow things down and reduce stimulation. For example, you might say, "Let's sit down and talk" or "Let's sit down and take a rest for a moment."

4. Speak slowly and in a normal voice. Use your communication strategies, such as validating and making neutral statements about what you see happening. For example, "I can see that you seem afraid and confused," or "I can see you are angry. Please tell me what is wrong."

5. Calmly repeat questions or statements when necessary, using the same words each time.

6. Allow your relative to have personal space in the room.

7. Recognize that too much emotion on your part can further upset your relative.

Don't

1. Shout.

2. Criticize.

3. Maintain continuous eye contact.

4. Argue with other people about what to do.

5. Make patronizing or authoritative statements such as "You are acting like a child," or "You'll do what I say."

Going to the hospital

1. If possible, your relative should go to the hospital voluntarily.

2. If your relative will not listen to you, ask someone else whom he or she trusts to convince him or her to go to the hospital. This should be part of your prearranged action plan.

3. Try to offer your relative a choice. For example, "Will you go to the hospital with me or would you prefer to go with John?" This reduces a person's sense that he or she is being coerced.

Concerns about violence

A plan for dealing with violence is essential. In the event of a violent situation, there will not be time to talk calmly or call for assistance.

If your relative threatens to harm him- or herself or you, or to seriously damage property, you must do whatever is necessary to protect yourself and others (including your relative) from harm.

You may need to leave the premises and call for help, or you may need to secure your relative in a room while you go for help. This is advisable only under extreme circumstances.

You may need to evaluate whether it is safe to drive alone with your relative to the hospital.

Calling the police

Understandably, families are reluctant to call the police. However, extreme circumstances may leave you no other option than to involve the police.

Often, merely telling the ill person that you are calling the police influences him or her to calm down.

When you call 911, tell the emergency operator that your relative needs emergency medical assistance and give the operator your relative's diagnosis. State that you need help getting him or her to the hospital.

Be prepared for a variety of responses from the police, depending on their knowledge of mental illnesses. It is helpful to document who the officers are, their badge numbers and their response time.

While the police are present, you may have time to call the doctor.

At the emergency department, speak directly with the doctor, social worker or nurse. Find out if your relative will be admitted, discharged and what follow-up treatment is recommended.

Dealing with suicidal episodes

One of the most terrifying aspects of a mood disorder is to hear your loved one talk about suicide. Although the topic is difficult to discuss, you should be knowledgeable about suicide and how to deal with it.

Remember that suicidal thinking and statements are a symptom of depression and are usually a temporary emotional state.

Most people do not want to end their life. Suicidal thinking, or suicide attempts, typically occur during a major depressive episode when the person feels helpless, hopeless and in a state of despair.

It is possible to prevent an escalation in suicidal thinking if you are aware of the warning signs. **At the same time, recognize that you do not have absolute control to change things and cannot be responsible for all of your relative's actions.**

Signs of suicidal thinking

Your relative talks about suicide and what it would be like to be gone; he or she makes comments such as "When I'm gone... ."

Your relative is concerned about having a will and about the distribution of his or her possessions. She or he begins to give away treasured possessions.

Your relative expresses feelings of worthlessness, such as "I'm no good to anybody."

Your relative shows signs of hopelessness about the future, making comments such as "What's the use?"

Your relative has distorted beliefs, such as thinking that a partner is having an affair or that money is being withheld.

Any mention of suicide must be taken seriously. If your relative speaks of suicide or inflicts wounds on him- or herself, contact the doctor immediately. If this is not possible, take your relative to the emergency department of your local hospital.

Long-term sufferers of depression can experience passive suicidal thinking. Thoughts of self-harm become a chronic feature of the depression, and it is difficult to differentiate between those statements that reflect a risk of self-harm and those statements that reflect the patient's fatigue with being depressed. In these cases, you must discuss the situation with the doctor in order to establish a management plan.

IF YOU DISCOVER YOUR RELATIVE AFTER A SUICIDE ATTEMPT:

1. Phone 911 immediately.

2. If you know first aid, administer it immediately.

3. Phone someone to accompany you to the hospital or be with you at home.

4. Do not try to handle the crisis alone. Contact a support group to help you with your feelings and reactions.

Limit-setting

Friends and family members should not tolerate the following behaviours, even if they are part of your relative's illness:

- physical aggression such as pushing, grabbing or pinching
- clear emotional abuse, such as yelling profanity or verbally aggressive threats
- sexual abuse
- property damage, such as damaging furniture or cars
- setting fires or creating fire hazards, such as by smoking in bed
- stealing from family, friends or others
- using non-prescribed drugs or alcohol, which complicate the psychiatric disorder
- financial mismanagement, such as engaging in spending sprees
- severely disruptive or tyrannical behaviours, such as insisting that all family members eat only certain foods, refusing to let anyone use the phone or barricading the doors.

Developing an Emergency Action Plan

Elements of an emergency action plan

1. Establish a list of phone numbers for the following:
   - doctor(s)
   - police
   - emergency department.

2. In advance, ask the doctor which hospital you should bring your relative to, should the need arise.

3. If possible, with your relative's consent, try to establish a strong relationship with the doctor.

4. Consider consulting with the police in advance. It can be helpful to know how your call will be received, and it is helpful for the police to know what they can expect should you need to call in an emergency.

5. Establish whom you can call, day or night, for support.

6. If you are the parent of young children, establish emergency child-care plans in case you must go to the hospital.

7. Know which relatives or friends your relative trusts in the event of an emergency.

8. Work out an emergency plan at a time when your relative is well and can participate and consent to the plan. Consider a Power of Attorney.

Your Emergency Action Plan

This form is designed to help you begin to develop an emergency action plan for your unique situation. Ask yourself the following questions:

1. Do I know the phone numbers for the following people?

        My relative's doctor(s)?   It is_____

        Police?   It is_____

2. Do I know which hospital my relative's doctor uses?

        It is   _____

        Hospital emergency department phone number   _____

        Crisis line/program number(s)   _____

                                              _____

3. Do I know my relative's medication(s)?   _____

                                              _____

                                              _____

4. Whom could I call day or night for support?

        Name _____   Phone Number(s)_____

5. For parents of small children: what child care could I use in case I had to accompany my relative to the hospital?

        Name _____   Phone Number(s)_____

        Name _____   Phone Number(s)_____

        Name _____   Phone Number(s)_____

6. Who are the relatives or friends whom my relative trusts in the event of an emergency?

        Name _____   Phone Number(s)_____

        Name _____   Phone Number(s)_____

        Name _____   Phone Number(s)_____

7. Have I discussed an emergency action plan with my relative during a stable time? If so, what are my relative's requests?

    1. _____

    2. _____

    3. _____

8. Are there additional steps that I could take to improve my emergency action plan? If so, list them here:

    1. _____

    2. _____

    3. _____

9. Do I need to revisit my plan? If so, how often?

_____

Working with the
Medical and Legal Systems

Historical background

To better understand mental health legislation, it is useful to look at its history. Today, the legislation in the United States and Canada sharply favours a patient's rights to refuse or accept treatment independent of his or her family and the state.

The roots of Canada's mental health legislation come from Britain's Parens Patriae Doctrine, which named the King as the Supreme Parent. Under this doctrine, the state intervened only when the family was unable or unavailable to provide care and protection for children of people with mental illness.

In Canada, from the 1870s until the 1960s, the state had the power to involuntarily hospitalize patients for treatment. Early on, people were committed to asylums and poor houses due to poverty, developmental delays or mental illness. Gradually, people with mental illness were separated out and hospitalized. To be released, patients had to undergo treatment and demonstrate improvement. As effective treatments were not available, many people were committed to institutions with little or no chance of improving or ever being released. Many individuals' civil rights were seriously compromised as a result.

In the 1960s, the development of antipsychotic medications led to more effective treatments of mental illness. At the same time, the civil rights movement challenged the historical approach to treating people with mental illness. These combined trends led to increased rights for patients and a wave of deinstitutionalization, where patients were discharged to the community. Deinstitutionalization assumed that community-based resources (housing, case management) would ensure that people with mental illnesses were adequately cared for. It was seen as a much less expensive means of care.

In the 1960s, judicial review of the mental health system led to new approaches for the involuntary committal of people with mental illness. The courts ruled that there were only two ways for the state to deprive a person of his or her liberty:

1. If someone broke the law, the state/police could arrest him or her and, if found guilty, the person would receive punishment.

2. The state could intervene if a parent failed to provide appropriate care of a child.

Treatment for a mental disorder was no longer viewed as a justifiable reason to deprive someone of his or her liberty unless the person was a threat to him- or herself or others. This is our current system.

While there is no doubt that changes were needed and were enacted with the best of intentions, our current system has created complex problems for families. As a result of these reforms, it is difficult for families to obtain care for relatives who will not agree to it because the ill person will not acknowledge his or her illness. Only extreme events allow involuntary intervention.

Throughout North America, families and communities have grappled with the problems associated with the new mental health laws. This has produced a pendulum swung toward legislation that would make it easier to obtain hospitalization and treatment for involuntary patients. These laws, which are now being enacted in some provinces and states, are called Community Treatment Orders. This is the latest step in society's attempts to balance individual and community rights in the treatment of people with mental illness.

The following is a description of the ways in which a person who has a mental illness can receive psychiatric inpatient care:

Criteria for inpatient admission to a psychiatric hospital in Ontario

A person can be admitted to a general or psychiatric hospital either voluntarily or involuntarily.

VOLUNTARY PATIENTS
With the recommendation of a physician and the consent of the patient, a person can be admitted voluntarily to a psychiatric hospital. Criteria for admission are that the person is in need of the observation, care and treatment provided by an inpatient psychiatric facility. This is the preferred situation, since the person is usually more likely to engage in a treatment plan with staff, and the family do not feel that they are acting against their relative's wishes.

The person wishing to be admitted to hospital can contact his or her doctor or mental health worker, if he or she has one, or go to the emergency department of a community hospital that has an inpatient psychiatric department, or to a psychiatric hospital directly. If family members are unsure of how to find one of these, they can contact a local distress centre or community mental health centre instead.

INVOLUNTARY PATIENTS
This is a much more difficult situation for all concerned. You will need to refer to the legislation for your own community, but, for most communities, these are the three ways allowed by law for a person to be admitted as an involuntary, or certified, patient:

1. The person must be considered to be a danger to him- or herself, or he or she is suicidal or self-harming.

2. The person is viewed as being a danger to others, or is homicidal.

3. The person is unable to care for him- or herself and is in imminent risk as a result, such as refusing to eat or drink.

HOW A PERSON CAN BE HOSPITALIZED ON AN INVOLUNTARY BASIS IN ONTARIO

A **form 1** is used by a physician who has seen your relative within the last seven days and has found the person to meet one or more of the three criteria listed above. Then the person can be brought into the psychiatric hospital and detained, restrained, examined and observed for up to 72 hours. At that time the person may be found to be sufficiently well as to no longer meet any of the three criteria and will be given voluntary status. The person then can choose to stay in hospital or to leave without medical approval.

A **form 2** is obtained when you go to a Justice of the Peace and provide information about the person's mental state. This information makes up an affidavit containing sufficient detail to satisfy the Justice of the Peace that the committal criteria (danger to self or others, inability to care for self and suffering from a mental illness) are met. Again the individual may be detained up to 72 hours, at which time the patient must be re-evaluated for certifiability.

You can ask the police to take your relative to the hospital. The police may independently take a person into custody in order to obtain a psychiatric assessment. The same conditions listed above apply.

A **form 3** is issued when a form 1 or a form 2 expires and the patient still meets conditions for certifiability. This lasts two weeks. If the patient is still deemed to be certifiable, a form 4 can be issued, which lasts for four weeks.

When someone is admitted involuntarily, he or she will automatically be visited by the Patient's Rights Adviser. The adviser will ask the patient if he or she wishes to appeal the form, and the adviser will assist the patient with the appeal process. Families are usually invited to the hearing by the patient or by the doctor to give information about the patient's condition.

Common problems for families

Here are some commonly asked questions:

• **My relative's doctor won't talk to me. How can I give the doctor information that I think is necessary for my relative's care and safety?**

Because the law does not allow a doctor to communicate with family without the patient's permission (except in the cases listed where there is a risk of immediate harm), the best way to be able to talk with your relative's doctor is for your relative to sign a Form 14 (Ontario), or an equivalent release-of-information form in the person's jurisdiction.

• **What if my relative won't sign a release-of-information form?**

This makes your situation more difficult. Here are some options:

1. Ask your relative to allow you to accompany him or her to an appointment with the doctor.

Discuss with your relative what you want to address during the session, so that he or she does not feel that you are trying to take away control of his or her life.

It may take some time to convince your relative of the importance of this and of your good intentions. Remember to use the communication skills learned in Session 4.

2. If your relative does not agree to this plan, you can call or write to the doctor on your own. Because of the laws of confidentiality, the doctor will not give you information about your relative, and usually will not even acknowledge that your relative is a patient. It can be helpful to acknowledge to your relative's doctor that you are aware of this at the beginning of the conversation.

You are not under the same confidentiality constraints as the doctor so you can provide the doctor with information that you think is important for him or her to know for your relative's care and safety. You can provide this information without jeopardizing the doctor's confidentiality.

Remember that the doctor needs to maintain a good, trusting relationship with your relative, and will likely feel the need to inform your relative that this communication has taken place. It is better to inform your relative yourself that you will be communicating one way with the doctor rather than having it come as a surprise to the patient from the doctor.

- **If I need to take my relative to the emergency department, how can I ensure that I have the chance to communicate the necessary information to the staff so that they understand the seriousness of the situation?**

When you accompany your relative to the emergency department, the staff should interview you, as well as your relative. You have information that staff need to make a good decision about your relative's treatment.

When you bring your relative in, inform the staff that you would also like to talk with them. Try to provide an organized account of the events leading up to the hospital visit. If safety is an issue, state this information clearly and emphatically.

- **What if I take my relative to the emergency department and they want to release him or her, and I don't think that my relative is safe to go home?**

If you fear that your relative will be released and that is not safe decision, you can ask to speak with the doctor who has seen your relative. You can then ask the doctor why he or she believes that your relative is safe to be released.

Ask for the doctor's reassurance that your relative and family will be safe before you agree to take your relative home. Inform the doctor if there are children in the home.

Treatment

This above section outlined the process and criteria to have someone admitted to hospital as either a voluntary or an involuntary patient. However, giving treatment requires a different set of consent requirements.

No patient, either voluntary or involuntary, may receive treatment without the consent of the patient or other authorized person, except in emergencies when life, limb or vital organ is endangered.

For consent to be valid, the consenting individual must

1. be competent to give the consent

2. have the intellectual capacity to make the decision

3. give the consent voluntarily

4. be given enough information to make an informed decision, including information relating to potential risks or side-effects.

Both voluntary and involuntary patients must be competent to consent to treatment. If a patient is involuntary and found to be mentally incompetent, the *Mental Health Act* (Ontario) outlines how the consent of the nearest relative must be obtained, starting with the spouse, children at the age of majority, siblings and next of kin. If the nearest relative does not consent to the treatment, a review board (made up of several different professionals) order for treatment must be obtained.

Beyond this, the patient has access to an appeals board if he or she objects to ongoing treatment. However, once a patient is stabilized, he or she no longer meets the criteria to remain an involuntary patient and, upon becoming voluntary, can once again refuse treatment if he or she chooses. Unfortunately, in some cases, this leads to discontinuation of medication/treatment and another relapse and involuntary admission to hospital.

Other types of intervention for involuntary patients include:

Public trustee (Ontario)

This is a government official who acts in the best interests of an individual. The individual may voluntarily appoint a trustee to administer his or her assets. If the person is incompetent and has not already appointed a trustee, a physician may issue a certificate of incompetence and refer the person to a public trustee who will act for the person or determine whether any family members can do so in a competent and just manner.

Power of attorney

This is a legal document and must be signed by an individual when he or she is mentally competent. This gives the person acting as power of attorney the right to act on behalf of the individual during any subsequent legal incapacity on the individual's part.

Wills

Parents or relatives may wish to leave a portion of their estate to a person who has a mental disability. It is advisable in some instances to appoint a trustee to handle the assets for the disabled relative.

This is intended as a brief overview of some legal issues pertaining to families and mental health issues. Legal issues can be complex and we recommend that family members seek legal advice for special legal problems.

Depression and bipolar disorder

CENTRE FOR ADDICTION AND MENTAL HEALTH (CAMH)
(416) 535-8501

MOOD DISORDERS ASSOCIATION OF ONTARIO
(416) 486-8046
(formerly the Manic-Depressive Association of Toronto)

Self-help association for clients experiencing depression or bipolar disorder; support group for relatives/friends; groups are held in various locations; telephone information and support; newsletter; library; advocacy.

SELF-HELP CLEARINGHOUSE OF METRO TORONTO
(416) 487-4355

Telephone referral to self-help groups; consultation, workshops and support for new or existing groups; assistance in forming groups; directory; volunteer speakers bureau; resource library; newsletter.

COMMUNITY RESOURCES CONSULTANTS OF TORONTO

Community mental health organization; direct support services for individuals and their families; advocacy; information and consultation services; publications.

a. Consultant services — information on mental health services including housing, treatment, self-help groups, social and recreational activities; education and training events.

b. Community rehabilitation services — outreach, assessment, case management, skill development, education and support to families.

c. Hostel outreach program — flexible, portable support to homeless women who have experienced significant mental health difficulties.

CANADIAN MENTAL HEALTH ASSOCIATION OF METRO TORONTO
(416) 789-7957

Information on, and referral to, mental health services, including psychiatrists in Metro Toronto; direct services for persons who have had, or are receiving, treatment for mental health problems; publications.

CONSUMER/SURVIVOR INFORMATION RESOURCE CENTRE
(416) 538-0203

Resource centre operated by consumers providing information on resources, agencies and services in Metro Toronto. Very user-friendly.

WOMEN'S COUNSELLING, REFERRAL AND EDUCATION CENTRE (WREC)
(416) 534-7501

Telephone counselling and referral services sensitive to women's needs, including screened therapists and counsellors on a sliding scale; alternative mental health resources; self-help groups; community resources; legal clinics; shelters.

FAMILY ASSOCIATION FOR MENTAL HEALTH EVERYWHERE (FAME)
(416) 744-3263

Education, information, support, advocacy for families and friends of persons who are mentally ill, newsletter.

GERSTEIN CENTRE
(416) 929-0149
Crisis Line: (416) 929-5200

24-hour non-medical crisis intervention for acute psychosocial crisis; concrete assistance with problems immediate to the crisis; brief stay at base facility when necessary; referrals for assistance with ongoing needs such as finances, housing, case management.

SCARBOROUGH MOBILE CRISIS PROGRAM
(416) 289-2434

Crisis intervention for persons aged 16 to 65 experiencing a psychiatric/psychosocial crisis; telephone support; mobile response in the home or other community setting (10:00 am to 1:00 am); crisis line.

DISTRESS CENTRE INCORPORATED
Distress Centre 1 (416) 598-1121
Distress Centre 2 (416) 486-1456

Telephone response to persons in need of immediate emotional support, crisis intervention or suicide prevention; linkage to other emergency services or professional help as appropriate.

HONG FOOK MENTAL HEALTH SERVICE
(416) 595-1103
(Serving the Chinese and Southeast Asian Communities)

Assessment and referral, supportive counselling, case management and advocacy for persons with chronic mental health problems; self-help group; counselling for spouses and families; family support group.

Family Service Agencies

Family Service Association of Metropolitan Toronto
(416) 922-3126

Counselling services — individual, couple, group and family counselling; education for living; culturally sensitive services focused on a range of psychosocial issues including anxiety, depression, separation and divorce, wife assault; services for abused women, abusive men, child witnesses; female survivors of childhood sexual abuse; parenting, including single, step and reconstituted families. Services available in a wide variety of different languages.

Fees on a sliding scale.

Call main office for phone number of your local branch.

Catholic Family Services of Toronto
(416) 362-2481

Individual, marriage and family counselling for persons of all ethnic, cultural, racial and religious backgrounds; group counselling for assaulted women and their children; group counselling for male batterers; individual, group and family counselling for incest victims, survivors and partners of survivors; stress management and self-esteem seminars.

Fees on a sliding scale.

Call main office for phone number of your local branch.

Jewish Family and Child Services of Metropolitan Toronto
(416) 638-7800

Range of services for persons with social and emotional problems; individual, couple, family and group counselling; family life education and life skills programs; assistance in finding employment and accommodation; separation, divorce and custody mediation; counselling, emergency financial assistance and court accompaniment for assaulted women; groups for assaulted women and abusive men.

Homewood Health Centre (Guelph)
(519) 824-1010

Inpatient and outpatient services for mental illnesses with some beds covered by OHIP and the rest by private insurance or private fees.

An eight-week inpatient program for bipolar disorder involving assessment and treatment with individually designed programs. OHIP ward coverage has four- to six-month wait; private coverage has four- to six-week wait.

Also have dual diagnosis (concurrent disorders) programs that treat alcohol abuse first in a four- to five-week inpatient program.

Patients must be stable and it is a voluntary program.

SAINT ELIZABETH HEALTH CARE
(416) 429-1234

Nursing, rehabilitation and related health care in the home provided by registered nurses and other health care providers; mental health care; can provide live-in services.

Fees on a sliding scale but may be covered by other sources.

MINISTRY OF THE ATTORNEY GENERAL
OFFICE OF THE PUBLIC GUARDIAN AND TRUSTEE
(416) 314-2800

Manages financial affairs of persons who are certified or declared mentally incompetent and who have no one willing, or able, to act on their behalf.

As a last resort, provides treatment decision for incapable persons over the age of 18.

Free power of attorney kits.

Have excellent, informative recorded messages regarding various legal situations (such as Ontario Substitute Decisions Act, Power of Attorney for Personal Care and Continuing Power of Attorney for Property).

Books about depression and bipolar disorder

Bartha, C., Parker, C., Thomson, C. & Kitchen, K. (1999). *Depressive Illness: An Information Guide.* Toronto: Centre for Addiction and Mental Health. (booklet)

Bipolar Clinic Staff. (2000). *Bipolar Disorder: An Information Guide.* Toronto: Centre for Addiction and Mental Health. (booklet)

*Burns, D. (1999). *Feeling Good: The New Mood Therapy.* New York: Avon.

Copeland, M.E. (1992). *The Depression Workbook: A Guide for Living with Depression and Manic Depression.* Oakland CA: New Harbinger.

Dowling, C. (1993). *You Mean I Don't Have to Feel this Way? New Help for Depression, Anxiety and Addiction.* New York: Bantam Books.

*Duke, P. & Hockman, G. (1993). *A Brilliant Madness: Living with Manic Depressive Illness.* New York: Bantam Books.

Elder, N. (1989). *Holiday of Darkness.* Toronto: Wall & Emerson.

*Fieve, R. (1997). *Moodswing.* New York: Bantam Books.

Gold, M. (1995). *The Good News About Depression.* New York: Bantam Books.

Greenberger, D. & and Padesky, C. (1995). *Mind over Mood: Change How You Feel by Changing the Way You Think.* New York: Guilford.

Healy, D. (1997). *Psychiatric Drugs Explained,* 2nd ed. St Louis, MO: Mosby Inc.

Lithium Information Centre. (1992). *Lithium and Manic Depression: A Guide.* Madison WI: Dean Foundation. (booklet)

Manning, M. (1996). *Undercurrents.* New York: HarperCollins.

Norden, M. (1995). *Beyond Prozac.* New York: HarperCollins.

Papolos D. & Papolos, J. (1997). *Overcoming Depression.* New York: HarperCollins.

Preston, J. (1996). *You Can Beat Depression: A Guide to Recovery.* Impact Publishers.

Redfield Jamison, K. (1997). *An Unquiet Mind.* New York: Random House.

Turkington, C. (1997). *Making the Prozac Decision: a Guide to Antidepressants.* Lowell House.

For families and partners

Berger, D. & Berger, L. (1992). *We Heard the Angels of Madness: A Guide to Coping with Manic Depression*. New York: Quill.

*Depaula, J.R. & Ablow, K. (1996). *How to Cope with Depression: A Guide for You and Your Family*. New York: Ballantine Books.

Gorman, J. (1998). *The Essential Guide to Psychiatric Drugs*. New York: St. Martin's Press.

Rosen, L.E. & Amador, X. (1996). *When Someone You Love is Depressed*. New York: Fireside.

*Available in mass market (inexpensive) paperback format

Online Resources — Depression

http://www.ndmda.org/
National Depressive and Manic-Depressive Association; information on depression and bipolar disorders.

http://www/nami.org
National Alliance for the Mentally Ill; depression in adults, children and adolescents.

http://www.yahoo.com/Health/Mental_Health/
Lists Web sites dealing with depression and bipolar disorder.

http://mentalhelp.net
Web resources on depression and bipolar disorders.

http://www.med.jhu.edu/drada/
Depression and Related Affective Disorders Association (DRADA).

http://www.nimh.nih.gov/
National Institute of Mental Health (US); information about depression.

http://www.healingwell.com/depression/
Resources for depression.

http://depression.com
Information on depression in teens, the elderly and those with chronic illnesses.

www.canmat.org
CANMAT (Canadian Network for Mood and Anxiety Treatments).

http://www.camh.net
Centre for Addiction and Mental Health (CAMH).

Online Resources — Bipolar Disorder

http://www.ndmda.org/
National Depressive and Manic-Depressive Association; information on depression and bipolar disorder.

http://www/nami.org
National Alliance for the Mentally Ill; depression in adults, children and adolescents.

http://www.yahoo.com/Health/Mental_Health/
Lists Web sites dealing with depression and bipolar disorder.

http://www.shscares.org/services/lrc/nih/bipolardisorder-nih.asp
National Institutes of Health (US) — Learning Resources Center articles on bipolar disorder.

http://thedailyapple.com/
Information about bipolar disorder.

http://mentalhelp.net
Web resources on depression and bipolar disorders.

http://www.med.jhu.edu/drada/
Depression and Related Affective Disorders Association (DRADA).

Handouts — French

Calendrier des huit sessions

	DATE DE LA RÉUNION	SUJET
Session 1		Introduction et aperçu des troubles
Session 2		Médicaments et traitements psychosociaux
Session 3		Gestion du stress
Session 4		Stratégies de communication
Session 5		Gestion des problèmes
Session 6		Gestion des situations de crise
Session 7		Système médical et juridique
Session 8		Sommaire et planification

Remarque : Les termes de genre masculin utilisés pour désigner des personnes englobent à la fois les femmes et les hommes. L'usage exclusif du masculin ne vise qu'à alléger le texte.

La dépression majeure — Aperçu

Prévalence

Entre 10 et 25 pour cent des femmes et cinq à 12 pour cent des hommes peuvent souffrir de dépression majeure.

SYMPTÔMES DE LA DÉPRESSION

On parle de dépression si une personne présente au moins cinq des symptômes suivants pendant une période de deux semaines :
• humeur déprimée la plupart de la journée ;
• perte d'intérêt à l'égard d'activités ;
• perte ou gain de poids notable ;
• perturbation du sommeil la plupart du temps (difficulté à dormir ou sommeil excessif) ;
• ralentissement des mouvements ou état d'agitation ;
• fatigue ou perte d'énergie ;
• difficulté à prendre une décision ou à se concentrer ;
• sentiment de dévalorisation ou de culpabilité excessive ;
• pensées suicidaires ou sur la mort fréquentes.

Ces symptômes interfèrent avec la capacité de la personne d'évoluer dans toutes les différentes situations de la vie ou dans la majeure partie d'entre elles. Voici quelques autres symptômes :
• hypersensibilité et exagération des préoccupations concernant sa propre personne ;
• pensées négatives ;
• indifférence aux encouragements, au soutien, aux réactions ou à la sympathie des autres ;
• diminution de la sensibilité aux sentiments des autres à cause de sa propre souffrance intérieure ;
• besoin de contrôler les rapports avec autrui ;
• incapacité de fonctionner normalement.

Les différentes catégories de dépression

DYSTHYMIE

Il s'agit d'un état dépressif chronique, qui persiste pendant au moins deux ans. Contrairement à une personne déprimée, celle qui souffre de dysthymie ne présente pas de déficience fonctionnelle grave ni de changements au niveau de ses mouvements ; elle n'a ni pensées suicidaires ni sentiment de dévalorisation.

DÉPRESSION POSTNATALE

Il s'agit d'une dépression qui survient après l'accouchement.

DÉPRESSION ATYPIQUE

Il existe une réactivité de l'humeur – la personne pourra réagir positivement à un événement agréable ; elle éprouve toutefois une sensation de lourdeur dans les bras et dans les jambes et une sensibilité de longue date au rejet.

MÉLANCOLIE

Humeur triste qui subsiste, même lors d'activités habituellement agréables ; la dépression est souvent plus prononcée le matin et s'accompagne de réveils très matinaux.

DÉPRESSION SECONDAIRE À UNE MALADIE

La dépression est causée par la présence d'une maladie.

DÉPRESSION INDUITE PAR L'ABSORPTION D'UNE SUBSTANCE

La dépression est causée par l'utilisation de drogues.

TROUBLE AFFECTIF SAISONNIER

La dépression survient à un moment particulier de l'année, en général en automne et en hiver, et disparaît au printemps et en été.

DÉPRESSION PSYCHOTIQUE

Elle est accompagnée de délires ou d'hallucinations.

Les causes de la dépression — Le modèle multidimensionnel

Il n'y a pas qu'une théorie pour expliquer pourquoi les gens développent des troubles dépressifs. La recherche a mis en évidence cinq facteurs qui prédisposent une personne à la dépression :
1. prédisposition biologique ;
2. prédisposition génétique ;
3. événements de la vie ;
4. type de personnalité ;
5. manque de soutien social.

Les gens qui souffrent de dépression luttent contre les sentiments suivants :
• peur ;
• gêne à demander de l'aide ;
• crainte que la prise de médicaments soit considérée comme un signe de faiblesse ;
• difficultés à réduire le stress et à modifier le mode de vie ;
• croyance qu'une amélioration de l'humeur signifie que le traitement n'est plus nécessaire.

Le trouble bipolaire — Aperçu

Prévalence

Environ un pour cent des adultes souffrent de trouble bipolaire. Ce trouble touche autant les femmes que les hommes.

Symptômes du trouble bipolaire

Il y a trois groupes de symptômes majeurs à retenir : la manie, l'hypomanie et la dépression.

1. Manie

SYMPTÔMES DE LA MANIE

Si une personne semble anormalement et continuellement exaltée, irritable ou euphorique pendant au moins une semaine, elle peut être en phase maniaque de la maladie. Toutefois, les personnes en état maniaque ne se sentent pas toutes euphoriques. Elles peuvent au contraire être très irritables, belligérantes ou très en colère, présenter un comportement extrêmement perturbateur et agressif et ne montrer aucun signe d'euphorie.

Outre les symptômes qui concernent l'humeur, les personnes doivent éprouver de façon notable au moins trois des symptômes suivants :

• sentiment exagéré d'estime de soi ou idées de grandeur ;
• réduction du besoin de sommeil ;
• logorrhée (discours trop abondant) ;
• fuite des idées ou pensées qui défilent ;
• hyperactivité ;
• manque de jugement ;
• symptômes psychotiques — les délires (croyances non fondées sur la réalité) et parfois les hallucinations (le plus souvent auditives) sont des symptômes fréquents de manie.

QU'ENTEND-ON PAR MANIE ?

Les personnes en état maniaque peuvent être très irritables et impatientes avec leur entourage. Elles peuvent être très impulsives et blessantes, rejeter autrui ou se comporter de manière impulsive, voire dangereuse.

La manie rend les gens extrêmement réactifs et émotifs. Si ces derniers sont incapables de maîtriser leur colère ou leurs frustrations, il peut en résulter des comportements violents.

2. Hypomanie (épisode hypomaniaque)

Bien que les symptômes de l'hypomanie soient moins graves que ceux de la manie, ils peuvent interférer avec la capacité de la personne d'affronter un certain nombre de situations. Historiquement, l'hypomanie était considérée comme une affection mineure. Plus récemment, on a reconnu qu'elle a davantage d'impact sur la vie et les rapports des sujets atteints que l'on ne pensait.

3. Épisode dépressif

Rappelez-vous que la dépression peut revêtir différentes formes et qu'elle survient souvent sans cause apparente. Les symptômes de la dépression dans le trouble bipolaire incluent au moins cinq des signes suivants qui doivent être présents pendant au moins deux semaines, presque chaque jour et pendant toute la journée :
• humeur déprimée la plupart de la journée ;
• perte d'intérêt à l'égard d'activités ;
• perte ou gain de poids notable ;
• perturbation du sommeil la plupart du temps (difficulté à dormir ou sommeil excessif) ;
• ralentissement des mouvements ou état d'agitation ;
• fatigue ou perte d'énergie ;
• difficulté à prendre une décision ou à se concentrer ;
• sentiment de dévalorisation ou de culpabilité excessive ;
• pensées suicidaires ou sur la mort fréquentes.

Ces symptômes interfèrent avec la capacité de la personne d'évoluer dans toutes les différentes situations de la vie ou dans la majeure partie d'entre elles.
Voici quelques autres symptômes :
• hypersensibilité et exagération des préoccupations concernant sa propre personne ;
• pensées négatives ;
• indifférence aux encouragements, au soutien, aux réactions ou à la sympathie des autres ;
• diminution de la sensibilité aux sentiments des autres à cause de sa propre souffrance intérieure ;
• besoin de contrôler les rapports avec autrui ;
• incapacité de fonctionner normalement.

Symptômes psychotiques — La personne peut croire à tort qu'on la persécute, qu'elle est punie pour ses péchés, qu'elle est atteinte d'une maladie incurable comme un cancer, ou dans certains cas graves, qu'elle n'existe pas réellement.

Il est important de réaliser que les symptômes de dépression incluent souvent une anxiété intense, des inquiétudes concernant des sujets insignifiants, des symptômes physiques, en particulier des douleurs, et d'autres pathologies imaginaires qui motivent de fréquentes visites chez le médecin de famille.

Types de trouble bipolaire

Certaines personnes présentent successivement des états maniaques, mixtes et déprimés, et vivent des périodes où elles se sentent bien ; on parle alors d'une « bipolarité I ». D'autres présentent une forme de manie moins grave appelée « hypomanie ». Les personnes qui traversent des périodes d'hypomanie et de dépression entrecoupées de périodes sans symptômes, et sans phases maniaques complètes, ont une « bipolarité II ».

ORDRE ET FRÉQUENCE DES DIFFÉRENTS ÉTATS

En règle générale, les états maniaques ou hypomaniaques, mixtes et dépressifs ne surviennent pas dans un ordre précis, et leur fréquence est imprévisible. Chez bien des gens, plusieurs années séparent chaque épisode ; chez d'autres, les épisodes sont plus fréquents. Une personne atteinte d'un trouble bipolaire subit environ une dizaine d'épisodes dépressifs, maniaques, hypomaniaques ou mixtes pendant sa vie. Plus la personne vieillit, plus les épisodes deviennent fréquents. Sans traitement, un état maniaque peut durer de deux à trois mois. Un état dépressif non traité persiste généralement plus longtemps, c'est-à-dire de quatre à six mois.

CYCLE RAPIDE

Dans environ 20 pour cent des cas le patient éprouve quatre épisodes ou plus par an (et parfois beaucoup plus), entre lesquels il ne présente pas de symptômes. Ce phénomène est appelé cycle rapide ; il s'agit d'un type de trouble bipolaire qui nécessite un traitement spécial. On en ignore la cause exacte. Parfois il peut être déclenché par certains antidépresseurs, selon un mécanisme inconnu. Parfois le patient revient à un cycle « normal » lorsqu'il cesse de prendre l'antidépresseur.

Les causes (étiologie) de la dépression majeure

HÉRÉDITÉ

La dépression semble toucher certaines familles, ce qui laisse supposer qu'il existe une composante héréditaire.

FACTEURS BIOLOGIQUES

On pense que la dépression est influencée par des déséquilibres chimiques au niveau cérébral et dans les systèmes endocrinien et immunitaire. Elle peut également être causée par une maladie grave ou un événement important.

ÉVÉNEMENTS DE LA VIE

Un traumatisme subi durant la petite enfance, comme la perte d'un parent, peut contribuer à l'apparition d'une dépression, de même qu'un stress important à l'âge adulte, comme le décès d'un conjoint ou la perte de son travail, ou un traumatisme important, comme un épisode de violence conjugale ou un bouleversement social.

TYPE DE PERSONNALITÉ

Les personnes qui sont plus introverties, dépendantes, inquiètes, méfiantes ou rigides sont plus susceptibles de développer une dépression.

SOUTIEN SOCIAL

L'absence de mécanismes de soutien entraîne un plus grand isolement qui peut contribuer à la dépression.

Le modèle de vulnérabilité au stress suggère que les causes de la dépression peuvent être diverses. Plus une personne présente de facteurs de risque, plus elle risque de connaître un épisode de dépression.

Les causes (étiologie) du trouble bipolaire

On ignore la cause précise du trouble bipolaire. Cependant, les recherches tendent à démontrer qu'il serait attribuable notamment à des facteurs génétiques. Cette maladie n'est pas nécessairement héréditaire ; les gènes en question pourraient être endommagés au moment de la conception.

Les gènes régissent la formation des cellules et de leur contenu. Les scientifiques sont d'avis que des changements génétiques peuvent causer la production de protéines défectueuses dans les cellules cérébrales. Ces protéines peuvent alors causer le trouble bipolaire. De nos jours, les chercheurs étudient différentes protéines qui pourraient intervenir dans cette maladie :
• les protéines qui entrent dans la production de substances chimiques dans le cerveau, appelées neurotransmetteurs ;
• les protéines qui utilisent des neurotransmetteurs pour donner des ordres aux cellules ;
• les gènes eux-mêmes.

Ce dont on est sûr, c'est qu'un excès de stress ou des problèmes familiaux ne peuvent pas causer à eux seuls cette maladie, mais peuvent « déclencher » un épisode chez les personnes qui en sont déjà atteintes. Le trouble bipolaire n'est pas non plus un simple déséquilibre des neurotransmetteurs comme la sérotonine ou la dopamine. Pourtant, une poussée de la maladie peut se répercuter sur ces neurotransmetteurs.

QU'EST-CE QUI PEUT « DÉCLENCHER » UN ÉPISODE BIPOLAIRE ?

Si tous les épisodes ne peuvent être attribués à un facteur déclencheur, beaucoup peuvent l'être. Les déclencheurs sont des situations qui peuvent provoquer un état maniaque ou dépressif chez une personne qui a une prédisposition génétique au trouble bipolaire. Un stress intense ou une perte continue de sommeil en sont des exemples. Certains déclencheurs sont chimiques ; ils comprennent des antidépresseurs qui fonctionnent « trop bien » et provoquent des états maniaques ; des médicaments courants comme les stéroïdes (par exemple, la prednisone employée dans le traitement de l'asthme ou de l'arthrite) ; et des drogues de rue telles la cocaïne et les amphétamines.

L'utilisation de médicaments dans le traitement de la dépression

Historique

Dans les années 1950, les médecins ont découvert que l'iproniazide, un médicament utilisé dans le traitement de la tuberculose, permettait aussi d'améliorer l'humeur des patients. On a, par la suite, découvert que l'iproniazide agit en stimulant plusieurs neurotransmetteurs. Les neurotransmetteurs sont les substances du cerveau qui permettent aux cellules de communiquer chimiquement entre elles et, dans certains cas, de régulariser notre humeur. Des recherches ont révélé que les personnes déprimées n'ont pas assez de neurotransmetteurs sérotoninergiques et que le fait d'aider le cerveau à produire plus de sérotonine semblait faire diminuer la dépression. Toutefois, le cerveau est très complexe et la sérotonine n'est qu'un de plus de 500 neurotransmetteurs. On doit effectuer d'autres recherches pour découvrir de quelle façon la chimie du cerveau contribue à la dépression.

Bien que de nombreuses questions subsistent, les antidépresseurs sont souvent utilisés et donnent des résultats positifs dans le traitement de la dépression, qu'ils soient pris seuls ou dans le cadre d'une psychothérapie. Grâce à une intervention précoce, les médicaments peuvent prévenir des épisodes dépressifs graves et permettre aux patients de conserver leurs capacités d'adaptation. Les médicaments permettent aussi une meilleure utilisation des dialogues pyschothérapeutiques lorsque les personnes déprimées sont renfermées sur elles-mêmes. Dans le cas de dépressions graves, les médicaments permettent de soulager les symptômes et de rétablir l'humeur des patients à un niveau plus acceptable, leur permettant ainsi de reprendre leurs activités quotidiennes.

Inquiétudes courantes exprimées à l'égard des antidépresseurs

Souvent, les gens craignent que les antidépresseurs créent une accoutumance ou une dépendance. Les antidépresseurs ne créent pas d'accoutumance et jouent un rôle important dans le traitement de la dépression.

Bon nombre de personnes hésitent à prendre des médicaments, car elles croient que le besoin d'en prendre est un signe de faiblesse. Cette perception des choses montre qu'elles considèrent la dépression comme une faiblesse de caractère plutôt que comme un trouble médical légitime. La dépression est une maladie qui, si elle n'est pas traitée, peut s'aggraver considérablement et mette la vie en danger.

Même les patients qui acceptent de prendre des médicaments peuvent trouver que les effets secondaires désagréables rendent difficile l'assiduité au traitement. Les effets secondaires courants des antidépresseurs de l'ancienne génération incluent la sécheresse de la bouche, la constipation, la difficulté à uriner et la vue trouble. Ces effets secondaires sont **anticholinergiques.** Bien que les anciens antidépresseurs donnent d'aussi bons résultats que les plus récents, les patients cessent souvent de les prendre en raison des effets secondaires.

C'est pourquoi un groupe de nouveaux médicaments a été conçu. Ces médicaments causent moins d'effets secondaires et sont plus tolérables, notamment : maux de tête, insomnie, anxiété, sédation et dysfonctionnement sexuel. Une partie importante de l'évaluation et du traitement consiste à déterminer quel médicament conviendra le mieux au patient. Très peu de personnes continueront de prendre un médicament si les effets secondaires sont intolérables. *Si un de vos proches ressent de tels effets, il est important qu'il consulte son médecin plutôt que de cesser de prendre ses médicaments. Bien que les antidépresseurs ne créent pas de dépendance, le fait d'arrêter soudainement de les prendre peut entraîner des réactions désagréables et éventuellement une moins bonne réaction aux prochains médicaments.*

Posologie

Pour obtenir les meilleurs résultats d'un médicament, le médecin augmentera progressivement la dose jusqu'à la quantité la plus élevée à laquelle le médicament produit un effet thérapeutique. On parle alors **d'optimisation**.

Contrairement à d'autres médicaments qui soulagent les symptômes très rapidement, les antidépresseurs prennent généralement deux semaines ou plus pour agir. Habituellement, les patients ressentent d'abord des effets secondaires, puis un soulagement par la suite, ce qui peut les décourager ou les démoraliser. Les effets secondaires peuvent être atténués par la prise d'autres médicaments, en modifiant la dose ou en changeant de médicament. Bien que les effets secondaires puissent être désagréables, ils indiquent que le corps absorbe le produit et que celui-ci commence à faire effet.

En plus d'optimiser la posologie, le médecin peut **intensifier** la dose d'un médicament, ou accroître ses effets en y ajoutant un autre médicament. À titre d'exemple, on peut donner du lithium pour augmenter les effets de l'antidépresseur principal.

Les recherches semblent indiquer que les patients réagissent tout aussi bien à toutes les catégories d'antidépresseurs, mais tolèrent certains médicaments mieux que d'autres. Il n'est pas rare que des patients essaient au moins deux médicaments avant d'en trouver un qui convienne. Pour certains patients qui ont une **forte sensibilité au dosage** (c'est-à-dire qu'ils réagissent même aux plus légères variations de la quantité de médicament dans leur organisme), il est important de prendre le médicament à la même heure, chaque jour. Une fois que le médicament a soulagé les symptômes de la dépression, on recommande souvent que les patients continuent de le prendre pendant au moins un an afin d'éviter les rechutes.

Différentes catégories d'antidépresseurs

La présente section fait le survol des médicaments en donnant des exemples de leurs noms géneriques, ainsi que de leurs noms commerciaux au Canada. Les dénominations commerciales varient d'un pays à l'autre. On peut trouver de plus amples renseignements dans les ouvrages de David Healy, *Psychiatric Drugs Explained* (Londres, Mosby, 1993) ou de Jack Gorman, *The Essential Guide to Psychiatric Drugs* (New York, St. Martin's Griffin, 1997).

Les médicaments de l'ancienne génération

IMAO — INHIBITEURS DE LA MONOAMINE-OXYDASE

Les inhibiteurs de la monoamine-oxydase (IMAO), comme le Nardil^{MD} (phénelzine) et le Parnate^{MD} (tranylcypromine) ont été les premiers antidépresseurs. Les IMAO bloquent l'action de la monoamine-oxydase, une enzyme qui dégrade certains neurotransmetteurs du cerveau. En contrant cette dégradation, les IMAO font *augmenter* le nombre et la disponibilité des neurotransmetteurs, ce qui aide au traitement de la dépression. On prescrit encore des IMAO, souvent pour le traitement de la dépression atypique.

Il est important de savoir que les IMAO affectent aussi le processus de la digestion et de la transformation des aliments qui contiennent de la tyramine, comme les fromages affinés et fermentés, les viandes fumées et certaines bières. En grande quantité, la tyramine peut être toxique et peut entraîner une élévation dangereuse de la tension artérielle. La monoamine-oxydase nous protège de la tyramine. Comme les IMAO entravent l'action de la monoamine-oxydase, les patients qui prennent ces médicaments doivent éviter de consommer les aliments susmentionnés. Cette restriction signifie qu'on prescrit les IMAO seulement lorsque d'autres médicaments n'ont pas été efficaces.

ANTIDÉPRESSEURS TRICYCLIQUES

Le deuxième groupe de médicaments, conçus pour traiter la dépression, se compose des antidépresseurs tricycliques ou imipraminiques. Ils comprennent l'Elavil^{MD} (amitriptyline), le Ludiomil^{MD} (maprotiline) et le Tofranil^{MD} (imipramine). Comme les médicaments de ce groupe ont tendance à causer plus d'effets secondaires que les médicaments plus récents et plus raffinés, on se tourne rarement vers eux comme première option de traitement. Cependant, certains patients tolèrent bien ces médicaments et les trouvent très efficaces. Les antidépresseurs tricycliques ont tendance à être plus sédatifs et sont associés aux effets secondaires anticholinergiques. Ces médicaments peuvent aussi causer une prise de poids et des étourdissements.

Les agents plus récents

LES INHIBITEURS SPÉCIFIQUES DU RECAPTAGE DE LA SÉROTONINE

Ce groupe de médicaments plus récents constitue habituellement le premier choix en matière de traitement de la dépression ; il comprend le Prozac^{MD} (fluoxétine), le Paxil^{MD} (paroxétine), le Luvox^{MD} (fluvoxamine) et le Zoloft^{MD} (sertraline). Ces médicaments ne causent habituellement pas d'effets secondaires anticholinergiques comme les antidépresseurs tricycliques. Bien que ces médicaments soient très efficaces, les patients peuvent ressentir au début des effets secondaires, comme des nausées, des problèmes de digestion, des maux de tête et un dysfonctionnement sexuel. D'autres patients peuvent développer des troubles du sommeil, comme de la difficulté à s'endormir ou des réveils fréquents durant la nuit.

Les autres catégories de médicaments plus récents

De nombreux médicaments plus récents se sont montrés efficaces pour le traitement de la dépression. Ces médicaments n'entrent pas dans une catégorie précise, car ils touchent plusieurs systèmes différents dans le cerveau. Ils comprennent l'Effexor^MD (venlafaxine), le Wellbutrin^MD (buprorion), le Manerix^MD (moclobémide) et le Serzone^MD (néfazodone) ; ils peuvent causer moins d'effets secondaires que les IMAO et les antidépresseurs tricycliques.

L'utilisation des médicaments dans le traitement du trouble bipolaire

Historique des médicaments

Le lithium, un psychorégulateur (régulateur de l'humeur), a été découvert dans les années 1800 et utilisé en médecine générale. Il était considéré comme un remède miracle pour traiter toutes sortes de malaises et de troubles. Son application à la psychiatrie date des années 1880. À cette époque « pré-scientifique », les cliniciens et les médecins n'avaient pas conscience des dangers dus à la toxicité du lithium et comme les patients tombaient malade, son usage diminua. Entre les années 1880 et 1950, le lithium fut abandonné et d'autres psychorégulateurs virent le jour dans les années 1970 et 1980. Fait étonnant, pendant la Guerre de sécession des États-Unis, un médecin qui traitait les patients atteints de troubles de l'humeur remarqua que le lithium semblait efficace dans le traite-ment du trouble bipolaire, mais il abandonna par la suite l'utilisation de ce médicament. Depuis quelques années, avec l'arrivée des tests pharmacologiques et la prise de conscience de la néces-sité de maintenir les médicaments à un niveau thérapeutique et non toxique, le lithium est redevenu un traitement de choix pour le trouble bipolaire.

COMMENT LE TROUBLE BIPOLAIRE EST-IL TRAITÉ ?

Le trouble bipolaire est traité par phases :
• traitement de la phase aiguë : il s'agit alors de traiter l'épisode de manie ou d'hypomanie ou l'épisode mixte en cours ;
• traitement préventif : il s'agit alors d'empêcher la survenue de nouveaux épisodes.

Psychorégulateurs

Les psychorégulateurs sont des médicaments qui atténuent les sautes d'humeur anormales. Ils peuvent également prévenir les nouveaux problèmes d'humeur.

Le **lithium**, un sel naturel, est le plus étudié de ces médicaments. On l'utilise depuis 50 ans. Le lithium est toujours employé couramment dans le traitement du trouble bipolaire.

La **carbamazépine**, un anticonvulsif, possède des propriétés psychorégulatrices découvertes dans les années 1970. Elle est prescrite de temps à autre.

L'**acide valproïque** (et ses dérivés tels que le valproate de sodium et le divalproex sodique) est un autre anticonvulsif que l'on a commencé à utiliser couramment dans les années 1990 comme psychorégulateur. Il est populaire, car de nombreux médecins estiment qu'il permet de soigner un plus vaste éventail de sautes d'humeur que le lithium, tout en ayant moins d'effets secondaires. Cependant, il n'est pas automatiquement « meilleur » que le lithium.

Comment le médecin choisit-il le traitement approprié ?

Le lithium et le valproate sont utilisés le plus souvent pour le traitement de la phase aiguë des épisodes maniaques. Les trois critères suivants influençant le choix de médicaments du médecin :
• le patient les a-t-il essayés avec succès lors d'un épisode précédent ?
• le patient a-t-il ressenti des effets secondaires précis pouvant l'entraîner à préférer un produit ?
• le type de trouble bipolaire présenté par le patient : le lithium est recommandé pour les patients présentant une humeur euphorique, et l'acide valproïque pour des patients associant épisode maniaque et humeur triste ou irritable ainsi que pour les malades à cycle rapide.

COMBIEN DE TEMPS LE TRAITEMENT INITIAL DES ÉPISODES AIGUS PREND-IL ?

Le plus souvent, on note une amélioration notoire dès les premières semaines du traitement, que ce soit avec le lithium ou avec l'acide valproïque. Si le premier traitement n'est pas efficace, ou si la réaction n'est que partielle, le médecin peut suggérer d'essayer un autre traitement ou une association médicamenteuse. La carbamazépine peut également être efficace, surtout pour les épisodes mixtes ou les cycles rapides.

Les anxiolytiques ou les antipsychotiques peuvent être utilisés pour atténuer les symptômes graves, le temps que les psychorégulateurs fassent effet.

Médicaments antipsychotiques

Les médicaments antipsychotiques sont utilisés couramment dans le traitement du trouble bipolaire pour maîtriser rapidement les symptômes maniaques (en tant que sédatif puissant) et pour traiter les symptômes psychotiques. Ces symptômes peuvent inclure un délire de grandeur, un sentiment de persécution et des hallucinations. Les antipsychotiques traditionnels peuvent également permettre de prévenir les épisodes maniaques, mais leur consommation à long terme peut occasionner des effets secondaires comme la dyskinésie tardive, un trouble moteur.

Les antipsychotiques plus récents se révèlent également utiles dans le traitement du trouble bipolaire. Ils comprennent l'olanzapine (Zyprexa^MD), la rispéridone (Risperdal^MD), la quétiapine (Seroquel^MD) et la clozapine (Clozaril^MD). L'action de ces nouveaux médicaments s'apparente peut être à celle des psychorégulateurs. Les recherches se poursuivent en vue de déterminer s'ils peuvent traiter non seulement la manie, mais également la dépression, et prévenir de nouveaux épisodes. Ces nouveaux médicaments comportent moins d'effets secondaires que les antipsychotiques traditionnels.

Anxiolytiques ou sédatifs légers

L'anxiété est un symptôme courant du trouble bipolaire. Les troubles du sommeil sont également très fréquents pendant les épisodes intenses. Les benzodiazépines comme le lorazépam (Ativan^MD) et le clonazépam sont souvent prescrits. Le patient peut en prendre pendant une courte période sans s'y accoutumer. Le clonazépam est particulièrement utile pour traiter l'excès d'énergie et l'insomnie typiques de l'hypomanie. Pour les problèmes d'anxiété plus graves, comme les crises de panique, la thérapie cognitivo-comportementale peut se révéler très utile et même essentielle, car les antidépresseurs qui servent parfois à traiter les troubles anxieux peuvent causer des épisodes maniaques.

Médicaments antidépresseurs

Parfois, dans la dépression du trouble bipolaire, un psychorégulateur seul n'est pas suffisant pour traiter les symptômes les plus graves de la dépression. Un antidépresseur adapté est alors associé au traitement. Si on l'administre seul, le traitement antidépresseur peut être dangereux dans le trouble bipolaire, car il peut parfois trop stimuler l'humeur du patient et entraîner de l'hypomanie ou de la manie.

Bien que souvent la première association antidépresseur/psychorégulateur soit efficace, il n'est pas inhabituel d'avoir à essayer plusieurs antidépresseurs avant de trouver une combinaison efficace. Pendant cette période d'essai, la personne peut bénéficier d'un traitement sédatif afin de l'aider à dormir et de calmer une anxiété ou une agitation.

De nombreux antidépresseurs sont efficaces, mais les suivants sont considérés comme des médicaments de choix par les experts :
• Lamotrigine^MD (un des plus efficaces) ;
• Buproprion^MD ;
• inhibiteurs spécifiques du recaptage de la sérotonine (comme la fluoxétine, la fluvoxamine, la paroxétine et la sertraline) ;
• IMAO (comme la phénelzine et la tranylcypromine) ;
• néfaxodone ;
• tricycliques (comme l'amitriptyline et l'imipramine) ;
• venlafaxine.

Traitement d'entretien

Le trouble bipolaire a fortement tendance à récidiver. La plupart des gens qui ne sont pas traités vont rechuteront en l'espace de quelques années. Les médicaments, en plus de traiter les symptômes, empêchent les rechutes. La chance de rester stable est nettement supérieure chez les personnes qui continuent le traitement.

Le traitement d'entretien doit-il être suivi à vie ?
Les recommandations sur le traitement d'entretien (à plus long terme) sont fonction de la nature de votre maladie. Certaines personnes ayant manifesté un seul épisode de légère intensité et sans grandes conséquences, peuvent se contenter de suivre un traitement pendant seulement un ou deux ans. Mais dans la majeure partie des cas, des traitements plus longs sont préconisés et parfois il s'agit d'un traitement à vie.

LE TRAITEMENT PRÉVENTIF AUX MÉDICAMENTS LA VIE DURANT EST-IL EFFICACE ?

Oui. Les psychorégulateurs (comme le lithium, le valproate et la carbamazépine) sont au cœur même des efforts de prévention. Ce type de prise en charge permet à environ le tiers des patients atteints de trouble bipolaire de ne ressentir aucun symptôme. Cependant, la plupart des patients qui présentent des symptômes verront ces derniers diminuer sensiblement et le nombre et la gravité des épisodes chuter de considérablement.

Arrêt du traitement aux médicaments

Il est normal que les personnes qui n'ont pas eu d'épisode de trouble bipolaire pendant plusieurs années espèrent pouvoir arrêter le traitement. Cependant, bien que les psychorégulateurs préviennent les épisodes, ils ne guérissent pas la maladie. Comme il existe un risque de rechute grave, parfois quelques mois après l'arrêt du traitement aux médicaments, toute décision concernant l'arrêt du traitement ne devrait être prise qu'après en avoir discuté longuement avec le médecin traitant.

Si l'on prend une pareille décision, on devrait arrêter le traitement progressivement (sur une période de plusieurs semaines ou mois). Le fait d'arrêter brusquement le traitement risque dans certains cas de le rendre moins efficace à la prochaine prise. C'est la raison pour laquelle la décision d'arrêter de prendre un médicament efficace devrait être prise en connaissance de cause, car il est possible que son administration éventuelle à une date ultérieure ne donne plus les effets attendus.

Électroconvulsivothérapie (ECT) pour le traitement du trouble bipolaire

L'électroconvulsivothérapie (ECT), appelée autrefois « électrochocs », est peut-être le plus controversé et le moins bien compris des traitements psychiatriques, en partie à cause du portrait sensationnaliste et trompeur qu'on en a fait dans les médias. En réalité, il s'agit d'un traitement sûr et très efficace pour les états dépressifs et maniaques du trouble bipolaire. Il est utilisé parfois comme traitement « d'entretien » à long terme pour éviter les rechutes.

PROCÉDURE

L'ECT consiste à administrer un bref stimulus électrique à la surface du cerveau, par l'entremise du cuir chevelu. Ce stimulus produit une convulsion de type épileptique, qui dure généralement de 15 secondes à deux minutes.

Une équipe composée d'un psychiatre, d'un anesthésiste et d'une ou de plusieurs infirmières est présente lors du traitement. Le patient reçoit une injection d'anesthésique qui l'endort brièvement pour la durée du traitement. On lui administre également un relaxant musculaire par voie intraveineuse pour réduire l'intensité des spasmes musculaires qui accompagnent les convulsions et l'empêcher ainsi de se blesser. Le patient reçoit de l'oxygène et on surveille son rythme cardiaque et sa tension artérielle. Bien que l'anesthésie ne dure que quelques minutes, le patient éprouve de la somnolence après le traitement et se repose ou dort pendant une heure environ.

Généralement, le traitement est effectué trois fois par semaine pendant trois ou quatre semaines, soit un total de neuf à 12 traitements. S'il s'agit d'un traitement d'entretien à long terme, on peut espacer les séances, par exemple, une fois par mois. Le traitement se poursuit tant que le patient et le médecin le jugent nécessaire. L'ECT est généralement administrée aux patients hospitalisés, mais les patients externes peuvent également recevoir ce traitement.

EFFETS SECONDAIRES

Après l'ECT, les patients peuvent avoir mal à la tête ou à la mâchoire. Un analgésique léger comme l'acétaminophène (Tylenol[MD]) suffit dans ce cas. Il y a généralement perte de mémoire des événements récents ou des problèmes de concentration (par exemple, les patients oublient ce qu'ils ont mangé au repas de la veille), mais ces symptômes s'estompent quelques semaines après la série de traitements. Certains patients signalent de légers problèmes de mémoire longtemps après le traitement, mais ceux-ci sont sans doute attribuables à leur dépression.

L'ECT peut être administrée de façon bilatérale (le courant électrique étant appliqué des deux côtés du cerveau) ou unilatérale (du côté droit du cerveau). Bien que l'ECT bilatérale provoque une perturbation plus grave de la mémoire que l'ECT unilatérale, elle est relativement plus efficace ; elle est donc habituellement privilégiée.

L'ECT DANS LE TRAITEMENT DU TROUBLE BIPOLAIRE

L'ECT est le traitement le plus efficace et probablement le plus rapide contre la dépression grave ; elle se révèle particulièrement utile chez les patients très agités ou suicidaires ou ceux qui éprouvent des symptômes psychotiques ou catatoniques. Certains patients reçoivent ce traitement au début d'un épisode en raison de l'urgence de leur situation ou des symptômes particuliers qu'ils ressentent, tandis que d'autres préfèrent y recourir uniquement si divers médicaments se sont révélés inefficaces. L'ECT permet également de traiter la manie grave.

Même si elle parvient très efficacement à mettre fin aux épisodes de dépression et de manie, l'ECT ne procure des effets bénéfiques que pendant quelques semaines ou quelques mois. Les patients doivent donc généralement commencer ou continuer à prendre des psychorégulateurs ou d'autres médicaments après le traitement. Un traitement d'entretien peut être administré lorsque les médicaments n'ont pas permis d'éviter une rechute ou ne sont pas tolérés en raison de leurs effets secondaires.

Médecine parallèle

Les remèdes naturels ont peut-être un rôle à jouer. Citons, entre autres, les huiles de poisson et l'inositol, un type particulier de sucre. Cependant, lorsque ces produits sont vendus dans des magasins d'alimentation naturelle, ils sont rarement fiables. Comme ils n'ont pas été dosés avec précision, on ne peut pas les recommander. Par ailleurs, ces produits n'ont fait l'objet que de quelques études. On a bien étudié les effets du millepertuis chez les personnes atteintes de dépression unipolaire, mais tel n'a pas été le cas pour le trouble bipolaire.

Traitement du trouble bipolaire réfractaire (patients « fragiles »)

Environ 30 pour cent des patients sont atteints d'une forme plus grave de la maladie nécessitant un traitement aux médicaments multiples de longue durée. Il est possible que ces particuliers ne réagissent pas bien aux traitements disponibles à l'heure actuelle et que l'on ait besoin de plus de temps pour trouver le bon équilibre médicamenteux (psychorégulateurs, médicaments antidépresseurs et anxiolytiques). Ceci peut avoir une incidence profonde sur de nombreuses facettes de leur existence, comme les activités professionnelles, les études ou les rapports familiaux.

Ces personnes ont également tendance à avoir plus de mal à rester en bonne santé. Ceci est dû au fait que, même après avoir trouvé la bonne combinaison de médicaments, des facteurs de stress légers ou des changements mineurs dans leur vie peuvent déclencher une rechute. Il faut donc éventuellement modifier partiellement ou radicalement le traitement aux médicaments, dont l'efficacité peut être longue à établir.

Les traitements psychosociaux —
Dépression et trouble bipolaire

Psychopédagogie et psychothérapie de soutien

La psychopédagogie et la psychothérapie de soutien sont constituées d'un dialogue psychothérapeutique, de courte ou de longue durée. Le but est d'assurer au patient un environnement favorable afin qu'il puisse apprendre à connaître sa maladie et à développer des stratégies pour la maîtriser et gérer. Ceci peut être particulièrement utile pour une personne qui cherche à s'adapter à un diagnostic qu'on vient de lui poser.

Objectifs du dialogue psychothérapeutique

1. Résoudre les problèmes du passé intervenant dans les problèmes actuels (comme les pertes majeures, les traumatismes de l'enfance, les changements de la vie et la gestion du stress).
2. Concevoir de nouveaux modes de réflexion et de nouvelles manières de résoudre les problèmes afin de favoriser ou de maintenir un certain bien-être.
3. Gérer les problèmes familiaux ou les difficultés relationnelles actuelles qui provoquent le stress et la rechute.

Le dialogue psychothérapeutique met l'accent sur certains problèmes que la personne essaie de surmonter, soit :
• accepter le diagnostic d'un trouble de l'humeur ;
• gérer les changements et les pertes liés au fait d'être atteint d'une maladie grave (travail, relations, objectifs futurs) ;
• planifier l'avenir ;
• gérer les événements stressants survenant au moment où la personne se sent particulièrement mal.

Le dialogue psychothérapeutique peut être très utile quand il est associé à un traitement aux médicaments. Les thérapies psychosociales s'adressent aux particuliers, aux couples, aux familles ou aux groupes. Le traitement choisi est fonction des besoins et des forces de tout un chacun et sur un plan pratique, des ressources disponibles dans certaines collectivités.

Traitements individuels - Les dialogues psychothérapeutiques

De nombreux cliniciens se basent sur une approche éclectique qui comprend des éléments provenant de différents modèles, comme la thérapie interpersonnelle, la thérapie cognitivo-comportementale et la psychothérapie par la compréhension de soi.

COMBINAISON DE PSYCHOTHÉRAPIE ET DE MÉDICAMENTS

Les familles et les patients demandent souvent s'il est judicieux d'associer à la psychothérapie ou au dialogue psychothérapeutique un traitement aux médicaments.

Le trouble bipolaire grave ou la dépression majeure doivent être traités par les deux techniques. Lorsque des patients sont très malades, il se peut qu'ils soient incapables de suivre une psychothérapie, car il leur est difficile de parler et d'écouter. Cependant, quand ils vont mieux, la psychothérapie peut permettre de cerner et de résoudre les problèmes qui peuvent avoir contribué à la maladie.

Le trouble bipolaire léger ou modéré nécessite également un traitement aux médicaments ; néanmoins, certains patients estiment que le dialogue psychothérapeutique est superflu. Leurs propres ressources intérieures sont parfois suffisantes pour les aider à récupérer et à se maintenir en bonne forme. Cependant, même ces personnes peuvent trouver les renseignements sur la maladie et sur les stratégies de gestion efficace extrêmement utiles. Ils peuvent, en effet, leur permettre de mieux connaître la maladie et les signes avant-coureurs de rechute et de mieux gérer le stress.

La dépression légère ou modérée peut être traitée uniquement par la psychothérapie. La thérapie interpersonnelle et la thérapie cognitivo-comportementale peuvent s'avérer très efficaces et, à long terme, peuvent contribuer à la prévention des rechutes.

THÉRAPIE INTERPERSONNELLE DANS LA DÉPRESSION

La thérapie interpersonnelle dans la dépression est de courte durée (12 à 16 semaines) et se concentre sur l'identification et la résolution des problèmes liés à la création de relations satisfaisantes. Ceci consiste éventuellement à apprendre à gérer les pertes, les changements survenant dans la vie et les conflits, et également à augmenter la capacité de se comporter en toute aisance dans les situations sociales. Ce modèle n'a pas fait l'objet de recherches parmi les malades atteints de trouble bipolaire (Klerman, G., Weissman, M., Rounsaville, B. et Chevron, E., 1997).

THÉRAPIE COGNITIVO-COMPORTEMENTALE DANS LA DÉPRESSION

Dans la dépression, la thérapie cognitivo-comportementale, qui est le type de thérapie le plus rigoureusement scientifique, est un traitement de courte durée, qui aide les gens à prendre conscience de la manière dont leurs pensées automatiques, leurs attitudes, leurs croyances et leurs attentes peuvent produire et entretenir une mauvaise humeur. Cette prise de conscience associée à la mise en pratique de nouveaux modes de pensée peut permettre de déboucher sur de nouveaux modes de comportement mieux adaptés.

La thérapie cognitivo-comportementale est actuellement à l'étape d'essai pour savoir si elle contribue au traitement de la dépression bipolaire et aide à prévenir les rechutes. Ce genre de traitement de courte durée (qui dure de 15 à 20 semaines) est pratiqué en association avec un psychorégulateur (Padesky, C. et Greenberger, D., 1995).

PSYCHOTHÉRAPIE PAR LA COMPRÉHENSION DE SOI

Ce genre de thérapie peut être de courte ou de longue durée. Le but est de comprendre comment les événements traumatisants de la vie ont influencé les mécanismes d'adaptation d'une personne, son estime de soi et son identité. La personne peut modifier sa situation en prenant conscience des causes et des effets de ces événements traumatisants et en adoptant de nouvelles stratégies de résolution de problèmes, avec l'aide d'un thérapeute de confiance.

Counselling professionnel

Il s'agit d'assurer un soutien lors de la reprise du travail, des études, du bénévolat et des activités de loisir en donnant des conseils structurés ou en proposant un programme officiel de réadaptation.

Responsables de la gestion des cas et intervenants communautaires en santé mentale

Lorsque l'évolution de la maladie d'un particulier est plus compliquée et dure plus longtemps, il peut être utile d'associer à la prestation des soins continue un responsable de la gestion de cas ou un intervenant communautaire en santé mentale. Les responsables de la gestion des cas s'occupent, entre autres, de la coordination des services (par exemple logement et finances) offerts aux patients, de même que de l'orientation des patients vers les services de traitement de jour, les services professionnels ou les services bénévoles. Ils peuvent également prêter leur concours dans le cadre des activités quotidiennes, comme les rendez-vous, l'établissement d'un budget, l'établissement d'un programme quotidien, le soutien affectif et le counselling. Dans certaines collectivités, il est possible d'avoir recours aux responsables de la gestion des cas et aux intervenants communautaires en santé mentale par l'entremise des organismes communautaires de santé mentale, des services de logement et des services de soins à domicile.

Thérapie de groupe

Des professionnels de la santé mentale dirigent des groupes de psychothérapie de huit à 12 personnes qui se soutiennent mutuellement en mettant en pratique de nouvelles stratégies d'adaptation. Ces groupes sont souvent fermés aux nouveaux membres et ont des contraintes de temps.

Groupes d'entraide

Les groupes d'entraide fournissent un soutien et des renseignements. Ils sont composés de personnes qui ont en commun un même problème ou une même maladie. Ces groupes sont le plus souvent ouverts (les gens peuvent se joindre au groupe ou le quitter à tout moment) et ils sont dirigés par des patients ou des proches qui connaissent bien le système de santé mentale. Certains organismes d'entraide offrent également des services aux familles.

Interventions familiales

Thérapie familiale et conjugale

Les recherches ont montré qu'en présence d'un climat émotionnel négatif (comme une perturbation, une critique ou un conflit), le rétablissement du patient est plus long et le risque de rechutes plus élevé. Le but de cette thérapie est de résoudre les situations conflictuelles afin de réduire l'intensité émotionnelle ressentie par le patient. La thérapie peut également permettre à la famille d'aider le patient à se conformer au traitement.

GROUPES DE SOUTIEN ET D'ÉDUCATION

Ces groupes, similaires aux groupes d'entraide pour patients, proposent des renseignements et un soutien aux membres des familles qui ont un parent malade. Ils peuvent être organisés par des hôpitaux, des organismes ou des associations d'entraide.

PROMOTION D'UN BON ÉTAT DE SANTÉ GÉNÉRAL

Bien que les thérapies aux médicaments et psychosociales soient spécifiquement adaptées au traitement de la maladie de votre proche, il est important de se souvenir que la promotion et le maintien d'un bon état de santé général sont primordiaux. Une alimentation saine et des exercices physiques sont importants tant pour le malade que pour sa famille, car ils doivent tous affronter un problème difficile.

Voici deux stratégies de réduction du stress :
• minimiser les facteurs de stress multiples qui favorisent la rechute – il s'agit d'une stratégie particulièrement importante pour le trouble bipolaire ;
• diminuer le niveau d'intensité émotionnelle dans la famille. Il est important de résoudre les conflits sans porter de jugement et sans être agressif verbalement ou physiquement.

Conseils

Votre proche est atteint d'un trouble qui ne le définit pas en tant que personne.
Quant leur état redevient stable, les personnes ayant un trouble de l'humeur doivent assumer la responsabilité de leurs actes, prendre leurs propres décisions et acquérir les compétences leur permettant d'être indépendantes.

La gestion du stress

La vie n'est pas un sprint, c'est un marathon. En apprenant à déceler et à gérer votre stress, vous saurez éviter l'épuisement causé par les troubles de l'humeur d'un proche.

Comment déceler le stress ?

Apprenez d'abord à reconnaître vos propres signes de stress. Notez-les, vous serez alors en mesure d'appliquer les stratégies d'adaptation préconisées par le groupe de gestion du stress. Voici quelques signaux d'alarme indiquant que votre niveau de tension est à la hausse :

SIGNES PHYSIQUES
- fatigue chronique
- tremblements
- doléances sur votre état de santé
- prise ou perte de poids
- mouvements corporels typiques des états d'angoisse, notamment taper des pieds
- paumes moites
- pupilles dilatées

SIGNES AFFECTIFS
- tristesse
- colère
- manque de concentration
- temps passé à rêvasser
- changements fréquents d'humeur

SIGNES COMPORTEMENTAUX
- troubles du sommeil
- brusques explosions de colère
- actes impulsifs
- plaintes répétées
- remarques négatives ou pleines de rancœur
- réflexions cyniques ou hostiles
- autocritique
- critiques excessives à l'égard d'autrui
- repli sur soi ou refus de communiquer avec autrui

- préoccupation avec le passé plutôt que l'avenir
- usage de drogues ou d'alcool
- difficulté à composer avec toute autorité supérieure
- altération de la productivité au travail
- négligence des détails
- difficulté à assumer les responsabilités habituelles

Stratégies de réduction du stress

Les stratégies suivantes vous aideront à réduire le stress, ou à éviter qu'il n'envahisse votre existence :

1. CRÉEZ UN RÉSEAU DE SOUTIEN RÉCONFORTANT.

Évitez l'isolement. Assurez-vous de la présence et de la disponibilité de quelques personnes auxquelles vous savez pouvoir vous adresser dès que vous vous sentez stressé. Comme vous le savez bien, les personnes capables de se mettre à votre place et de témoigner de l'empathie à votre égard sont rares. Il vous faudra donc consacrer temps et efforts pour trouver celles qui vous seront d'un certain secours.

Adressez-vous à des associations d'entraide, à des groupes de soutien, à des spécialistes, à des parents et à des amis en qui vous avez confiance, qui ne se poseront pas en juges et qui sauront vous écouter.

2. INTÉRESSEZ-VOUS À DES ACTIVITÉS EXTRA-FAMILIALES.

- Bien-être physique — Faites de l'exercice, inscrivez-vous à un club de sport, marchez aussi souvent que possible, joignez-vous à une équipe sportive.
- Bien-être affectif — Définissez vos besoins. Passez du temps avec des amis. N'oubliez pas de penser aussi à vous-même : lisez, rédigez votre journal ou livrez-vous à un nouveau passe-temps. Prévoyez à l'avance et de façon régulière les moments où vous rechargerez vos batteries affectives.
- Bien-être spirituel — Tâchez de vous épanouir sur le plan spirituel. Prenez le temps de respirer. Écoutez des cassettes-audio de relaxation ou faites de la méditation. Les recherches prouvent que la pratique régulière de méthodes de relaxation et de méditation permet d'atténuer le stress physique.

3. CRÉEZ UN ENVIRONNEMENT SEREIN.

Communiquer calmement avec autrui contribuera à réduire votre stress. Les recherches prouvent qu'en agissant ainsi, vous parviendrez à diminuer les risques de rechute de vos proches.

Cette petite prière de sagesse, la **Prière de sérénité**, vous aidera dans ce sens :

Mon Dieu, accorde-moi
la sérénité d'accepter ce que
je ne peux pas changer ;
le courage de changer ce que je peux changer ; et
la sagesse de faire la différence.

4. Ne jouez pas les martyrs.

- Souvenez-vous que les sentiments négatifs sont naturels.
- Donnez-vous la liberté de vous fixer des limites. Soyez tolérant à l'égard de vous-même lorsque vous les dépassez et repartez à zéro.
- Trouvez un juste équilibre entre vos propres besoins et ceux de vos proches.
- Faites appel à un service de relève pour vous ménager quelques moments de répit. Nul n'est censé être disponible 24 heures sur 24.

Souvenez-vous que le niveau de stress diminue à mesure que vos capacités d'adaptation augmentent.

Votre réseau de soutien

Où le trouver ?

Dressez la liste des personnes susceptibles de vous soutenir dans les domaines suivants :

SOUTIEN AFFECTIF
Qui peut comprendre à quel point il est difficile de vivre avec une personne atteinte de maladie mentale ?

_____

_____

RÉSOLUTION DES PROBLÈMES
Qui peut vous aider à gérer une situation particulièrement délicate ?

_____

_____

ENCOURAGEMENT

Qui peut vous encourager et de vous remonter le moral quand vous vous sentez accablé ?

_____

_____

AIDE PHYSIQUE
Qui peut faire des courses ou accompagner votre proche chez le médecin ?

_____

_____

SOUTIEN SPIRITUEL
Qui vous aidera dans des moments critiques ?

_____

_____

Les exercices de relaxation

Choisissez la position qui vous est la plus confortable. Assis, décroisez vos jambes et placez vos deux pieds à plat sur le sol. Posez les mains sur les cuisses. Arrangez-vous pour que votre épine dorsale soutienne naturellement la partie supérieure de votre corps. Inspirez, expirez, et penchez la tête vers l'avant de façon à ce que votre menton s'appuie sur votre poitrine. Si vous en ressentez le besoin, fermez les yeux. Laissez retomber naturellement vos épaules.

Inspirez et expirez lentement et profondément en suivant les mouvements de votre diaphragme et reposez-vous un instant dans cette position. Une fois de plus, inspirez et expirez lentement et profondément.

Commençons par les pieds. Concentrez votre attention sur leur tension, de façon à mieux l'éliminer. À mesure que vous vous concentrez, vous allez constater que la tension est remplacée par de la relaxation, vous ressentirez une agréable lourdeur, ou peut-être aurez-vous l'impression que la tension s'échappe de votre corps et disparaît dans le sol. Continuez à inspirer et à expirer profondément.

Passez maintenant aux jambes, d'abord aux mollets, aux genoux, puis aux cuisses. Si vous vous laissez distraire pendant ces exercices de détente, ne vous en faites pas et souvenez-vous simplement que vous vous exercez : il n'y a pas de bonne ou de mauvaise manière de vous détendre.

Respirez profondément avant de faire passer ce sentiment de relaxation au fessier, aux reins et à l'abdomen. Prenez votre temps, respirez lentement et profondément et reposez-vous.

C'est au tour de vos mains, de vos avant-bras et de vos bras de se relâcher tout doucement, tandis que vous continuez à respirer lentement et profondément.

Respirez à partir de votre diaphragme, votre abdomen se soulève et s'affaisse chaque fois que vous inspirez et expirez. Constatez que vos épaules restent statiques même si vous respirez plus profondément qu'à l'ordinaire. La relaxation atteint à présent votre poitrine et vos épaules, vous vous sentez lourd, une douce chaleur envahit votre corps, le siège sur lequel vous êtes assis vous soutient parfaitement.

Tout en continuant à respirer profondément et avec aisance, laissez ce bien-être se répandre à votre cou, votre visage, vos mâchoires, vos yeux, votre front, toute la tête.

Continuez à respirer profondément, à ressentir cette agréable lourdeur, et dites-vous que vous pouvez atteindre cet état de détente tous les jours, et qu'il est important de consacrer quelques minutes par jour à votre respiration.

Quand vous vous sentez prêt, respirez une dernière fois profondément, ouvrez les yeux et étirez-vous.

Rappel. Si vous pratiquez cet exercice de détente chez vous, vous préférerez peut-être la position allongée qui vous procurera une détente plus profonde. Certaines personnes pratiquent des méthodes de relaxation musculaire pour mieux s'endormir. Il reste que la pratique de la relaxation en position assise décrite plus haut est particulièrement utile puisqu'on peut l'utiliser à tout moment et en tout lieu.

Évitez cependant d'y avoir recours quand vous avez besoin de toute votre vigilance, notamment quand vous conduisez un véhicule.

Reproduit avec l'autorisation de Kate Kitchen. Edmund Jacobson est à l'origine de l'utilisation des techniques de relaxation. Pour de plus amples renseignements, consulter Jacobson, E. *Progressive Relaxation*. Chicago, The University of Chicago Press, Midway, réimpression, 1974.

La capacité de communiquer et la dépression

Que faire pour améliorer la capacité de communication avec les personnes déprimées ?

1. N'évoquez qu'un sujet à la fois.

2. Parlez doucement et calmement, votre dialogue gagnera en sérénité.

3. Exprimez vos observations et vos désirs de façon concise, simple et positive. Dites par exemple : « Ce serait agréable de sortir aujourd'hui ».

4. Exprimez-vous à la première personne, ce qui permettra à votre interlocuteur de focaliser son attention sur vos sentiments et besoins personnels, plutôt que d'utiliser la deuxième personne « Tu » ou « Vous », qui pourrait être perçue comme une accusation ou une critique, et le mettra sur la défensive. Ainsi, la phrase « J'ai vraiment besoin de savoir quand tu passes une mauvaise journée » est préférable à « Tu aurais dû me dire que tu te sentais particulièrement mal aujourd'hui ».

5. Quand vous vous adressez à votre interlocuteur, soyez direct et positif ; utilisez la formule : « J'aimerais vraiment que tu me dises ... »

6. Soyez le plus clair possible. Efforcez-vous de faire usage de mots, d'expressions du visage et de gestes qui transmettent tous le même message. Ainsi, quand vous souhaitez exprimer vos réserves quant à une suggestion, ne faites pas « non » de la tête en même temps que vous dites « D'accord, nous allons essayer... »

7. Associez discours positif et discours négatif, en veillant à ce que la partie positive de votre réaction constitue la première moitié de votre phrase, et la partie négative la seconde. De cette façon vous communiquez à votre interlocuteur que vous avez bien entendu et compris son point de vue, tout en lui présentant une autre idée. Exemple : « Je sais que tu es très fatigué ces derniers temps, mais j'aimerais beaucoup que tu rapportes ta tasse à café à la cuisine ».

8. Combinez les suggestions précédentes avec des phrases commençant par « Je », de sorte que votre interlocuteur prenne conscience que vous ne faites qu'exprimer vos propres pensées et vos sentiments personnels. Proposez des solutions de compromis, afin que votre interlocuteur comprenne qu'il fait partie intégrante de la solution proposée.

   Exemple : « Le fait que tu dormes pendant la journée et que tu sois réveillé au milieu de la nuit me perturbe ». Puis immédiatement après proposez votre solution : « Tu pourrais par exemple aller au lit une heure plus tôt chaque soir, afin de reprendre un rythme de sommeil normal ».

9. Revenez à plusieurs reprises sur vos réflexions et suggestions, en vous souvenant que les troubles de l'humeur affaiblissent les facultés d'écoute et de compréhension de votre interlocuteur. Cette technique est intitulée « technique du disque rayé ».

10. Utilisez la technique de l'« écoute active » : hochez de la tête de temps à autre afin que votre interlocuteur se rende compte que vous suivez attentivement ce qu'il vous dit.

11. N'hésitez pas à le féliciter, même pour de toutes petites réalisations. Les changements sont difficiles, pour chacun d'entre nous.

Ce qu'il NE faut PAS faire quand on souhaite communiquer efficacement avec des proches souffrant de dépression ou de manie.

1. Évitez d'introduire l'expression « il faut » dans vos phrases. Votre interlocuteur ne manquera pas de les percevoir comme exprimant un jugement négatif ou une critique.

2. Évitez de vous précipiter sur des formules banales de réconfort. Souvenez-vous que votre proche a un long chemin à parcourir. Le rassurer de façon intempestive lui donnera le sentiment que vous n'avez pas confiance en sa capacité de guérison et compliquera la résolution des problèmes. Préférez des formules du genre : « Je ne sais ni quand ni comment les choses vont s'arranger, mais j'ai confiance que ça arrivera ».

   C'est par l'écoute, plutôt que par le réconfort systématique, que vous parviendrez à comprendre les pensées, les angoisses et les plans de votre interlocuteur.

   Si vous avez des difficultés dans ce domaine, tâchez de garder votre calme et de vous souvenir que la guérison est une entreprise de longue haleine.

3. Évitez de vous montrer systématiquement disponible et positif. Vous n'êtes pas censé posséder les solutions à tous les problèmes. Parfois, les gens ont simplement besoin d'être écoutés.

4. Évitez de prendre à cœur les commentaires de votre interlocuteur ; les troubles de l'humeur se traduisent parfois par de l'agressivité, des paroles hostiles que l'auteur regrettera une fois guéri.

5. Évitez de débattre de sujets graves ou décisifs quand vous êtes fatigué, contrarié ou frustré.

Les conseils des Alcooliques Anonymes s'appliquent à la lettre :
> **Cessez immédiatement d'évoquer des sujets graves quand :**
> - **vous avez faim ;**
> - **vous êtes en colère ;**
> - **vous vous sentez seul ;**
> - **vous êtes fatigué.**

Comment améliorer la communication au sein de son réseau de soutien ?

1. Prenez conscience du fait que les membres de la famille élargie, les amis et les collègues savent fort peu de choses concernant les maladies mentales. Les gens partagent généralement des données désuètes et des mythes. N'hésitez pas à leur fournir des données et des renseignements de base.

2. Si les campagnes d'information ont à l'évidence attiré l'attention du public sur les maladies mentales, les préjugés sont encore là. Ne vous confiez pas à n'importe qui. Choisissez des personnes ouvertes et réceptives à ce genre de confidences.

3. En tant que proche, vous ressentez le besoin de vous confier à vos amis, parfois même à les mobiliser autour du problème que vous vivez. Les preuves d'amitié reposent sur la réciprocité. Veillez donc à maintenir l'équilibre et à préserver vos facultés d'écoute de leurs problèmes et intérêts personnels.

4. Enfin, lorsque vous ressentez le besoin pressant de vous faire aider et soutenir moralement par des amis, exprimez clairement ce dont vous avez besoin (un entretien, une séance de cinéma en leur compagnie). Vos amis se montreront probablement plus disponibles s'ils savent exactement ce que vous attendez d'eux.

La capacité de communiquer et le trouble bipolaire

Que faire pour améliorer la capacité de communication avec les personnes atteintes de dépression et de manie ?

1. N'évoquez qu'un sujet à la fois.

2. Parlez doucement et calmement, votre dialogue gagnera en sérénité.

3. Exprimez vos observations et vos désirs de façon concise, simple et positive. Dites par exemple : « Ce serait agréable de sortir aujourd'hui ».

4. Exprimez-vous à la première personne, ce qui permettra à votre interlocuteur de focaliser son attention sur vos sentiments et besoins personnels, plutôt que d'utiliser la deuxième personne « Tu » ou « Vous », qui pourrait être perçue comme une accusation ou une critique, et le mettra sur la défensive. Ainsi, la phrase « J'ai vraiment besoin de savoir quand tu passes une mauvaise journée » est préférable à « Tu aurais dû me dire que tu te sentais particulièrement mal aujourd'hui ».

5. Quand vous vous adressez à votre interlocuteur, soyez direct et positif ; utilisez la formule : « J'aimerais vraiment que tu me dises... »

6. Soyez le plus clair possible. Efforcez-vous de faire usage de mots, d'expressions du visage et de gestes qui transmettent tous le même message. Ainsi, quand vous souhaitez exprimer vos réserves quant à une suggestion, ne faites pas « non » de la tête en même temps que vous dites « D'accord, nous allons essayer... »

7. Associez discours positif et discours négatif, en veillant à ce que la partie positive de votre réaction constitue la première moitié de votre phrase, et la partie négative la seconde. De cette façon vous communiquez à votre interlocuteur que vous avez bien entendu et compris son point de vue, tout en lui présentant une autre idée. Exemple : « Je sais que tu es très fatigué ces derniers temps, mais j'aimerais beaucoup que tu rapportes ta tasse à café à la cuisine ».

8. Combinez les suggestions précédentes avec des phrases commençant par « Je », de sorte que votre interlocuteur comprenne que vous ne faites qu'exprimer vos propres pensées et vos sentiments personnels. Proposez des solutions de compromis, afin que votre interlocuteur comprenne qu'il fait partie intégrante de la solution proposée. Exemple : « Le fait que tu dormes pendant la journée et que tu sois réveillé la nuit me perturbe. » Puis immédiatement après proposez votre solution : « Tu pourrais par exemple aller au lit une heure plus tôt chaque soir, afin de reprendre un rythme de sommeil normal ».

9. Revenez à plusieurs reprises sur vos réflexions et suggestions, en vous souvenant que les troubles de l'humeur affaiblissent les facultés d'écoute et de compréhension de votre interlocuteur. Cette technique est intitulée « technique du disque rayé ».

10. Utilisez la technique de l'« écoute active » : hochez de la tête de temps à autre afin que votre interlocuteur se rende compte que vous suivez attentivement ce qu'il vous dit.

11. N'hésitez pas à le féliciter, même pour de toutes petites réalisations. Les changements sont difficiles, pour chacun d'entre nous.

Ce qu'il NE faut PAS faire quand on souhaite communiquer efficacement avec des proches souffrant de dépression et de manie.

1. Évitez d'introduire l'expression « il faut » dans vos phrases. Votre interlocuteur ne manquera pas de les percevoir comme exprimant un jugement négatif ou une critique.

2. Évitez de vous précipiter sur des formules banales de réconfort. Souvenez-vous que votre proche, qui est malade, a un long chemin à parcourir. Le rassurer de façon intempestive lui donnera le sentiment que vous n'avez pas confiance en sa capacité de guérison et compliquera la résolution des problèmes. Préférez des formules du genre : « Je ne sais ni quand ni comment les choses vont s'arranger, mais j'ai confiance que ça arrivera ».

   C'est par l'écoute, plutôt que par le réconfort systématique, que vous parviendrez à comprendre les problèmes, les angoisses et les plans de votre interlocuteur.

   Si vous avez des difficultés dans ce domaine, tâchez de garder votre calme et de vous souvenir que la guérison est une entreprise de longue haleine.

3. Évitez de vous montrer systématiquement disponible et positif. Vous n'êtes pas censé posséder les solutions à tous les problèmes. Parfois les gens ont simplement besoin d'être écoutés.

4. Évitez de prendre à cœur les commentaires de votre interlocuteur ; les troubles de l'humeur se traduisent parfois par de l'agressivité, des paroles hostiles que l'auteur regrettera une fois guéri.

5. Évitez de débattre de sujets graves ou décisifs quand vous êtes fatigué, contrarié ou frustré.

   Les conseils des Alcooliques Anonymes s'appliquent à la lettre :

   Cessez immédiatement d'évoquer des sujets graves quand :
   - **vous avez faim ;**
   - **vous êtes en colère ;**
   - **vous vous sentez seul;**
   - **vous êtes fatigué.**

6. Si votre proche est atteint de manie, évitez de commenter ses idées ou de le convaincre de leur manque de logique. Vous provoqueriez inévitablement un conflit.

La communication avec les personnes atteintes de manie

CE QU'IL FAUT FAIRE

1. Réduisez le nombre de stimuli, les personnes souffrant de manie sont vite trop stimulées. Il n'est pas exclu que vous ayez à limiter le nombre de personnes qui viennent lui rendre visite au même moment. Veillez à minimiser le bruit et les activités à votre domicile.

2. N'engagez que de brèves conversations avec le malade.

3. Ne vous occupez que des problèmes immédiats. Ne tentez ni de raisonner, ni d'argumenter.

4. Évitez de parler de sentiments.

5. Efforcez-vous d'être ferme, pratique et réaliste, sans être autoritaire.

CE QU'IL NE FAUT PAS FAIRE

1. Vous précipiter pour satisfaire les exigences du malade.

2. Vous laisser entraîner par ses accès d'euphorie ou ses attentes irréalistes.

3. Tenter de le convaincre que ses plans ne sont pas réalistes. Cependant, prenez les mesures adéquates pour garantir sa sécurité (ne lui laissez pas les clés de la voiture ou une carte de crédit, par exemple).

Comment améliorer la communication au sein de votre réseau de soutien ?

1. Prenez conscience du fait que les membres de la famille élargie, les amis et les collègues savent fort peu de choses sur les maladies mentales. Les gens partagent généralement des données désuètes et des mythes. N'hésitez pas à leur fournir des données et des renseignements de base.

2. Si les campagnes d'information ont à l'évidence attiré l'attention du public sur les maladies mentales, les prejugés sont encore là. Ne vous confiez pas à n'importe qui. Choisissez des personnes ouvertes et réceptives à ce genre de confidences.

3. En tant que proche, vous ressentez le besoin de vous confier à vos amis, parfois même à les mobiliser autour du problème que vous vivez. Les preuves d'amitié reposent sur la réciprocité. Veillez donc à maintenir l'équilibre et à préserver vos facultés d'écoute de leurs problèmes et intérêts personnels.

4. Lorsque vous ressentez le besoin pressant de vous faire aider et soutenir moralement par des amis, exprimez clairement ce dont vous avez besoin (un entretien, une séance de cinéma en leur compagnie). Vos amis se montreront probablement plus disponibles s'ils savent exactement ce que vous attendez d'eux.

Comment expliquer aux enfants les troubles de l'humeur de leurs parents ?

Le parent en bonne santé est souvent inquiet de l'influence qu'exerce sur ses enfants la maladie de son partenaire. Il faut tenir compte des facteurs suivants lorsqu'on explique la situation aux enfants.

Le dialogue avec les enfants

1. Expliquez-leur la maladie dont souffre votre conjoint, en tenant compte de leur âge et de leur faculté de compréhension. Vous n'avez pas besoin de fournir des détails précis sur le diagnostic médical. Limitez-vous à leur expliquer la raison pour laquelle leur parent se comporte de cette manière.

2. Les enfants doivent bien comprendre qu'ils ne sont pas personnellement responsables de cette situation. Déculpabilisez-les en insistant sur le fait que l'état de votre partenaire a été déclenché par une maladie, et expliquez-leur que leur parent n'est pas fâché contre eux ou que la maladie n'est pas une façon de les punir.

3. Ce n'est pas à l'enfant de résoudre le problème, ou de jouer un rôle d'adulte pour remplacer son parent malade. Rassurez-le dans ce domaine : ce sont des adultes qui vont se charger du problème.

4. Pendant les périodes où le parent se sent mieux, faites en sorte que le parent malade puisse avouer son état aux enfants, en insistant sur le fait qu'ils n'y sont pour rien.

Les parents peuvent aider les enfants à vivre avec la maladie mentale de leur parent. Nous vous donnons ci-dessous une liste d'« amortisseurs » qui ont fait les preuves de leur efficacité.

Comment ramener les enfants au calme

1. **Par la présence d'un parent en bonne santé chez eux,** qui continuera à se montrer attentif et affectueux, et à inspirer l'entière confiance de ses enfants. Ce parent servira de modèle qui les inspirera dans leur vie d'adultes.

2. **En encourageant leurs activités en dehors de la famille** pour éviter qu'ils ne soient plongés jour et nuit dans les problèmes vécus à la maison.

Comment gérer votre problème ?
Une petite séance de remue-méninges

Quelques conseils pour gérer le problème

• Se concentrer sur une seule facette du problème à la fois.
• Définir le problème avec autant de précision que possible.
• Exprimer la raison pour laquelle vous trouvez la situation problématique.

Une fois que vous avez sélectionné un problème spécifique, faites un **remue-méninges** afin d'envisager toutes les solutions possibles.

Les éléments à prendre en compte au cours de votre séance de remue-méninges

1. Définissez le problème.
Pourquoi considérez-vous la situation actuelle comme problématique ? Quelle est la partie du problème que vous souhaiteriez résoudre à l'heure actuelle ? (Vous pourrez vous attaquer à une autre facette de ce problème plus tard.)

2. Passez en revue les mesures que vous avez déjà prises pour tenter de résoudre ce problème.
Vous ne voulez sûrement pas « réinventer la roue ». Il reste qu'il est frustrant de continuer à essayer des solutions qui n'ont jamais fonctionné. Savez-vous ce que disait Mae West à ce sujet : « Quand il me faut choisir entre deux maux, je choisis toujours celui que je n'ai pas encore essayé. »

3. Dressez une liste d'idées que vous n'avez pas encore essayé d'appliquer.
Incluez toutes les idées qui pourraient avoir un impact sur le problème auquel vous êtes confronté, aussi insignifiantes ou irréalistes soient-elles. Ne vous censurez pas systématiquement, vous ne faites que réfléchir à de nouvelles solutions. Vous n'allez pas nécessairement les appliquer toutes et vous n'êtes pas tenu d'en appliquer une seule.

L'avantage d'un remue-méninges, c'est que les idées s'enchaînent. Toute nouvelle idée est fondée sur l'idée précédente. Il ne s'agit pas, dans cet exercice de remue-méninges, d'évaluer ni de procéder à la critique de vos idées. Prenez tout le temps qu'il vous faut pour dresser votre liste.

4. Faites une pause après avoir dressé votre liste de possibilités.
Décidez alors du plan que vous souhaitez appliquer en premier. Ne vous arrêtez pas là. Choisissez une seconde option, puis une troisième. La gestion d'un problème est un marathon, pas un sprint. Avec le temps, il est fort probable que vous mettiez en œuvre nombre de vos idées.

Facteur tout aussi important, souvenez-vous qu'en mettant en pratique une idée, vous pouvez l'abandonner en cours de route si elle s'avère inefficace. La gestion des problèmes consiste précisément à essayer beaucoup d'idées différentes.

5. Revenez à votre liste en cas d'échec.
Ajoutez-y vos idées nouvelles et supprimez celles qui n'ont pas été utiles.

Comment agir en situation de crise ?

Il peut être très difficile de réfléchir calmement et de se montrer efficace dans des moments de crise soudaine et inattendue. Le meilleur moyen de s'y préparer est de planifier à l'avance, à un moment où votre proche est en forme, quelques stratégies d'urgence et de s'exercer avec les méthodes de communication enseignées antérieurement.

Quelques conseils pour bien gérer une situation de crise

CE QU'IL FAUT FAIRE

1. Restez aussi calme que possible et diminuez le nombre d'éléments de distraction.

2. Si la situation l'exige, demandez aux personnes présentes de quitter la pièce ou la maison.

3. Parlez à tour de rôle, gardez votre calme et réduisez les stimuli le plus possible. Proposez de vous asseoir pour parler ensemble, ou pour vous reposer un moment.

4. Parlez lentement, sur un ton naturel. Appliquez les stratégies de communication : approuvez ce que vous entendez et faites des observations neutres sur la situation. Dites par exemple : « Je vois que tu es effrayé et confus », ou bien « Je vois que tu es en colère. Dis-moi ce qui ne va pas ».

5. Répétez calmement vos questions ou vos phrases, en utilisant toujours les mêmes mots.

6. Ménagez à votre proche un espace suffisant dans la pièce où vous vous trouvez.

7. Sachez que toute expression émotionnelle incontrôlée de votre part risque d'accroître l'état de tension de votre proche.

CE QU'IL NE FAUT PAS FAIRE

1. Crier.

2. Critiquer.

3. Maintenir à tout prix le contact visuel.

4. Se disputer avec les autres sur ce qu'il faut faire.

5. Faire des réflexions autoritaires ou condescendantes telles que « Tu te comportes comme un enfant », ou «Tu vas faire ce que je te dis ».

Le départ pour l'hôpital

1. Dans la mesure du possible, votre proche devrait y consentir.

2. Si votre proche refuse de vous écouter, demandez à une personne en qui il a confiance de le convaincre d'aller à l'hôpital. Cette éventualité doit faire partie intégrante de votre plan d'urgence.

3. Efforcez-vous de laisser le choix à votre proche, notamment en lui proposant : « Préfères-tu que je t'accompagne moi-même à l'hôpital ou que ce soit Jean qui le fasse ? », de sorte qu'il aura moins le sentiment d'être forcé.

En cas de violence

Il faut absolument que vous ayez mis au point un plan d'action en cas de violence, car, vous n'aurez pas le loisir de discuter calmement ou de demander de l'aide.

Si votre proche menace de se faire ou de vous faire du mal, ou d'endommager des biens, agissez immédiatement de façon à l'en empêcher et à vous protéger vous-même, ainsi que les autres (y compris votre proche).

Vous devrez peut-être quitter les lieux pour demander de l'aide ou devoir enfermer votre proche dans l'une des pièces de votre maison pendant que vous allez chercher de l'aide. Ce genre de mesure ne doit être prise que dans des cas extrêmes.

Si vous décidez de le conduire à l'hôpital, assurez-vous que vous ne courez aucun risque à conduire votre véhicule en sa présence.

S'il vous faut appeler la police

Il va de soi que c'est là une décision difficile. Cependant, dans les cas extrêmes, il n'y a souvent pas le choix.

Essayez tout d'abord de dire au malade que vous allez appeler la police ; il se peut que cette éventualité suffise à le calmer.

Si vous n'avez pas le choix, composez le 911 et dites à la téléphoniste que votre proche est dans un état requérant d'urgence une assistance médicale. Précisez la nature de sa maladie et n'hésitez pas à demander de l'aide pour le conduire à l'hôpital.

La réponse que vous risquez de recevoir de la part de la personne qui répondra à votre coup de téléphone dépendra de sa connaissance des maladies mentales. Notez le nom des policiers, leur numéro d'insigne et le délai qui s'est écoulé entre votre appel et leur arrivée.

Une fois la police présente, vous aurez le temps d'appeler le médecin traitant de votre proche.

Au service des urgences de l'hôpital, adressez-vous directement au médecin, à un travailleur social ou à une infirmière. Demandez si votre proche va être hospitalisé ou s'il va sortir de l'hôpital, et le traitement de suivi recommandé.

Que faire en cas d'épisodes suicidaires ?

Il est terrifiant d'entendre une personne chère parler de suicide. Malgré l'aspect traumatisant de cette éventualité, vous devez vous renseigner sur le suicide et savoir comment vous comporter dans ce cas.

Souvenez-vous que les pensées et les réflexions suicidaires sont des symptômes de dépression, passagers la plupart du temps.

La grande majorité des personnes qui en parlent n'ont pas l'intention réelle de mettre fin à leur existence. Les pensées suicidaires, voire les tentatives de suicide, adviennent pendant les épisodes de dépression majeure, quand le malade se sent impuissant, découragé, désespéré.

Dans la majorité des cas, vous parviendrez à éviter les intentions suicidaires, à condition d'être attentif à leurs signes avant-coureurs. **Mais sachez que vous n'êtes pas en mesure de changer la situation à vous seul, et vous n'êtes pas personnellement responsable des actes de votre proche.**

Les signes des pensées suicidaires

Votre proche évoque la possibilité de se suicider et se demande ce qu'il adviendra « après » ; il fait des réflexions du genre : « Quand je ne serai plus là... »

Votre proche se préoccupe de son testament, de la répartition de ses biens. Il commence à distribuer ceux auxquels il tient le plus.

Votre proche a l'impression d'être inutile, il fait des remarques du genre « Je ne sers plus à rien... »

Votre proche donne des signes de découragement concernant l'avenir et fait des réflexions du genre « À quoi bon ?...»

Votre proche exprime des convictions erronées ; il s'imagine que son partenaire le trompe ou qu'on lui cache son argent.

Prenez au sérieux toutes les mentions de suicide. Si votre proche parle de suicide ou s'inflige des blessures, appelez immédiatement son médecin. Si vous n'arrivez pas à le contacter, conduisez votre proche immédiatement au service des urgences de l'hôpital.

Les dépressifs de longue date ont souvent des pensées suicidaires passives. L'idée de se faire du mal est récurrente dans la dépression, et il est difficile de faire la distinction entre les réflexions qui sont de réels signaux d'alarme et celles qui ne font qu'exprimer la lassitude d'un malade qui souffre. Dans ces cas, n'hésitez pas à discuter la situation avec le médecin et à mettre au point un plan efficace d'intervention.

Si vous découvrez votre proche après une tentative de suicide :

1. Appelez immédiatement le 911.

2. Si vous avez suivi un cours de secourisme, administrez immédiatement le traitement approprié.

3. Demandez par téléphone à quelqu'un de vous accompagner à l'hôpital ou de rester avec vous à la maison.

4. N'essayez pas de gérer seul cette situation de crise. Contactez un groupe de soutien qui vous aidera à exprimer vos sentiments et vos réactions.

Sachez poser des limites

Qu'il s'agisse d'amis ou de membres de la famille, nul ne doit tolérer les comportements suivants, quand bien même ils seraient la conséquence directe de la maladie d'un proche :

• une agression physique : votre proche vous bouscule, vous empoigne ou vous pince ;

• des cruautés mentales : votre proche hurle des injures ou vous menace verbalement ;

• des abus sexuels ;

• des dommages à des biens (meubles, voiture, etc.) ;

• une tentative d'incendie ou le risque de provoquer un incendie : fumer des cigarettes au lit par exemple ;

• des vols à des membres de votre famille, à des amis ou à d'autres personnes ;

• l'emploi de médicaments qui n'ont pas été prescrits ou d'alcool, risquant d'aggraver l'état psychiatrique du malade ;

• une mauvaise gestion des finances, comme la des dépenses incontrôlées ;

• des comportements manifestement perturbateurs ou tyranniques, tels que contraindre tous les membres de la famille à manger seulement certains aliments, les empêcher d'utiliser le téléphone ou barricader les portes de la maison.

Comment mettre au point un plan d'intervention d'urgence ?

Éléments du plan

1. Dressez la liste des numéros de téléphone suivants :
   - le ou les médecin(s) ;
   - la police ;
   - le service des urgences.

2. Demandez à l'avance au médecin traitant à quel hôpital vous devez conduire votre proche en cas de besoin.

3. Dans la mesure du possible, et avec l'assentiment de votre proche, efforcez-vous de créer des liens solides avec le médecin traitant.

4. Envisagez de consulter la police à l'avance. Vous avez en effet tout intérêt à savoir comment la police répondra à votre appel au moment critique. La police a également tout intérêt à anticiper comment elle pourra vous assister si vous l'appelez en cas d'urgence.

5. Dressez la liste des personnes que vous pouvez appeler, jour et nuit.

6. Si vous avez de jeunes enfants, prenez des dispositions en vue de leur garde au cas où vous soyez contraint d'aller à l'hôpital.

7. Réfléchissez aux personnes, parmi vos amis ou votre famille, à qui votre proche ferait confiance.

8. Mettez au point votre plan d'urgence à un moment où votre proche se sent bien, et faites-le participer et consentir à vos décisions. Demandez-lui de vous signer une procuration.

Votre plan d'intervention d'urgence

Ce formulaire vise à vous aider à mettre au point un plan d'intervention d'urgence adapté à votre situation particulière. Posez-vous les questions suivantes :

1. Est-ce que je connais les numéros de téléphone suivants ?

Le(s) médecin(s) traitant(s) de mon proche?   N°(s) _____

La police ?   N°(s) _____

2. Quel est l'hôpital que le médecin traitant de mon proche m'a recommandé ?

Nom de l'hôpital _____

N° de téléphone du service des urgences de cet hôpital _____

Numéro(s) de la ligne d'urgence ou du programme   _____

_____

3. Quels sont les médicaments pris par mon proche ?   _____

_____

_____

4. Qui puis-je appeler à l'aide jour et nuit ?

Nom_____ N°(s) de téléphone _____

5. Si vous avez de jeunes enfants : qui puis-je appeler d'urgence pour garder mes enfants si je dois accompagner mon proche à l'hôpital ?

Nom_____ N°(s) de téléphone _____

Nom_____ N°(s) de téléphone _____

Nom_____ N°(s) de téléphone _____

6. Quels sont les parents ou amis à qui mon proche ferait confiance en cas d'urgence ?

Nom_____ N°(s) de téléphone _____

Nom_____ N°(s) de téléphone _____

Nom_____ N°(s) de téléphone _____

7. Ai-je déjà discuté d'un plan d'intervention d'urgence avec mon proche à un moment où il se sentait mieux ? Si oui, que souhaitait-il ?

1. _____

2. _____

3. _____

8. Y a-t-il d'autres mesures que je pourrais prendre pour améliorer mon plan d'intervention d'urgence ? Si oui, quelles sont-elles :

1. _____

2. _____

3. _____

9. Dois-je réviser mon plan ? Si oui, avec quelle fréquence ?

_____

Collaboration avec les les systèmes médical et juridique

Historique

Pour mieux comprendre la législation sur la santé mentale, il est bon de se pencher sur son histoire. De nos jours, la législation en vigueur aux États-Unis et au Canada privilégie nettement les droits du patient d'accepter ou de refuser un traitement, sans tenir compte de ce que sa famille et l'État désirent.

La législation canadienne sur la santé mentale puise son origine dans la doctrine *Parens Patriae* de Grande-Bretagne qui désignait le roi comme Parent Souverain. Conformément à cette doctrine, l'État n'intervenait que lorsque la famille n'était pas capable d'assurer soins et protection aux enfants de personnes atteintes de maladie mentale ou n'était pas disponible.

Au Canada, entre les années 1870 et 1960, l'État avait le pouvoir d'hospitaliser les patients contre leur gré, pour leur faire suivre un traitement. Auparavant, les gens étaient internés dans des asiles d'aliénés et dans des hospices, soit en raison de leur pauvreté, de retards dans leur développement ou encore de maladie mentale. Peu à peu, les personnes atteintes de maladie mentale furent mises à l'écart et hospitalisées. Les patients n'étaient autorisés à quitter l'hôpital qu'après avoir suivi un traitement et lorsqu'il était prouvé que leur état de santé s'était amélioré. Dans la mesure où il n'existait pas de traitements efficaces, de nombreuses personnes internées dans les asiles n'avaient pratiquement aucune chance de voir leur état s'améliorer et donc d'être autorisées à quitter l'hôpital. Par conséquent, les droits civiques de nombreux citoyens furent violés.

Dans les années 1960, le développement des médicaments antipsychotiques permit de traiter plus efficacement les personnes atteintes de maladie mentale. À la même période, l'approche historique des traitements traditionnels fut remise en question par le mouvement pour la défense des droits de la personne, ce qui a permis d'accroître les droits des patients et a suscité une vague de mises en congé par les hôpitaux, entraînant la prise en charge des malades mentaux par la communauté. Ces mesures présupposaient que les ressources communautaires (logement, gestion des cas) seraient suffisantes pour permettre aux personnes atteintes de maladie mentale d'être convenablement soignées. On voyait là un moyen d'accorder des soins à moindre frais.

Dans les années 1960, l'examen judiciaire du système de santé mentale a débouché sur une révision des méthodes relatives à l'internement forcé des personnes atteintes de maladie mentale. Les tribunaux ont décrété qu'il n'existait, en fait, que deux raisons autorisant l'État à priver quelqu'un de sa liberté :

1. En cas de violation de la loi, l'État ou la police avait le pouvoir d'arrêter une personne et si cette dernière était jugée coupable, elle se voyait infliger une peine.

2. L'État pouvait intervenir dans le cas où un parent ne prodiguait pas à son enfant les soins appropriés.

Être traité pour des troubles mentaux n'était plus considéré comme une raison justifiant l'internement d'une personne, à moins que cette personne ne constitue une menace pour elle-même ou pour autrui. Tel est notre système actuel.

S'il ne fait aucun doute qu'il était nécessaire d'apporter des changements et que ces changements ont été mis en œuvre avec les meilleures intentions du monde, notre système actuel a néanmoins engendré de sérieux problèmes pour les familles. Il est, en effet, difficile pour les familles d'obtenir des soins pour des parents n'ayant pas conscience de leur maladie et qui, de ce fait, refusent les soins. Une intervention, contre le gré d'une personne, ne peut se produire que dans des cas extrêmes.

Dans toute l'Amérique du Nord, les familles et les communautés se sont débattues avec les problèmes liés à la nouvelle législation sur la santé mentale, ce qui a produit un mouvement de balancier entre une législation rigide et une législation plus souple qui faciliterait l'hospitalisation et les traitements pour les malades en cure obligatoire. Ces lois, promulguées actuellement dans quelques provinces et dans quelques États, sont appelées Ordonnances de traitement en milieu communautaire. Il s'agit des dernières tentatives de la part de la société pour obtenir un équilibre entre les droits des particuliers et ceux de la communauté en matière de traitement des personnes atteintes de maladie mentale.

Voici une description des conditions dans lesquelles une personne ayant une maladie mentale peut être hospitalisée dans un établissement psychiatrique.

Critères d'admission dans un hôpital psychiatrique en Ontario

Une personne peut être admise dans un hôpital général ou dans un hôpital psychiatrique soit en cure volontaire, soit en cure obligatoire.

MALADES EN CURE VOLONTAIRE

Un patient peut être admis dans un hôpital psychiatrique, sur recommandation du médecin traitant et avec le consentement du patient lui-même. Le critère d'admission est le besoin qu'a la personne d'être mise en observation ou de recevoir des soins et un traitement en hôpital psychiatrique. Il s'agit de la situation idéale, car la personne concernée sera généralement mieux disposée à suivre un plan de traitement avec du personnel médical, et de ce fait, la famille n'aura pas le sentiment d'agir à l'encontre des désirs du proche.

La personne souhaitant être admise à l'hôpital peut, soit contacter son médecin traitant ou un travailleur en santé mentale, si elle en a un, soit se rendre au service des urgences d'un hôpital communautaire doté d'un service psychiatrique pour malades hospitalisés, ou encore se rendre directement à un hôpital psychiatrique. Si les membres de la famille ne savent pas exactement comment trouver un de ces centres, ils peuvent s'adresser à un centre de crise local ou à un centre communautaire de santé mentale.

MALADES EN CURE OBLIGATOIRE

Il s'agit d'une situation beaucoup plus compliquée pour toutes les personnes concernées. Vous devrez vous référer à la législation en vigueur dans votre communauté. Dans la plupart des communautés, voici les trois options légales d'admission d'une personne comme malade en cure obligatoire ou malade certifié :

1. La personne doit présenter un danger pour elle-même, ou avoir des tendances suicidaires ou autodestructrices.

2. La personne est considérée comme dangereuse pour les autres ou comme ayant des tendances meurtrières.

3. La personne est dans l'incapacité de s'occuper d'elle-même et se trouve donc en danger imminent, car elle refuse, par exemple, de s'alimenter ou de boire.

MODE D'HOSPITALISATION D'UNE PERSONNE EN CURE OBLIGATOIRE, EN ONTARIO

La **formule 1** est utilisée par un médecin qui a examiné votre parent au cours des sept derniers jours et qui a décelé chez cette personne un ou plusieurs des trois critères énumérés ci-dessus. Ensuite, cette personne peut-être emmenée à l'hôpital psychiatrique et y être détenue, maîtrisée, examinée et mise en observation pour une période maximale de 72 heures. Si, à l'issue de cette période, la personne se porte suffisamment bien et ne répond plus à aucun des trois critères cités, elle sera alors traitée dans le cadre d'une cure volontaire et pourra, dans ce cas, choisir de rester à l'hôpital ou de quitter ce dernier sans autorisation médicale.

La **formule 2** est obtenue lorsque vous vous rendez chez le juge de paix et que vous lui fournissez des renseignements sur l'état de santé mentale de la personne. Ces informations constitueront un affidavit contenant suffisamment de détails pour convaincre le juge de paix que les critères de mise sous garde (danger pour la personne elle-même ou pour autrui, incapacité de la personne de prendre soin d'elle-même et preuve que la personne souffre d'une maladie mentale) sont respectés. Encore, la personne peut être détenue pendant au maximum 72 heures à l'issue desquelles elle devra être réexaminée pour déterminer son statut.

Vous pouvez demander à la police d'emmener votre parent à l'hôpital. Indépendamment de votre demande, la police a le droit de placer une personne en garde à vue, afin d'obtenir un avis psychiatrique. Les même conditions que celles énumérées plus haut sont applicables.

La **formule 3** est utilisée lorsque la formule 1 ou la formule 2 arrive à expiration et que le patient continue à répondre aux critères de mise sous garde. Cette situation dure deux semaines. Si au bout de ces deux semaines, le patient continue de nécessiter une mise sous garde, on émettra alors la **formule 4** qui, elle, sera valable durant quatre semaines.

Lorsqu'une personne est admise en cure obligatoire, elle recevra automatiquement la visite d'un **conseiller en matière de droits des patients.** Ce conseiller demandera au patient s'il désire interjeter appel contre la formule utilisée et, dans l'affirmative, il l'aidera dans la procédure. Les familles sont généralement invitées à l'audience par le patient ou par le médecin, afin de fournir des renseignements concernant l'état de santé du patient.

Problèmes courants pour les familles

Voici quelques questions généralement posées :

• Le médecin de mon proche refuse de me parler. Comment puis-je lui transmettre les renseignements que je juge nécessaires pour le traitement ou la sécurité de mon proche ?

Comme la loi n'autorise pas un médecin à communiquer avec la famille sans l'autorisation du patient (sauf dans les cas cités plus haut où il existe un risque de danger immédiat), le meilleur moyen pour parler au médecin de votre proche est d'obtenir que ce dernier signe la formule 14 (Ontario) ou qu'il signe un formulaire équivalent d'autorisation de divulguer des renseignements en vigueur dans le territoire dans lequel il réside.

• Qu'arrivera-t-il s'il refuse de signer la formule d'autorisation de divulguer des renseignements ?

Cela compliquera votre situation. Voici quelques options :

1. Demandez à votre proche de vous autoriser à l'accompagner à son rendez-vous chez le médecin. Discutez avec lui de ce que vous souhaitez dire durant la consultation, afin qu'il n'ait pas le sentiment que vous voulez prendre le contrôle de son existence.

   Convaincre votre parent de l'importance de ce qui précède et de vos bonnes intentions peut prendre un certain temps. N'oubliez pas d'utiliser les capacités de communication dont il est question dans la partie 4 du présent document.

2. Si votre proche n'accepte pas votre proposition, vous pouvez téléphoner ou écrire au médecin, de votre propre chef. En raison des lois sur la confidentialité, le médecin ne vous donnera aucun renseignement concernant votre parent et normalement ne confirmera même pas qu'il est son patient. Il peut être utile de faire savoir au médecin, dès le début de la conversation, que vous êtes conscient de ce fait.

   Vous n'êtes pas astreint à la même confidentialité que le médecin, ce qui vous permet de lui fournir des renseignements concernant les soins ou la sécurité de votre proche qu'il vous semble important de porter à sa connaissance. Vous pouvez fournir ces informations sans que le secret professionnel du médecin soit mis en cause.

N'oubliez pas que le médecin doit maintenir, avec votre proche, une bonne relation, basée sur la confiance, et qu'il éprouvera donc certainement la nécessité de lui faire savoir que vous avez eu un entretien tous les deux. Il est donc préférable que vous informiez vous-même votre proche de l'entretien que vous aurez avec son médecin traitant, plutôt qu'il ne l'apprenne par surprise de la bouche du médecin.

• **Si je dois emmener mon proche au service des urgences, comment puis-je être sûr que j'aurais la possibilité de communiquer les renseignements nécessaires au personnel médical, afin qu'il comprenne la gravité de la situation ?**

Quand vous accompagnez un proche au service des urgences, le personnel médical vous posera à tous les deux des questions. Vous possédez des renseignements dont le personnel médical aura besoin pour prendre la bonne décision concernant le traitement qui sera dispensé.

En arrivant, informez le personnel médical que vous souhaiteriez vous entretenir avec lui. Essayez de fournir un rapport clair et précis des événements qui ont conduit à cette visite à l'hôpital. S'il s'agit de la sécurité du patient, expliquez la situation de façon claire et nette.

• **Que se passera-t-il si j'emmène mon proche au service des urgences et que ce service est prêt à le laisser quitter l'hôpital alors que je pense qu'il ne sera pas en sécurité à la maison ?**

Si vous craignez que votre proche reçoive l'autorisation de sortir et que ce ne soit pas dans son intérêt, vous pouvez demander à parler au médecin qui l'a examiné. Demandez-lui pourquoi il estime que votre proche sera en sécurité s'il quitte l'hôpital.

Avant d'accepter de ramener votre proche chez vous, demandez au médecin de vous confirmer que votre proche et votre famille seront en sécurité. Faites savoir au médecin s'il y a des enfants à la maison.

Le traitement

La partie précédente décrit le processus et les critères d'admission à l'hôpital d'une personne, soit comme malade en cure volontaire, soit comme malade en cure obligatoire. Cependant, prescrire un traitement exige un ensemble de conditions différentes.

Aucun patient, que ce soit en cure volontaire ou en cure obligatoire, ne peut recevoir de traitement sans qu'il en donne lui-même l'accord, ou sans l'accord d'une personne habilitée à prendre une telle décision, sauf en cas d'urgence, c'est-à-dire quand la vie, un membre ou un organe vital sont en danger.

Pour que le consentement soit valide, la personne consentante doit :

1. être en état de donner son consentement ;

2. avoir la capacité intellectuelle de prendre la décision ;

3. donner son consentement de son plein gré ;

4. posséder suffisamment d'informations, y compris des renseignements relatifs à des risques éventuels ainsi qu'à des effets secondaires possibles, pour être à même de prendre une décision en connaissance de cause.

Les malades en cure volontaire, tout comme les malades en cure obligatoire, doivent être capables de consentir au traitement. Si un malade en cure obligatoire est considéré comme incapable mentalement de prendre une décision, la *Loi sur la santé mentale* (Ontario) précise comment le consentement du parent le plus proche (en commençant par le conjoint, les enfants majeurs, les frères et sœurs, pour finir par le plus proche parent) doit être obtenu. Si le parent le plus proche refuse le traitement, il faut obtenir une ordonnance de traitement de la part d'une commission de révision (constituée de différents professionnels). Outre ce qui précède, le patient, s'il conteste le traitement en cours, a le droit d'interjeter appel devant une commission qui réexaminera son cas. Toutefois, une fois que l'état de santé du patient se sera stabilisé, il ne répondra donc plus aux critères de cure obligatoire, et comme il deviendra, par conséquent, malade en cure volontaire, il pourra de nouveau refuser le traitement s'il le désire. Une telle situation peut malheureusement conduire, dans certains cas, à l'interruption de la prise de médicaments ou du traitement avec le risque d'entraîner une rechute et la réadmission à l'hôpital en cure obligatoire.

Voici quelques autres types d'intervention pour les patients en cure obligatoire :

Le curateur public (Ontario)

Le curateur public est un fonctionnaire agissant dans l'intérêt d'une personne. Cette personne peut désigner de son plein gré un fiduciaire qui administrera ses biens. Si la personne est incapable de prendre une décision et n'a pas encore désigné de fiduciaire, un médecin peut rédiger une attestation d'incompétence et adresser cette personne à un curateur public qui agira pour son bien ou qui déterminera si un membre de la famille peut le faire de façon équitable.

La procuration

Il s'agit d'un document légal qui doit être signé par une personne saine d'esprit. Ce document donnera le droit à la personne ayant procuration d'agir au nom de la personne malade durant une période d'incapacité légale qui pourrait survenir ultérieurement.

Les testaments

Des parents ou des proches peuvent souhaiter léguer une partie de leurs biens à quelqu'un souffrant de maladie mentale. Il est recommandé, dans certains cas, de nommer un fiduciaire pour s'occuper des biens de la personne souffrant de maladie mentale.

L'objet du présent document est de donner une brève vue d'ensemble de quelques questions d'ordre juridique relatives aux familles et à la santé mentale. Les questions juridiques peuvent être complexes. Nous recommandons donc aux familles d'obtenir des conseils juridiques pour résoudre certains problèmes particuliers.

Liste de référence à l'intention des clients et des familles

Dépression et trouble bipolaire

CENTRE DE TOXICOMANIE ET DE SANTÉ MENTALE (CTSM)
(416) 535-8501

AMI QUÉBEC
150-5253, boul. Décarie, Montréal (Québec) H3W 3C3
(515) 486-1448

ASSOCIATION DES DÉPRESSIFS ET DES MANIACO-DÉPRESSIFS DU QUÉBEC
801, rue Sherbrooke Est, Montréal (Québec) H2L 1K7
(514) 529-7552

MOOD DISORDERS ASSOCIATION OF ONTARIO
(416) 486-8046
(Anciennement Manic-Depressive Association of Toronto)

Association d'entraide à l'intention des clients souffrant de dépression ou de trouble bipolaire ; groupe de soutien destiné aux proches et aux amis (les groupes se réunissent à divers endroits) ; renseignements et soutien au téléphone ; circulaire ; bibliothèque ; défense des intérêts.

SELF-HELP CLEARINGHOUSE OF METRO TORONTO
(416) 487-4355

Orientation téléphonique vers des groupes d'entraide ; consultation, ateliers et soutien accordé à de nouveaux et à d'anciens groupes ; aide en matière de création de groupes ; répertoire ; bureau de conférenciers bénévoles ; bibliothèque de documentation ; circulaire.

COMMUNITY RESOURCES CONSULTANTS OF TORONTO

Organisme communautaire de santé mentale ; services de soutien direct offerts aux familles et aux particuliers ; défense des intérêts ; renseignements et services de consultation ; publications.

a. Services de consultants — renseignements sur les services de santé mentale, y compris le logement, les traitements, les groupes d'entraide, les activités sociales et de loisir, les activités d'éducation et de formation.

b. Services de réadaptation communautaires — sensibilisation, évaluation, gestion de cas, perfectionnement des compétences, éducation et soutien aux familles

c. Programme d'approche dans les foyers d'accueil — soutien souple et adaptable offert aux femmes sans abri qui ont été aux prises avec de graves troubles mentaux.

ASSOCIATION CANADIENNE POUR LA SANTÉ MENTALE — TORONTO
(416) 789-7957

Renseignements sur les services de santé mentale et orientation vers ces services, y compris des psychiatres de Toronto ; services directs offerts aux personnes qui ont suivi ou qui suivent des traitements en raison de problèmes de santé mentale ; publications.

CONSUMER/SURVIVOR INFORMATION RESOURCE CENTRE
(416) 538-0203

Centre de ressources exploité par des consommateurs offrant des renseignements sur les ressources, les organismes et les services de Toronto. Service très convivial.

WOMEN'S COUNSELLING, REFERRAL AND EDUCATION CENTRE (WREC)
(416) 534-7501

Conseils et services d'orientation offerts au téléphone pour répondre aux besoins des femmes, y compris l'orientation vers des thérapeutes et des conseillers présélectionnés (honoraires selon une échelle mobile); autres ressources de santé mentale ; groupes d'entraide ; ressources communautaires ; cliniques d'aide juridique ; abris.

FAMILY ASSOCIATION FOR MENTAL HEALTH EVERYWHERE (FAME)
(416) 744-3263

Éducation, information, soutien, défense des intérêts des familles et des amis de personnes atteintes de maladie mentale ; circulaire.

CENTRE GERSTEIN
(416) 929-0149
Ligne d'écoute téléphonique : (416) 929-5200

Intervention non médicale offerte 24 heures sur 24 en cas de crise psychosociale aiguë ; aide concrète offerte aux personnes ayant des problèmes liés à leur état de crise ; bref séjour dans des installations de base, le cas échéant ; orientation vers des services de soutien pour les besoins permanents comme les finances, le logement et la gestion de cas.

SCARBOROUGH MOBILE CRISIS PROGRAM
(416) 289-2434

Services d'intervention d'urgence à l'intention des personnes âgées de 16 à 65 ans qui traversent une crise de nature psychiatrique ou psychosociale ; soutien au téléphone ; réponse mobile au domicile ou dans un cadre communautaire (de 10 h à 1 h du matin) ; ligne d'écoute téléphonique.

Distress Centre Incorporated
Centre de détresse 1 (416) 598-1121
Centre de détresse 2 (416) 486-1456

Service téléphonique destiné aux personnes ayant besoin d'un soutien affectif immédiat ; intervention d'urgence ou prévention du suicide ; liens avec d'autres services d'urgence ou de l'aide professionnelle, selon le cas.

Hong Fook Mental Health Service
(416) 595-1103
(Organismes servant les communautés chinoise et d'Asie du Sud-Est)

Service d'évaluation et d'orientation, counseling d'appoint, gestion de cas et défense des intérêts de personnes atteintes de problèmes chroniques de santé mentale ; groupe d'entraide ; counseling à l'intention des conjoints et des familles ; groupe de soutien à la famille

Organismes de services familiaux
Family Service Association of Metropolitan Toronto
(416) 922-3126

Services de counselling — offerts aux particuliers, aux couples, aux groupes et aux familles ; éducation à la vie ; services adaptés aux différences culturelles concernant tout un éventail de problèmes psychosociaux, y compris l'anxiété, la dépression, la séparation et le divorce, les voies de fait contre une conjointe ; services destinés aux femmes victimes de violence, aux hommes violents et aux enfants témoins ; femmes victimes de violence sexuelle durant l'enfance ; cours de compétence parentale à l'intention des familles monoparentales, des beaux-pères et des belles-mères et des familles reconstituées. Services offerts dans une variété de langues.

Honoraires selon une échelle mobile.

Contacter le bureau central pour obtenir le numéro du bureau local.

Catholic Family Services of Toronto
(416) 362-2481

Services de counselling individuel, conjugal et familial à l'intention des personnes de toutes les origines ethniques, culturelles, raciales et de toutes les religions ; counselling de groupe à l'intention des femmes victimes de voies de fait et de leurs enfants ; counselling de groupe à l'intention des hommes violents ; counselling individuel, de groupe et familial à l'intention des personnes victimes d'inceste, des survivants et des partenaires de survivants ; séances sur la gestion du stress et l'estime de soi.

Honoraires selon une échelle mobile.

Contacter le bureau central pour obtenir le numéro du bureau local.

JEWISH FAMILY AND CHILD SERVICES OF METROPOLITAN TORONTO
(416) 638-7800

Toute une gamme de services à l'intention des personnes ayant des problèmes sociaux et affectifs ; counselling individuel, familial, conjugal et de groupe ; programmes d'éducation à la vie familiale et programmes de dynamique de la vie ; aide en matière de recherche d'emploi et d'un logement ; médiation en matière de séparation, de divorce et de garde des enfants ; counselling, aide financière d'urgence et accompagnement au tribunal pour les femmes victimes de violence ; groupes à l'intention des femmes victimes de violence et des hommes violents.

HOMEWOOD HEALTH CENTRE (GUELPH)
(519) 824-1010

Services aux malades hospitalisés et externes qui sont atteints de maladies mentales ; le coût de certains lits est payé par l'Assurance-santé de l'Ontario et le reste par des assurances privées ou des frais privés.

Programme de huit semaines sur le trouble bipolaire à l'intention des malades hospitalisés comportant des services d'évaluation et de traitement dans le cadre de programmes individuellement conçus. La période d'attente pour les services en salle commune couverts par l'Assurance-santé de l'Ontario est de quatre à six mois ; la période d'attente pour une protection d'assurance privée est de quatre à six semaines.

En outre le centre offre des programmes de traitement des cas de double diagnostic (troubles concomitants) qui soignent l'abus d'alcool en premier lieu dans le cadre d'un programme en milieu hospitalier qui dure de quatre à cinq semaines.

Les patients doivent être stables et en cure volontaire.

SAINT ELIZABETH HEALTH CARE
(416) 429-1234

Services infirmiers et de réadaptation et soins de santé connexes offerts à domicile par des infirmières autorisées et d'autres fournisseurs de soins de santé ; soins de santé mentale ; possibilité d'obtenir des services d'une personne logeant à domicile.

Honoraires selon une échelle mobile et pouvant être payés par d'autres sources.

MINISTÈRE DU PROCUREUR GÉNÉRAL
BUREAU DU TUTEUR ET CURATEUR PUBLIC
(416) 314-2800

Responsable de la gestion des affaires financières des personnes qui sont certifiées ou déclarées mentalement incompétentes et qui n'ont personne capable d'agir en leur nom ou disposé à le faire.

Service de dernier recours, pouvant prendre des décisions en matière de traitement au nom des personnes incapables, âgées de plus de 18 ans.

Trousses de procuration gratuites.

Excellents messages enregistrés offrant des renseignements sur les différentes situations légales (par exemple *Loi sur la prise de décisions au nom d'autrui,* Procuration relative au soin de la personne, Procuration perpétuelle relative aux biens).

Liste d'ouvrages à l'intention des clients et des familles

Livres sur la dépression et le trouble bipolaire

Bartha, C., C. Parker, C. Thomson, K. Kitchen. *La dépression : Guide d'information,* Toronto, Centre de toxicomanie et de santé mentale, 1999. (livret)

Personnel de la clinique des troubles bipolaires. *Le trouble bipolaire : Guide d'information,* Toronto, Centre de toxicomanie et de santé mentale, 2000. (livret)

*Burns, D. *Feeling Good : The New Mood Therapy.* New York, Avon, 1999.

Copeland, M.E. *The Depression Workbook : A Guide for Living with Depression and Manic Depression.* Oakland (Californie), New Harbinger, 1992.

Dowling, C. *You Mean I Don't Have to Feel this Way ? New Help for Depression, Anxiety and Addiction.* New York, Bantam Books, 1993.

*Duke, P. et G. Hockman. *A Brilliant Madness : Living with Manic Depressive Illness.* New York, Bantam Books, 1993.

Elder, N. *Holiday of Darkness.* Toronto, Wall & Emerson, 1989.

*Fieve, R. *Moodswing.* New York, Bantam Books, 1997.

Gold, M. *The Good News About Depression.* New York, Bantam Books, 1995.

Greenberger, D. et C. Padesky. *Mind over Mood : Change How You Feel by Changing the Way You Think.* New York, Guilford, 1995.

Healy, D. *Psychiatric Drugs Explained,* 2e éd. St Louis (Missouri), Mosby Inc., 1997.

Lithium Information Centre. *Lithium and Manic Depression : A Guide.* Madison (Wisconsin), Dean Foundation, 1992. (livret)

Manning, M. *Undercurrents.* New York, HarperCollins, 1996.

Norden, M. *Beyond Prozac.* New York, HarperCollins, 1995.

Papolos D. et J. Papolos. *Overcoming Depression.* New York, HarperCollins, 1997.

Preston, J. *You Can Beat Depression : A Guide to Recovery.* Impact Publishers, 1996.

Redfield Jamison, K. (1997). *An Unquiet Mind,* New York : Random House.

Turkington, C. *Making the Prozac Decision : a Guide to Antidepressants.* Lowell House, 1997.

À l'intention des familles et des partenaires

Berger, D. et L. Berger. *We Heard the Angels of Madness : A Guide to Coping with Manic Depression*, New York, Quill, 1992.

*Depaula, J. R. et K. Ablow. *How to Cope with Depression : A Guide for You and Your Family*, New York, Ballantine Books, 1996.

Gorman, J. *The Essential Guide to Psychiatric Drugs*, New York, St. Martin's Press, 1998.

Rosen, L.E. et X. Amador. *When Someone You Love is Depressed*, New York, Fireside, 1996.

*Disponible sous forme de livre de poche à grande diffusion (bon marché)

Ressources en ligne — Dépression

www-fhs.mcmaster.ca/direct/francais/fran.html
Centre de ressources, d'information et d'éducation de la dépression.

http://www.ndmda.org/
National Depressive and Manic-Depressive Association; renseignements sur la dépression et le trouble bipolaire.

http://www/nami.org
National Alliance for the Mentally Ill ; dépression chez les adultes les enfants et les adolescents.

http://www.yahoo.com/Health/Mental_Health/
Listes des sites Web traitant de la dépression et du trouble bipolaire.

http://mentalhelp.net
Ressources sur Internet sur la dépression et le trouble bipolaire.

http://www.med.jhu.edu/drada/
Depression and Related Affective Disorders Association (DRADA).

http://www.nimh.nih.gov/
National Institute of Mental Health (É.-U.) ; renseignements sur la dépression.

http://www.healingwell.com/depression/
Ressources sur la dépression.

http://depression.com
Renseignements sur la dépression chez les adolescents, les personnes âgées et les personnes atteintes de maladies chroniques.

www.canmat.org
CANMAT (Canadian Network for Mood and Anxiety Treatments).

http://www.camh.net
Centre de toxicomanie et de santé mentale (CTSM).

Ressources en ligne — Trouble bipolaire

www-fhs.mcmaster.ca/direct/francais/fran.html
Centre de ressources, d'information et d'éducation de la dépression.

http://www.ndmda.org/
National Depressive and Manic-Depressive Association ; renseignements sur la dépression et le trouble bipolaire.

http://www/nami.org
National Alliance for the Mentally Ill ; dépression chez les adultes, les enfants et les adolescents.

http://www.yahoo.com/Health/Mental_Health/
Listes des sites Web traitant de la dépression et du trouble bipolaire.

http://www.shscares.org/services/lrc/nih/bipolardisorder-nih.asp
National Institutes of Health (É.-U.) — Articles du Centre de ressources éducatives sur le trouble bipolaire.

http://thedailyapple.com/
Renseignements sur le trouble bipolaire.

http://mentalhelp.net
Ressources sur Internet sur la dépression et le trouble bipolaire.

http://www.med.jhu.edu/drada/
Depression and Related Affective Disorders Association (DRADA).